The Fire
of
Liberty

The Boston massacre

THE FIRE OF LIBERTY

Compiled, edited and with an introduction by
Esmond Wright

HAMISH HAMILTON
LONDON

First published in Great Britain 1984
by Hamish Hamilton Limited
Garden House 57–59 Long Acre London WC2E 9JZ

© The Folio Society Limited 1983

ISBN 0–241–11110–2

Printed in Great Britain by
Jolly & Barber Ltd, Rugby

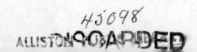

Contents

Introduction   7

1774–5 The people are ripe for mischief.   9

1775 Things are now come to a crisis.   21

1776 Life, Liberty and the pursuit of Happiness.   47

1777 Oh fatal ambition! Poor General Burgoyne!   80

1778 You cannot conquer America.   119

1779 The dance of death.   157

1780 Washington is certainly to be bought – honours will do it.   178

1781 Your Lion shall growl – but never bite more.   211

1782–3 There never was a good war – or a bad peace.   240

Index   252

Illustrations

'A Monumental Inscription on the Fifth of March'. A coloured contemporary print showing the Boston Massacre. 1770. (The Mansell Collection) *frontispiece*

Miniature of General Thomas Gage. Jeremiah Meyer. (National Portrait Gallery, London)

A contemporary view of the British landing their troops in Boston Harbour, 1768. (The Mansell Collection) *facing page 16*

'Noddle Island, or How★ we are deceived'. A contemporary lampoon of the withdrawal of British troops in 1776. London, 12 May 1776. Coloured engraving. (Trustees of the British Museum)

The Boston Tea Party. Drawing by Johann Ramberg for a German publication covering the American Revolution. This is the earliest known drawing of the Tea Party itself. 1784. (The Metropolitan Museum of Art, Bequest of Charles Allen Munn, 1924) 17

Contemporary engravings showing the battles of Lexington and Concord, 19 April 1775. (Connecticut Historical Society, Hartford) 32

Hugh, Earl Percy. Painting by Pompeo Batoni. Before 1776. (The Duke of Northumberland, Alnwick) 33

'A Perspective View of the Blockade of Boston Harbour'. Watercolour by Christian Remick, *c.* 1768. (Massachusetts Historical Society, Boston)

The Battle of Bunker Hill. Painting by John Trumbull, *c.* 1786. (Copyright Yale University Art Gallery) 48

Engraving of Benedict Arnold. (Mary Evans Picture Library)

Engraving of General William Howe. (Mary Evans Picture Library)

Montgomery killed during the attack on Quebec. Painting by John Trumbull. (Mary Evans Picture Library) 49

George III as Commander-in-Chief of the Army. Painting by Benjamin West, 1779. (Reproduced by Gracious Permission of Her Majesty the Queen) 80

4

Lord North. Painting by Nathaniel Dance, *c.* 1770. (The Earl of
Rosebery)

Lord George Germain. Painting by Thomas Gainsborough, 1783–5.
(The Lord Sackville, Courtesy of the Courtauld Institute of
Art)   *81*

Engraving of General John Burgoyne. (The Mansell Collection)

Major John André. Painting attributed to Sir Joshua Reynolds.
(Major-General Sir Allan Adair, Courtesy of the Courtauld
Institute of Art)

Engraving of General Burgoyne addressing the Indians in Canada.
(The Mansell Collection)   *96*

Joseph Brant, Chief of the Mohawks. Painting by George Romney,
c. 1776. (National Gallery of Canada)   *97*

Benjamin Franklin. Painting by Joseph Wright, 1782. (Pennsylvania Academy of Fine Arts, Philadelphia)   *128*

Miniature of Silas Deane. Watercolour on ivory by Charles
Willson Peale, 1776. (Connecticut Historical Society,
Hartford)

The Marquis de Lafayette. Painting by Thomas Fully, *c.* 1825–6.
(Independence National Historical Park, Philadelphia)   *129*

'Lord Howe and the Comte d'Estaing off Rhode Island, August
9th, 1778'. Painting by R. Wilkins. (The Earl Howe)

The Collapse of the Earl of Chatham, by John Singleton Copley,
c. 1779. (Trustees of the Tate Gallery)   *144*

Miniature of Sir Henry Clinton. Watercolour on ivory by John
Smart, 1777. (National Army Museum, London)

Miniature of John Paul Jones. Watercolour on ivory by Constance
de Lowendal Turpin de Crisse, 1780. (National Portrait
Gallery, Smithsonian Institute, Washington)

The French attack on St Lucia is thrown back. Watercolour by
Pierre Ozanne, 1778. (Reproduced from the Collections of the
Library of Congress)   *145*

Six Pence a Day. 'Exposed to the Horrors of War, Pestilence and
Famine for a Farthing an Hour'. Engraving of 1775. (Trustees
of the British Museum)

The *Bonhomme Richard* and the H.M.S. *Serapis*. (United States Naval
Academy Museum)   *176*

Henry ('Light-Horse Harry') Lee. Painting by Charles Willson
Peale. (Independence National Historical Park, Philadelphia)

5

Casimir Pulaski. Painting by Jan Styka. (Fort Pulaski National Monument)

Nathanael Greene. Painting by Charles Willson Peale. (Independence National Historical Park, Philadelphia)   *177*

Lieutenant-Colonel Banastre Tarleton. Painting by Sir Joshua Reynolds, 1782. (The Trustees of the National Gallery London)   *192*

General Horatio Gates at Saratoga. Painting by James Peale, *c*. 1799. (Maryland Historical Society, Baltimore)   *193*

The execution of John André. Contemporary engraving. (The Mary Evans Picture Library)   *208*

The Comte de Rochambeau. Portrait by Charles Willson Peale. (Independence National Historical Park, Philadelphia)

General Daniel Morgan. Painting by Charles Willson Peale. (Independence National Historical Park, Philadelphia)   *209*

Charles, Earl Cornwallis. Painting by Thomas Gainsborough, 1783. (National Portrait Gallery, London)   *224*

Washington and his generals at Yorktown. Painting by James Peale, *c*. 1781. (Colonial Williamsburg Foundation)

The surrender of Cornwallis at Yorktown. Contemporary engraving. (The Mary Evans Picture Library)   *225*

Contemporary coloured engraving of the attack on Bunker Hill and the burning of Charlestown. (The Mansell Collection)   *front endpaper*

Contemporary coloured engraving of the Battle of Bunker Hill. (The Mansell Collection)   *back endpaper*

Introduction

'Who shall write the history of the American Revolution? Who can write it? Who will ever be able to write it?'

So ex-President John Adams wrote to ex-President Thomas Jefferson on 30 July 1815. To Adams the Revolution was 'a radical change in the principles, opinions, sentiments and affections of the people', and it began 'in the minds and hearts of the people'.

It was that certainly – and more. It led to a War of Independence that was waged on land and sea, and along a savage thousand-mile-long unmapped frontier. It was a civil war, rich in suffering and in exiles (one in five of all Americans in 1776 stayed loyal to George III). It was – until the Vietnam War – the longest war in American history; it saw the first use of combined operations, and was marked by extensive use of guerillas. Sir John Moore, of later fame at Corunna, said that he had learned in it the importance of the rifle, of fire-power and of mobility; the Virginia and Kentucky riflemen were described as 'the most fatal widow- and orphan-makers in the world'. It became part of a wider, and older, struggle between Britain and France; Lafayette and some 10,000 other Frenchmen – many of them volunteers – saw service in America, and when Lafayette sent to Washington the key of the demolished Bastille in 1789, he did so, he said, 'as a tribute which I owe . . . as a Missionary of Liberty to its Patriarch'.

As in any war, fact soon becomes legend, and legend becomes folk-lore. So it is the story of colonists unskilfully disguised as Mohawk Indians hurling tea into Boston harbour; of Paul Revere awaiting the signal from the Old North Church steeple, even if he lost his horse and never reached Concord – more a hero in verse perhaps than he ever was in prose; of Captain Parker mustering his uneasy band in a cold dawn on Lexington Green; of Arnold's bravery on the Chaudière and his skill at Valcour Island; of Washington crossing the Delaware amid its ice floes (even if Leutze's painting shows him with his mount peering forwards on the crowded barge, which seems, given the weather, to have been both unlikely and unwise for horse and rider); of Nathan Hale beneath the gallows; of John Paul Jones' cry, 'I have not yet begun to fight', as his *Bonhomme Richard* grappled with the *Serapis* (a cry so made for history that it, too, sounds apocryphal); of Clark's riflemen wading the swollen

7

waters of the Wabash on the march to Vincennes; of Washington's emotional farewell to his officers at Fraunces' Tavern.

To this add the matching and less-chronicled legends of the lost; Earl Percy's rescue column at Lexington, expertly handled; the massive combined operations of Howe's landing at Staten Island in July 1776; Major André's execution after Arnold's treachery at West Point; the 'world turned upside down' at Yorktown. The British record is thinner than the American, though rich in senior officers' apologia and vindictiveness. Apart from the narratives of Sergeant Lamb, of Frederick Mackenzie, James Murray and Ambrose Serle, it is a less documented tale.

The War of American Independence, a civil and ideological as well as a military struggle, was, however, rich in incidents, and rich in brave and hesitant men, in timidity and in treachery. Their own accounts and their diaries, British and American, French and Loyalist, are the best testament to their courage, their hesitations and their cowardice. It was from this long and bitter struggle, fought out as much by mercenaries as by heroes, that a republican government emerged for a territory still unmapped and so extensive that few thought that it could survive united and republican for very long. The importance of the war was not confined to North America. Washington in his First Inaugural Address saw his country's destiny not only as the preservation of 'the republican model of government', but also as 'the preservation of the sacred fire of liberty'.

ESMOND WRIGHT

A NOTE ON THE TEXT

In the interests of historical accuracy all the source material quoted in this book has been reprinted in its original form. This means that spelling and punctuation vary considerably from passage to passage, but it was felt that any attempt at consistency would involve sacrificing too much of the colour and flavour of the writing. The author of each passage is identified in the text; a detailed list of sources is available from the Institute of United States Studies at the University of London.

Professor Wright would like to thank Sheila Thompson for her invaluable help on the text.

1774-5

The people are ripe for mischief

All beginnings are arbitrary. It could be argued that American independence was implicit from the founding of the first permanent settlements in Virginia and Massachusetts early in the seventeenth century, or that it began with the first major constitutional clash over the Stamp Act in 1765. The first shots, however, were not fired until 5 March 1770, in the so-called Boston Massacre, when five men died from shots fired by British sentries after a snowball fight. The soldiers were defended by John Adams, two were found guilty of manslaughter and the rest were acquitted; and, despite the annual celebration of the Massacre thereafter by speeches of an inflammatory colour, the years 1770 to 1773 were nevertheless years of peace. There were two British regiments at hand, but they were confined to Castle William in Boston harbour to avoid provocation; there was only one tax levied, a threepenny tax on a pound of tea, but ninety per cent of the tea consumed was smuggled.

In May 1773, however, in order to help a near-bankrupt East India Company, Lord North's government allowed the passage of East India Company tea directly from India to America — eliminating the duties and the middlemen's profits in England. It was to be sent to a selected group of merchants for distribution, thus giving them a monopoly. The Hutchinson family — one of whom, Thomas, was the native-born Governor of Massachusetts — was prominent among the privileged consignees. This tea would pay a tax, however small; if the price were low, reasoned Lord North, the Americans, especially their female tea addicts, would not object to the tax, 'a peppercorn of principle'. There 'was no purpose making objections, the king would have it so,' said Lord North. But the Prime Minister was 3000 miles away and misread the omens.

Consignments of tea were intended for Boston, Philadelphia, Charleston and New York. Four tea-ships were ordered for Boston, the Dartmouth, Eleanor, Beaver *and* William. *One was cast away on Cape Cod; the other three reached harbour and tied up at Griffin's Wharf. Governor Hutchinson was on the spot and saw the situation all too clearly. But then, unlike Lord North, he was a proud and stubborn man. The tea, he said, must be landed.*

9

The crowd assembling at the wharf took a different view. They were not only from Boston but from surrounding towns and villages, and they were in an ugly mood. An unsigned pamphlet was circulated among them.

Friends! Brethren! Countrymen! – That worst of plagues, the detested tea, shipped for this port by the East India Company, is now arrived in this harbour – the hour of destruction or manly opposition to the machinations of tyranny stare you in the face. Every friend to his country, to himself, and posterity, is now called upon to meet at Faneuil Hall, at nine o'clock this day, at which time the bells will ring, to make an united and successful resistance to this last, worst, and most destructive measure of administration.

Three bands of Mohawk Indians boarded the three ships and threw 342 chests of tea over the side. George Hewes was among them.

It was now evening, and I immediately dressed myself in the costume of an Indian, equipped with a small hatchet, which I and my associates denominated the tomahawk, with which, and a club, after having painted my face and hands with coal dust in the shop of a blacksmith, I repaired to Griffin's Wharf, where the ships lay that contained the tea. When I first appeared in the street after being thus disguised, I fell in with many who were dressed, equipped and painted as I was, and who fell in with me and marched in order to the place of our destination . . . We then were ordered by our commander to open the hatches and take out all the chests of tea and throw them overboard, and we immediately proceeded to execute his orders, first cutting and splitting the chests with our tomahawks, so as thoroughly to expose them to the effects of the water . . .

During the time we were throwing the tea overboard, there were several attempts made by some of the citizens of Boston and its vicinity to carry off small quantities of it for their family use. To effect that object, they would watch their opportunity to snatch up a handful from the deck, where it became plentifully scattered, and put it into their pockets. One Captain O'Connor, whom I well knew, came on board for that purpose, and when he supposed he was not noticed, filled his pockets, and also the lining of his coat. But I had detected him and gave information to the captain of what he was doing. We were ordered to take him into custody, and just as he was stepping from the vessel, I seized him by the skirt of his coat and in attempting to pull him back, I tore it off; but, springing forward, by a rapid effort he made his escape.

He had, however, to run a gauntlet through the crowd upon the wharf, each one, as he passed, giving him a kick or a stroke . . .

Local Loyalists saw it differently, as did Peter Oliver, nephew of Thomas Hutchinson, Chief Justice of the colony of Massachusetts:

The Teas at last arrived, in the latter End of Autumn, & now Committee Men & Mob Men were buzzing about in Swarms, like Bees, with every one their Sting. They applied first to the Consignees, to compel them to ship the Teas back again. The Mob collected with their great Men in Front. They attacked the Stores & dwelling Houses of the Consignees, but they found them too firm to flinch from their Duty; the Mob insisted that the Teas should be sent to England. The Consignees would not take such a Risque upon theirselves, for had the Teas been lost, they must have been the Losers. At last, the Rage of the Mob, urged on by the Smugglers & the Heads of the Faction, was increased to such an Height, that the Consignees were obliged to fly for Protection to the Castle; as the King's Ship in the Harbor, which was ordered to give them Protection, refused it to them. There was no Authority to defend any Man from Injury.

The Faction did what was right in their own Eyes; they accordingly planned their Manoeuvre, & procured some of the Inhabitants of the neighboring Towns to assist them; this they did, in Order to diffuse the Odium of the Action among their Neighbors. The Mob had, partly, Indian Dresses procured for them, & that the Action they were about to perpetrate might be sanctified in a peculiar Manner, Adams, Hancock & the Leaders of the Faction, assembled the Rabble in the largest Dissenting Meeting House in the Town, where they had frequently assembled to pronounce their Annual Orations upon their Massacre, & to perpetrate their most atrocious Acts of Treason & Rebellion – thus, literally, 'turning the House of God into a Den of Thieves'.

Thus assembled, on December 14th, they whiled away the Time in Speech-making, hissing & clapping, cursing & swearing untill it grew near to Darkness; & then the signal was given, to act their Deeds of Darkness. They crowded down to the Wharves where the Tea Ships lay, & began to unlade. They then burst the Chests of Tea, when many Persons filled their Bags & their Pockets with it; & made a Tea Pot of the Harbor of Boston with the Remainder; & it required a large Tea Pot for several hundred Chests of Tea to be poured into, at one Time. Had they have been prudent enough to have poured it into fresh Water instead of Salt Water, they & their Wives, & their Children; & their

11

little ones, might have regaled upon it, at free Cost, for a twelve Month; but now the Fish had the whole Regale to theirselves. Whether it suited the Constitution of a Fish is not said; but it is said, that some of the Inhabitants of Boston would not eat of Fish caught in their Harbor, because they had drunk of the East India Tea.

After the Affair was over, the town of Boston, finding that it was generally condemned, said it was done by a Crew of Mohawk Indians; but it was the Rule of Faction to make their Agents first look like the Devil, in Order to make them Act like the Devil. This villainous Act soon grew into serious Consideration. Some of the Country Towns, as well as some of the Inhabitants of Boston, thought that Justice demanded Indemnification to the owners of the Tea; but the Faction was great; & it prevailed; it had so repeated Success, in Impunity, from their other Disorders, that the Power of Great Britain did not weigh a Feather in their Consideration: but it at last shut up their Port; & deprived them of some other Priviledges, as the Sequel will relate.

The British reaction was prompt. Since 1769 it had been considering an inquiry into Massachusetts; the rendezvous of the navy had already been moved from Halifax to Boston. But half-measures would no longer suffice. The so-called 'Coercive' or 'Intolerable' Acts were passed: the port of Boston was closed until the tea was paid for; the Massachusetts Charter was annulled; the council was appointed rather than elected; the Quartering Act was re-enacted for the contumacious town.

FROM THE MASSACHUSETTS GOVERNMENT ACT

20 May 1774

An Act for the better regulating the Government of the Province of the Massachusetts-Bay in New England

. . . Be it therefore enacted [that so much of the said Charter which relates to the election of Councillors] is hereby revoked . . . [and that from 1 August 1774] the Council, or Court of Assistants of the said Province for the time being, shall be composed of such of the inhabitants or proprietors of lands within the same as shall be thereunto nominated and appointed by His Majesty, his heirs and successors, from time to time, by warrant under his or their signet or sign manual, and with the advice of the Privy Council . . .

And it is hereby further enacted, that the said Assistants or Counsellors . . . shall hold their offices respectively, for and during the pleasure of His Majesty . . .

It shall and may be lawful for His Majesty's Governor . . . of the said

Province . . . to nominate and appoint, under the seal of the Province, from time to time, and also to remove, without the consent of the Council, all judges of the inferior courts of common pleas, commissioners of oyer and terminer, the attorney general, provosts, marshals, justices of the peace, and other officers to the Council or courts of justice belonging; and . . . to nominate and appoint the sheriffs without the consent of the Council, and to remove such sheriffs with such consent, and not otherwise.

Upon every vacancy of the offices of Chief Justice and Judges of the Superior Court of the said Province . . . the Governor for the time being, or, in his absence, the Lieutenant-Governor, without the consent of the Council, shall have full power and authority to nominate and appoint the persons to succeed to the said offices, who shall hold their commission during the pleasure of His Majesty . . .

And whereas, by several acts of the General Court . . . the freeholders and inhabitants of the several townships . . . are authorized to assemble together annually or occasionally, upon notice given, in such manner as the said acts direct, for the choice of selectmen, constables, and other officers, and for the making and agreeing upon such necessary rules, orders, and bye-laws, for the directing, managing, and ordering, the prudential affairs of such townships . . . and whereas a great abuse has been made of the power of calling such meetings, and the inhabitants have, contrary to the design of their institution, been misled to treat upon matters of the most general concern, and to pass many dangerous and unwarrantable resolves: for remedy whereof, be it enacted; that no meeting shall be called . . . without the leave of the Governor, or in his absence of the Lieutenant-Governor, in writing expressing the special business of the said meeting, first had and obtained, except the annual meeting in the months of March or May for the choice of select men, constables, and other officers, or except for the choice of persons to fill up the offices aforesaid . . . and also, except any meeting for the election of a representative or representatives in the General Court; and that no other matter shall be treated of at such meetings, except the election of their aforesaid officers or representatives, nor at any other meeting, except the business expressed in the leave given by the Governor, or, in his absence, by the Lieutenant-Governor.

And whereas the method at present used in the Province of Massachusetts-Bay, in America, of electing persons to serve on grand juries, and other juries, by the freeholders and inhabitants of the several towns, affords occasion for many evil practices, and tends to pervert the free and impartial administration of justice: for remedy whereof, be it

further enacted . . . the jurors to serve at the superior courts of judi-
cature, courts of assize, general gaol delivery, general sessions of the
peace, and inferior court of common pleas, in the several counties
within the said Province . . . shall be summoned and returned by the
sheriffs of the respective counties within the said Province . . .

*For Charles Van, MP for the Brecon, and for Lord George Germain, also an
MP, it was not enough. During a debate in the Commons on the Boston Port Bill on
23 March 1774, Mr Van said he agreed —*

to the flagitiousness of the offence in the Americas, and therefore was
of opinion that the town of Boston ought to be knocked about their ears
and destroyed. *Delenda est Carthago.* Said he, I am of opinion you will
never meet with that proper obedience to the laws of this country until
you have destroyed that nest of locusts.

*Five days later, during a debate on the bill for regulating the government of
Massachusetts Bay, Lord George Germain had this to say:*

I could have wished that the noble lord, when he was forming this
scheme of salvation to this country, would have at least considered that
there were other parts of the internal government necessary to be put
under some regulation. I mean particularly the internal government of
the province of Massachusetts Bay. I wish to see the council of that
country on the same footing as other colonies. There is a degree of
absurdity, at present, in the election of the council. I cannot, Sir, dis-
agree with the noble lord, nor can I think he will do a better thing than
put an end to their town meetings. I would not have men of a mercantile cast every day collecting themselves together and debating about
political matters; I would have them follow their occupations as merchants, and not consider themselves as ministers of that country. I
would also wish that all corporate powers might be given to certain
people in every town, in the same manner that corporations are formed
here; I should then expect to see some subordination, some authority
and order. I do not know by what power those are to be formed, but I
wish that they may be formed by some . . .

I would wish to bring the constitution of America as similar to our
own as possible. I would wish to see the council of that country similar
to a House of Lords in this. I would wish to see chancery suits determined by a court of chancery, and not by the assembly of that province.
At present, their assembly is a downright clog upon all the proceedings

of the governor, and the council are continually thwarting and opposing any opposition he may make for the security and welfare of that government. You have, Sir, no government, no governor; the whole are the proceedings of a tumultuous and riotous rabble, who ought, if they had the least prudence, to follow their mercantile employment and not trouble themselves with politics and government, which they do not understand.

News of the Act travelled fast from Boston. Carried by express riders, it reached New York on 25 April.

A true copy, received in New York, two o'clock, PM, Tuesday, April 25, 1775. Isaac Low, Chairman, New York Committee.

Elizabethtown, seven o'clock in the evening, Tuesday, April 25, 1775.

A true copy received at Woodbridge, ten of the clock in the evening, Tuesday, April 25, 1775.

The above received at New-Brunswick, the 25th April, 1775, twelve o'clock at night.

A true copy received at Princetown, April 26, 1775, half past three in the morning.

The above received at Trenton on Wednesday morning, about half after six o'clock and forwarded at seven o'clock.

Philadelphia, twelve o'clock, Wednesday, received, and forwarded at the same time. April 26, 1775.

Many towns — like Kingston, New Hampshire — rallied to Boston's aid:

To the Overseers of the Town of Boston   14 September 1774
GENTLEMEN,

The inhabitants of Kingston, in the Province of New Hampshire, see with deep concern the unhappy misunderstanding and disagreement that now subsists between Great Britain and these American Colonies, being fully sensible the happiness of both countries depend on an union, harmony and agreement to be established between them on a just, equitable and permanent foundation. But when we consider the new, arbitrary and unjust claims of our brethren in Great Britain to levy taxes upon us at their sovereign will and pleasure, and to make laws to bind us in all cases whatsoever, we view and consider ourselves and our posterity under the operations of these claims as absolute slaves; for what is a slave but one who is bound in all cases whatsoever by the will

15

and command of another? An we look on the late unjust, cruel, hostile and tyrannical acts of the British Parliament, respecting the Massachusetts Bay in general, and the Town of Boston in particular, as consequences of these unrighteous claims, and from them clearly see what the whole continent has to expect under their operation . . .

William Lee of Virginia, the only American ever to hold the office of alderman of the City of London, was a close observer of the political scene, and a friend of Burke, Fox and Wilkes. He wrote to his brother, Richard Henry Lee, in Virginia.

London, 17 March 1774

The intention of this act is totally to annihilate the town of Boston, which will most effectively be done, if the people there permit it to be carried into execution. Lord North, Dartmouth and, some say, Lord Mansfield have been against these measures; but the King with his usual obstinacy and tyrannical disposition is determined, if it be possible, to inslave you all; the Bedford Party, Lord Temple and the remnant of the Grenville Party, Lord Suffolk and Wedderburne, wish the same as well as to make their court to the King, so that Lords North and Dartmouth have been over ruled in the cabinet, where the whole business is settled, and Parliament made the instrument when it is thought convenient; for the mode of business is quite changed in this country from what it was formerly. Neither King nor Minister ever do anything wrong, because Parliament is very ready to sanctify what the King or Minister determines to be right.

10 September 1774

. . . Every nerve will be exerted to subdue your spirit, and make you first bow your necks to the yoke, which will prove a useful example to the people at home. The plan is deeply laid by the King, Lords Bute, Mansfield and Wedderburne; for which purpose they employ the most useful tools in the kingdom: Lord North, a tyrant from principle, cunning, treacherous and persevering, a perfect adept; and his brother-in-law, Lord Dartmouth, who will whine, preach and cry, while he is preparing privately a dagger to stab you to the heart. Under this direction, the several acts against Boston, the Massachusetts Bay and Quebec act, have passed the last sessions; to enforce them soldiers and ships of war have already been sent to Boston, and many more will follow on the least occasion. General Carleton, the ablest officer in the British service, is sent to his Government of Quebec, to embody 30,000 Roman Catholics there. The Ministers have offered to General Amherst the command in chief of America, and to General Sir William Draper,

General Thomas Gage, commander-in-chief

The British fleet in Boston harbour

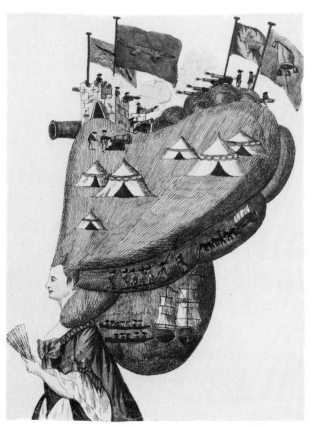

'Noddle Island, or How★ we are deceived.'

The earliest known drawing of the Boston tea party

the government of New York. General Amherst has not yet agreed to accept, but has it now in consideration. Amherst, Gage, Carleton and Draper are to be employed against you.

Back in Boston, it was not easy to be a British officer in what was virtually an occupied town. By November 1774, eleven British regiments were quartered in the city, in private homes as well as taverns and empty buildings. The diary of an anonymous British officer recounts the trials — and the boredom — of service life in Boston.

1775 Jany. 1st Nothing remarkable but the drunkenness among the soldiers which is now got to a very great pitch; owing to the cheapness of the liquor, a man may get drunk for a copper or two. Still a hard frost . . .

21st Last night there was a riot in King Street in consequence of an officer having been insulted by the watchmen, which has frequently happened, as those people suppose from their employment that they may do it with impunity; the contrary, however, they experienced last night. A number of officers as well as townsmen were assembled, and in consequence of the watch having brandished their hooks and other weapons, several officers drew their swords and wounds were given on both sides, some officers slightly; one of the watch lost a nose, another a thumb, besides many others by the points of swords, but less conspicuous than those above mentioned. A court of enquiry is ordered to sit next Monday, consisting of five field officers, to enquire into the circumstances of the riot . . .

March 6th 1775 This day an oration was delivered by Dr Warren, a notorious Whig, at the great South Meeting opposite the Governor's House; it was in commemoration of what they term the Massacre on the 5th of March, 1770. It was known for some days that this was to be delivered; accordingly a great number of officers assembled at it, when after he had finished a most seditious, inflammatory harangue, John Hancock stood up and made a short speech in the same strain, at the end of which some of the officers cried out, 'Fie! Fie!' which being mistaken for the cry of fire an alarm immediately ensued, which filled the people with such consternation that they were getting out as fast as they could by the doors and windows. It was imagined that there would have been a riot, which if there had been would in all probability have proved fatal to Hancock, Adams, Warren and the rest of those villains, as they were all up in the pulpit together, and the meeting was crowded with officers and seamen in such a manner that they could not have escaped; however, it luckily did not turn out so. It would indeed have been a pity for them to have made their exit in that way, as I hope we shall have the pleasure before long of seeing them do it by the hands of the hangman.

But George III had no doubts of his policy, as he made plain to Lord North in a letter from Queen's House dated 18 November 1774 and timed at 12.48 p.m.

I am not sorry that the line of conduct seems now chalked out, which the enclosed dispatches thoroughly justify; the New England governments are in a state of rebellion, blows must decide whether they are to be a subject to this country or independent.

He went even further in a letter the following day.

19 November 1774, 3:17 P M

LORD NORTH,

I return the private letters received from Lieut.-General Gage; his idea of suspending the Acts appears to me the most absurd that can be suggested. The people are ripe for mischief, upon which the mother-country adopts suspending the measures she has thought necessary: this must suggest to the colonies a fear that alone prompts them to their present violence; we must either master them or totally leave them to themselves and treat them as aliens. I do not by this mean to insinuate that I am for advice [*sic*; advising] new measures but I am for supporting those already undertaken.

British opinion rallied round the king, and Samuel Johnson spoke for many when he wrote in 1774:

He that wishes to see his country robbed of its rights cannot be a patriot.

That man, therefore, is no patriot, who justifies the ridiculous claims of American usurpation; who endeavours to deprive the nation of its natural and lawful authority over its own colonies; those colonies, which were settled under English protection; were constituted by an English charter; and have been defended by English arms.

To suppose, that by sending out a colony, the nation established an independent power; that when, by indulgence and favour, emigrants are become rich, they shall not contribute to their own defence, but at their own pleasure; and that they shall not be included, like millions of their fellow-subjects, in the general system of representation; involves such an accumulation of absurdity, as nothing but the show of patriotism could palliate.

He that accepts protection, stipulates obedience. We have always protected the Americans; we may, therefore, subject them to government.

The less is included in the greater. That power which can take away life, may seize upon property. The parliament may enact, for America, a law of capital punishment; it may, therefore, establish a mode and proportion of taxation.

Contemptuous opinions were expressed in Parliament of American fighting qualities. Benjamin Franklin heard some of them, including the views of the Earl of Sandwich, as they were expounded on 10 February 1775:

The noble Lord mentions the impracticality of conquering America; I cannot think the noble Lord can be serious on this matter. Suppose the Colonies do abound in men, what does that signify? They are raw, undisciplined, cowardly men. I wish instead of forty or fifty thousand of these *brave* fellows they would produce in the field at least two hundred thousand; the more the better, the easier would be the conquest; if they did not run away, they would starve themselves into compliance with our measures . . . Are these the men to fright us from the post of honour? Believe me, my Lords, the very sound of a cannon would carry them off . . . as fast as their feet could carry them. This is too trifling a part of the argument to detain your Lordships any longer.

The king interviewed General Gage and seemed impressed by his emphasis on duty and obedience, as he reported to Lord North:

Since you left me this day, I have seen Lieutenant General Gage, who came to express his readiness though so lately come from America to return at a day's notice if the conduct of the Colonies should induce the directing coercive measures, his language was very consonant to his Character of an honest determined Man; he says they will be Lyons, whilst we are Lambs but if we take the resolute part they will undoubtedly prove very meek; he thinks the four Regiments intended to Relieve as many Regiments in America if sent to Boston are sufficient to prevent any disturbance; I wish You would see him and hear his ideas as to the mode of compelling Boston to submit to whatever may be thought necessary; indeed all men seem now to feel that the fatal compliance in 1766 has encouraged the Americans annually to encrease in their pretensions that thorough independency which one State has of another, but which is quite subversive of the obedience which a Colony owes to its Mother Country.

All the preliminaries are here: obstinacy masquerading as firmness in the king and his ministers; readiness in America to confront the Mother Country on what a few saw as an issue of principle, and which others could exploit; and a few — too few — 'friends of America' in Britain, like Charles James Fox, Edmund Burke, Richard Price and Joseph Priestley, Dr Shipley, the Bishop of St Asaph, John Wilkes, Henry Seymour Conway and Isaac Barré. They were not powerful or numerous enough, but they remained pro-American until the end.

1775

Things are now come to a crisis

By the spring of 1775, armed militia from the New England countryside surrounded Boston, and revolutionary organisations existed colony by colony. The Continental Congress had afforded evidence of a nation coming together, and had recommended an intercolonial parliament, though still seeking a peaceful solution. General Gage, the British commander-in-chief and (since 1774) military governor, was under orders to destroy military stores and, if possible, to capture the two leading rebels, Samuel Adams and John Hancock. Accordingly, he sent out his column on the night of 18 April 1775.

Paul Revere was a stocky Boston silversmith, an habitué of the Green Dragon where plots were hatched and intelligence assembled, a post-rider for the Massachusetts Provincial Congress and, by calling, a patriot. Many years later he gave an account of the events of that night, which, thanks more to Longfellow than to Revere himself, had since passed into legend.

In the winter, towards the spring, we frequently took turns, two and two, to watch the soldiers, by patrolling the streets all night. The Saturday night preceding the 19th of April, about 12 o'clock at night, the boats belonging to the transports were all launched, and carried under the sterns of the men-of-war . . . We likewise found that the grenadiers and light infantry were all taken off duty.

About 10 o'clock, Dr Warren sent in great haste for me, and begged that I would immediately set off for Lexington, where Messrs Hancock and Adams were and acquaint them of the movement, and that it was thought they were the objects.

When I got to Dr Warren's house, I found he had sent an express by land to Lexington – a Mr William Dawes. The Sunday before, by desire of Dr Warren, I had been to Lexington, to Messrs Hancock and Adams, who were at the Rev Mr Clark's. I returned at night through Charlestown; there I agreed with a Colonel Conant, and some other gentlemen, that if the British went out by water, we would show two lanthorns in the North Church steeple; and if by land, one, as a signal, for we were apprehensive it would be difficult to cross Charles River, or get over Boston neck. I left Dr Warren, called upon a friend, and desired him to make the signals.

I then went home, took my boots and surtout, went to the north part of town, where I had kept a boat; two friends rowed me across Charles River, a little to the eastward where the *Somerset* man-of-war lay. It was then young flood, the ship was winding, and the moon was rising. They landed me on the Charlestown side . . . I got a horse of Deacon Larkin . . .

In Medford, I awakened the captain of the minute-men; and after that, I alarmed almost every house, till I got to Lexington. I found Messrs Hancock and Adams at the Rev Mr Clark's; I told them my errand, and enquired for Mr Dawes. They said he had not been there. I related the story of the two officers, and supposed that he must have been stopped, as he ought to have been there before me.

After I had been there about half an hour, Mr Dawes came. We refreshed ourselves, and set off for Concord to secure the stores, &c there. We were overtaken by a young Dr Prescott, whom we found to be a high son of liberty . . .

We had got nearly half way. Mr Dawes and the Doctor stopped to alarm the people of a house. I was about one hundred rods ahead when I saw two men, in nearly the same situation as those officers were near Charlestown. I called for the Doctor and Mr Dawes to come up; in an instant I was surrounded by four. They had placed themselves in a straight road that inclined each way. They had taken down a pair of

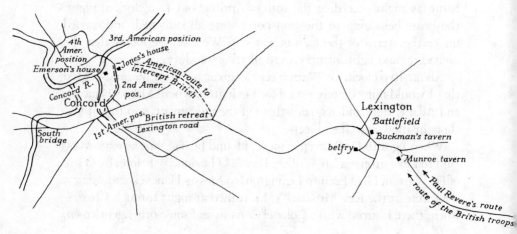

bars on the north side of the road, and two of them were under a tree in the pasture. The Doctor, being foremost, he came up and we tried to get past them; but they being armed with pistols and swords, they forced us into the pasture. The Doctor jumped his horse over a low stone wall and got to Concord.

The British column was commanded by Lieutenant-Colonel Smith, a fat and slow-moving officer, and Major Pitcairn led the six companies of its advance corps. They found a group of 'rebels' drawn up on Lexington Green. Who first shouted 'Fire!' is still a mystery, but it all began on Lexington Green. Lieutenant William Sutherland went along as a volunteer and wrote a report for General Gage on his return:

I went on with the front party which consisted of a sergeant and six or eight men. I shall observe here that the road before you go into Lexington is level for about 1,000 yards. Here we saw shots fired to the right and left of us, but as we heard no whissing of balls, I conclude they were to alarm the body that was there of our approach.

On coming within gunshot of the village of Lexington, a fellow from the corner of the road on the right hand, cocked his piece at me, but burnt priming. I immediately called to Mr Adair and the party to observe this circumstance which they did and I acquainted Major Pitcairn of it immediately. We still went on further when three shots more were fired at us, which we did not return, and this is the sacred truth as I hope for mercy. These three shots were fired from a corner of a large house to the right of the church. When we came up to the main body, which appeared to me to exceed 400 in and about the village, who were drawn up in a plain opposite to the Church, several officers called out, 'Throw down your arms, and you shall come to no harm', or words to that effect.

They refusing to act instantaneously, the gentlemen who were on horseback rode in amongst them of which I was one, at which instant I heard Major Pitcairn's voice call out, 'Soldiers, don't fire, keep your ranks, form and surround them.' Instantly some of the villains who got over the hedge fired at us which our men for the first time returned, which set my horse a-going who galloped with me down a road above 600 yards, among the middle of them before I turned him . . . In consequence of their discovering themselves, our Grenadiers gave them a smart fire.

The same events take a different shape as recalled fifty years later by Sylvanus Wood, a shoemaker from Woburn, Massachusetts, who was twenty-four years old

23

when the battle took place. There is no evidence in his account of 400 men on Lexington Green.

The British troops approached us rapidly in platoons, with a general officer on horseback at their head. The officer came up to within about two rods of the center of the company where I stood, the first platoon being about three rods distant. There they halted. The officer then swung his sword, and said, 'Lay down your arms, you damned rebels, or you are all dead men – Fire!' Some guns were fired by the British at us from the first platoon, but no person was killed or hurt, being probably charged only with powder.

Just at this time, Captain Parker ordered every man to take care of himself. The company immediately dispersed; and while the company was dispersing and leaping over the wall, the second platoon of the British fired, and killed some of our men. There was not a gun fired by any of Captain Parker's company, within my knowledge. I was so situated that I must have known it, had anything of the kind taken place before a total dispersion of our company. I have been intimately acquainted with the inhabitants of Lexington, and particularly with those of Captain Parker's Company, and, on one occasion, and, with one exception, I have never heard any of them say or pretend that there was any firing at the British from Parker's Company, or any individual in it, until within a year or two. One member of the Company told me, many years since, that, after Parker's company had dispersed, and he was at some distance, he gave them 'the guts of his gun'.

For Jonas Clark, the forty-five-year-old bell-voiced Harvard graduate serving as pastor at Lexington, eight of whose parishioners died on the Green before his eyes, the clash served as rich material. He entitled his 1776 sermon 'The Fate of Blood Thirsty Oppressors and God's Tender Care of His Distressed People', and he thought the British

. . . more like *murderers* and *cutthroats* than the troops of a *Christian king*, without provocation, without warning, when no war was proclaimed, they draw the *sword of violence* upon the inhabitants of this town, and with a *cruelty* and *barbarity* which would have made the most innocent savage blush, they *shed* INNOCENT BLOOD! – But, O *my* God! – How shall I speak! – or how describe the distress, the *horror* of that *awful morn*, that *gloomy day!* – *Yonder* [representation of a hand pointing] *field* can witness the *innocent blood* of our *brethren slain!* And from thence does *their blood* cry unto God for vengeance from the ground!

24

Among those awaiting the British at Concord was Amos Barrett, a twenty-two-year-old corporal of David Brown's Concord minutemen company.

We at Concord heard they was a-coming. The Bell rung at 3 o'clock for an alarm. As I was then a Minuteman, I was soon in town and found my captain and the rest of my company at the post. It wasn't long before there was other minute companies. One company, I believe, of minutemen was raised in almost every town to stand at a minute's warning. Before sunrise there was, I believe, 150 of us and more of all that was there . . .

When we was on the hill by the bridge, there was about eighty or ninety British came to the bridge and there made a halt. After a while they begun to tear up the plank of the bridge. Major Buttrick said if we were all of his mind, he would drive them away from the bridge; they should not tear that up. We all said we would go. We then wasn't loaded; we were all ordered to load – and had strict orders not to fire till they fired first, then to fire as fast as we could . . .

They stayed about ten minutes and then marched back, and we after them. After a while we found them a-marching back towards Boston. We was soon after them. When they got about a mile and a half to a road that comes from Bedford and Billerica, they was waylaid and a great many killed. When I got there, a great many lay dead and the road was bloody.

A relief column came out from Boston under Lord Percy and awaited the weary and wounded men at Lexington to escort them on the return. Lieutenant John Barker of the King's Own Regiment had no illusions about the horror of that return march, remembering shots from many houses and every hedgerow.

We were fired on from all sides, but mostly from the rear, where people had hid themselves in houses till we had passed and then fired. The country was an amazing strong one, full of hills, woods, stone walls, &c, which the rebels did not fail to take advantage of, for they were all lined with people who kept up an incessant fire upon us, as we did too upon them but not with the same advantage, for they were so concealed there was hardly any seeing them. In this way we marched between nine and ten miles, their numbers increasing from all parts, while ours was reducing by deaths, wounds and fatigue, and we were totally surrounded with such an incessant fire as it's impossible to conceive; our ammunition was likewise near expended.

In this critical situation we perceived the 1st Brigade coming to our assistance: it consisted of the 4th, 23rd, and 47th regiments and the battalion of marines, with two field pieces, 6-pounders . . .

We were now obliged to force almost every house in the road, for the Rebels had taken possession of them and galled us exceedingly, but they suffered for their temerity, for all that was found in the houses were put to death.

Lieutenant Frederick Mackenzie (later Captain) was a quiet, studious officer of the Royal Welch Fusiliers, and proved to be one of the most assiduous — and careful — of British diarists of the war. His account agrees with that of Barker.

During the whole of the march from Lexington, the Rebels kept an incessant irregular fire from all points on the column, which was more galling as our flanking parties, which at first were placed at sufficient distances to cover the march of it, were at last, from the different obstructions they occassionally met with, obliged to keep almost close to it. Our men had very few opportunities of getting good shots at the Rebels, as they hardly ever fired but under cover of some stone wall, from behind a tree, or out of a house; and the moment they had fired they lay down out of sight until they had loaded again, or the column had passed. In the road indeed in our rear, they were most numerous, and came on pretty close, frequently calling out, 'King Hancock forever'.

Many of them were killed in the houses on the road side from whence they fired; in some, seven or eight men were destroyed. Some houses were forced open in which no person could be discovered, but when the column had passed, numbers sallied forth from some place in which they had lain concealed, fired at the rear guard, and augmented the numbers which followed us. If we had had time to set fire to those houses, many rebels must have perished in them, but as night drew on, Lord Percy thought it best to continue the march. Many houses were plundered by the soldiers, notwithstanding the efforts of the officers to prevent it. I have no doubt that this inflamed the Rebels, and made many of them follow us farther than they otherwise would have done. By all accounts some soldiers who stayed too long in the houses, were killed in the very act of plundering by those who lay concealed in them.

An anonymous observer, writing from the British ships in Boston harbour, wrote of the retreat all too vividly.

. . . even women had firelocks. One was seen to fire a blunderbuss between her father and her husband from their windows. There they

26

three, with an infant child, soon suffered the fury of the day. In another house which was long defended by eight resolute fellows, the grenadiers at last got possession, when after having run their bayonets into seven, the eighth continued to abuse them with all the [beastlike rage] of a true Cromwellian, and but a moment before he quitted this world applied such epithets as I must leave unmentioned . . .

The British soldiers were horrified at the scale of the attack; the Americans were equally appalled. Deacon Joseph Adams escaped during the hubbub, leaving his wife Hannah in bed to face the British bayonets.

. . . divers of them entered our house by bursting open the doors, and three of the soldiers broke into the room in which I was laid on my bed, being scarcely able to walk from my bed to the fire and not having been to my chamber door from my time being delivered in childbirth to that time. One of the said soldiers immediately opened my [bed] curtains with his bayonet fixed and pointing . . . to my breast. I immediately cried out, 'For the Lord's sake, don't kill me!'

He replied, 'Damn you.'

One that stood near said, 'We will not hurt the woman if she will go out of the house, but we will surely burn it.'

I immediately arose, threw a blanket over me, went out, and crawled into a corn-house near the door with my infant in my arms, where I remained until they were gone. They immediately set the house on fire, in which I had left five children and no other person; but the fire was happily extinguished when the house was in the utmost danger of being utterly consumed.

The redcoats raided Cooper's Tavern, and made no distinction between minutemen and customers, as this unsigned account describes:

The King's Regular troops . . . fired more than one hundred bullets into the house where we dwell, through doors, windows, etc. Then a number of them entered the house where we and two aged gentlemen were, all unarmed. We escaped with our lives into the cellar. The two aged gentlemen were immediately most barbarously and inhumanely murdered by them, being stabbed through in many places, their heads mauled, skulls broke, and their brains beat out on the floor and walls of the house.

There was little of these excitements in Gage's laconic description of the event in his

27

account of 22 April to Lord Barrington, the Secretary of War.

. . . I have now nothing to trouble your lordship with, but of an affair that happened here on the 19th instant. I having intelligence of a large quantity of military stores, being collected at Concord, for the avowed purpose, of supplying a body of troops, to act in opposition to his Majesty's government; I got the grenadiers, and light infantry out of town, under the command of Lieutenant Colonel Smith of the 10th Regiment, and Major Pitcairne of the Marines, with as much secrecy as possible, on the 18th at night; and the next morning, by eight companys of the 4th the same number, of the 23d 47th, and Marines under the command of Lord Percy. It appears from the firing of alarm guns and ringing of bells, that the march of Lieutenant Colonel Smith was discovered, and he was opposed, by a body of men, within six miles of Concord: some few of whom first began to fire upon his advanced companys, which brought on a fire from the troops, that dispersed the body opposed to them, and they proceeded to Concord, where they destroyed all the military stores they could find. On the return of the troops, they were attacked from all quarters, where any cover was to be found, from whence it was practicable to annoy them; and they were so fatigued with their march, that it was with difficulty they could keep out their flanking partys, to remove the enemy at a distance, so that they were at length, a good deal pressed. Lord Percy then arrived opportunely to their assistance, with his brigade, and two pieces of cannon. And not withstanding a continual skirmish for the space of fifteen miles, receiving fire from every hill, fence, house, barn &c his lordship kept the enemy off and brought the troops to Charles Town, from whence they were ferryed over to Boston. Too much praise cannot be given to Lord Percy, for his remarkable activity and conduct, during the whole day. Lieutenant Colonel Smith, and Major Pitcairne, did everything men could do, as did all the officers in general, and the men behaved with their usual intrepidity.

The whole country was assembled in arms with surprizing expedition, and several thousand are now assembled about this town, threatening an attack, and getting up artillery: and we are very busy in making preparations to oppose them . . .

At Lexington and Concord the British lost seventy-three men with 200 wounded, the Americans forty-nine, with forty-six wounded; and an eleven-month siege of Boston began. By June, 7000 men, drawn from all New England, had formed a ring around the town, from Charlestown and the Mystic River on the north, to

Roxbury and Dorchester Heights on the south. They dug themselves in, sniped at British sentries and fired on British guard ships; occasionally a cannon shot thudded into their lines. They did not always react wisely, as the shy and delicate nineteen-year-old John Trumbull, son of the Governor of Connecticut, recounts:

The entire army, if it deserved the name, was but an assemblage of brave, enthusiastic, undisciplined country lads; the officers in general, quite as ignorant of military life as the troops, excepting a few elderly men, who had seen some irregular service among the provincials, under Lord Amherst. Our first occupation was to secure our positions, by constructing fieldworks for defense . . .

Nothing of military importance occurred for some time; the enemy occasionally fired upon our working parties, whenever they approached too nigh to their works; and in order to familiarize our raw soldiers to this exposure, a small reward was offered in general orders, for every ball fired by the enemy, which should be picked up and brought to head-quarters. This soon produced the intended effect — a fearless emulation among the men; but it produced also a very unfortunate result; for when the soldiers saw a ball, after having struck and re-bounded from the ground several times (*en ricochet*) roll sluggishly along, they would run and place a foot before it, to stop it, not aware that a heavy ball retains a sufficient impetus to overcome such an obstacle. The consequence was, that several brave lads lost their feet, which were crushed by the weight of the rolling shot. The order was of course withdrawn, and they were cautioned against touching a ball, until it was entirely at rest.

On 25 May, the Cerberus *dropped anchor and General Gage welcomed his reinforcements, three of whom were major-generals come to assist him, and eventually to replace him.*

> Behold the Cerberus the Atlantic plough,
> Her precious cargo, Burgoyne, Clinton, Howe.
> Bow, wow, wow!

Sir William Howe had already served in America — indeed, in 1759, as a lieutenant he led Woolfe's troops up the Heights to seize Quebec. He was a skilled tactician and had pioneered the use of light infantry. He had won a reputation as a professional but he was ultra-cautious and disapproved of this particular war. Howe was a big, heavy — and heavily indulgent — man, popular with his men and, like many a popular commander, unwilling to risk their lives. He replaced Gage as commander-in-chief in September.

Henry Clinton was timid, distrustful of others — and even more of himself. 'Gentleman' Johnny Burgoyne, eldest in years at fifty-nine but junior in service, made up for both of them in colour and rodomontade. He was a playwright, a parliamentarian and a man-about-town. Horace Walpole in his diary calls him General Hurlothrombo and General Swagger.

All three were Members of Parliament, and there were twenty more generals, not unlike them, in the House of Commons. Not all British generals, it should be added, were willing to serve against the Americans, notably Amherst, Harvey and Admiral Augustus Keppel.

The Americans had a commander of a very different kind. When the Second Continental Congress met at Philadelphia a month later, it appointed George Washington. He accepted the call reluctantly, as he admitted to his wife.

MY DEAREST,

I am now set down to write to you on a subject which fills me with inexpressible concern, and this concern is greatly aggravated and increased, when I reflect upon the uneasiness I know it will cause you. It has been determined in Congress that the whole army raised for the defense of the American cause shall be put under my care, and that it is necessary for me to proceed immediately to Boston to take upon me the command of it.

You may believe me, my dear Patsy, when I assure you in the most solemn manner that, so far from seeking this appointment, I have used every endeavour in my power to avoid it, not only from my unwillingness to part with you and the family, but from a consciousness of its being a trust too great for my capacity, and that I should enjoy more real happiness in one month with you at home than I have the most distant prospect of finding abroad, if my stay were to be seven times seven years. But as it has been a kind of destiny that has thrown me upon this service, I shall hope that my undertaking it is designed to answer some good purpose. You might, and I suppose did, perceive, from the tenor of my letters, that I was apprehensive I could not avoid this appointment, as I did not pretend to intimate when I should return. That was the case. It was utterly out of my power to refuse this appointment, without exposing my character to such censure as would have reflected dishonour upon myself, and have given pain to my friends . . . I shall rely, therefore, confidently on that Providence which has heretofore preserved and been bountiful to me, not doubting but that I shall return safe to you in the fall. I shall feel no pain from the toil or the danger of the campaign, my unhappiness will flow from the uneasiness I know you will feel from being left alone . . .

PS Since writing the above I have received your letter of the fifteenth and have got two suits of what I was told was the prettiest muslin. I wish it may please you. It cost 50/– a suit, that is 20/– a yard.

There was nothing automatic in the choice of Washington. It was all John Adams' contriving and, as always, he took pleasure in the intrigue.

Mr Hancock himself had an ambition to be appointed commander-in-chief. Whether he thought an election a compliment due to him, and intended to have the honor of declining it, or whether he would have accepted, I know not. To the compliments he had some pretensions, for, at that time, his exertions, sacrifices, and general merits in the cause of his country had been incomparably greater than those of Colonel Washington. But the delicacy of his health, and his entire want of experience in actual service, though an excellent militia officer, were decisive objections to him in my mind. In canvassing the subject, out of doors, I found too that even among the delegates of Virginia there were difficulties. The apostolical reasonings among themselves which should be greatest, were not less energetic among the saints of the Old Dominion than they were among us of New England. In several conversations, I found more than one very cool about the appointment of Washington, and particularly Mr Pendleton was very clear and full against it.

Full of anxieties concerning these confusions, and apprehending daily that we should hear very distressing news from Boston, I walked with Mr Samuel Adams in the State Yard, for a little exercise and fresh air, before the hour of Congress, and there represented to him the various dangers that surrounded us. He agreed to them all, but said, 'What shall we do?' I answered him that he knew I had taken great pains to get our colleagues to agree upon some plan, that we might be unanimous; but he knew that they would pledge themselves to nothing; but I was determined to take a step which should compel them and all the other members of Congress to declare themselves for or against something. 'I am determined this morning to make a direct motion that Congress should adopt the army before Boston, and appoint Colonel Washington commander of it.' Mr Adams seemed to think very seriously of it, but . said nothing.

Accordingly, when Congress had assembled, I rose in my place, and in as short a speech as the subject would admit, represented the state of the Colonies, the uncertainty in the minds of the people, their great expectation and anxiety, the distresses of the army, the danger of its dissolution, the difficulty of collecting another, and the probability that the British army would take advantage of our delays, march out of Boston, and spread desolation as far as they could go. I concluded with a motion, in form, that Congress would adopt the army at Cambridge, and appoint a General; that though this was not the proper time to nominate a General, yet as I had reason to believe this was a point of the greatest difficulty, I had no hesitation to declare that I had but one gentleman in my mind for that important command, and that was a gentleman from Virginia who was among us and very well known to all of us, a gentleman whose skill and experience as an officer, whose independent fortune, great talents, and excellent universal character would command the approbation of all America, and unite the cordial exertions of all the Colonies better than any other person in the Union.

Mr Washington, who happened to sit near the door, as soon as he heard me allude to him, from his usual modesty darted into the library-room. Mr Hancock — who was our President, which gave me an opportunity to observe his countenance while I was speaking on the state of the Colonies, the army at Cambridge, and the enemy — heard me with visible pleasure, but when I came to describe Washington for the commander, I never remarked a more sudden and striking change of countenance. Mortification and resentment were expressed as forcibly as his face could exhibit them. Mr Samuel Adams seconded the motion, and that did not soften the President's physiognomy at all.

The subject came under debate, and several gentlemen declared themselves against the appointment of Mr Washington, not on account of any personal objections against him, but because the army were all from New England, had a General of their own, appeared to be satisfied with him, and had proved themselves able to imprison the British army in Boston which was all they expected or desired at that time. Mr Pendleton of Virginia, Mr Sherman of Connecticut, were very explicit in declaring this opinion: Mr Cushing and several others more faintly expressed their opposition, and their fears of discontents in the army and in New England . . .

The subject was postponed to a future day. In the meantime, pains were taken out of doors to obtain a unanimity, and the voices were generally so clearly in favor of Washington that the dissentient members were persuaded to withdraw their opposition, and Mr Washington was nominated, I believe by Mr Thomas Johnson of Maryland, unanimously elected, and the army adopted.

Before Washington set off (he was to be away from home, with one visit excepted, not for the six months he foresaw, but for eight years) he heard of the second battle of

The British column found a group of 'rebels' on Lexington Green

'When we was on the hill by the bridge, there was about eighty or ninety British came up and there made a halt . . .'

Lord Percy

the war at Bunker Hill, where the British lost 1150 men, out of 2500 engaged, and 92 officers — one in four of the British officers killed in the whole war.

Gage had decided to seize and fortify Dorchester Heights and Charlestown which, if taken by the Americans, would make Boston quite untenable. The Committee of Safety, hearing rumours of this, decided, on 15 June, to occupy Bunker Hill, 110 feet high, and — just behind it — Breed's Hill, seventy-five feet high, inside Charlestown Neck. From Breed's Hill, small cannon could threaten Boston and its shipping.

Howe was ordered by Gage to dislodge them. He succeeded, but only after three frontal attacks up a slope held by accurate sharp-shooters.

It was a cloudless June afternoon. Howe's twenty companies of light infantry and grenadiers, supported by the 43rd and 52nd Foot under Brigadier Robert Pigot, toiled over uneven ground, some of it knee deep in grass. Each man was loaded with full kit of knapsack, blanket and ammunition, a deadweight of 125 pounds. General Howe marched at their head.

The American militia followed not only the advice of Gustavus Adolphus to his reiters — 'Wait till you can see the whites of their eyes' — but of their own commander, cheerful old Rufus Putnam — 'When you fire, aim at the gorgets and fancy vests of the officers.'

But again it needs a skilful interpreter of General Gage's official prose to guess at the scale of the disaster.

You will receive an account of some success against the rebels, but attended with a long list of killed and wounded on our side; so many of the latter that the hospital has hardly hands sufficient to take care of them. These people shew a spirit and conduct against us, they never shewed against the French, and every body has judged them from their former appearance, and behaviour, when joyned with the kings forces in the last war; which has led many into great mistakes.

They are now spirited up by a rage and entousiasm, as great as ever people were possessed of, and you must proceed in earnest or give the business up. A small body acting in one spot, will not avail, you must have large army's, making divertions on different sides, to divide their force.

I dont find one province in appearance better disposed than another, tho' I think if this army was in New York, that we should find many friends, and be able to raise forces in that province on the side of the Government . . .

The American versions were quite different, more detailed and more vivid. Among them are those of the tall, blue-eyed Amos Farnsworth, a pious farmer-turned-corporal from Groton in the Massachusetts militia, who was twice wounded.

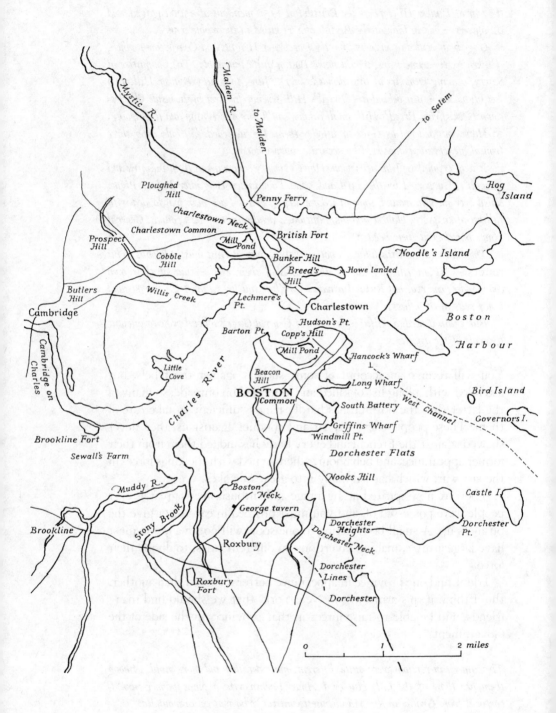

As the enemy approached, our men was not only exposed to the attack of the very numerous musketry, but to the heavy fire of the battery on Corps-Hill, 4 or 5 men of war, several armed boats or floating batteries in Mistick-River, and a number of field pieces. Not with standing we within the intrenchment, and at a breast work without, sustained the enemy's attacks with great bravery and resolution, kiled and wounded great numbers, and repulsed them several times; and after bearing, for about 2 hours as sever and heavy a fire as perhaps was ever known, and many having fired away all their ammunition, and having no reinforsement, althoe thare was a great boddy of men nie by, we ware overpowered by numbers and obliged to leave the intrenchment, retreating about sunset to a small distance over Charlestown Neck.

NB I did not leave the intrenchment until the enemy got in. I then retreated ten or fifteen rods; then I receved a wound in my rite arm, the bawl gowing through a little below my elbow breaking the little shel bone. Another bawl struck my back, taking a piece of skin about as big as a penny. But I got to Cambridge that night. The town of Charlestown supposed to contain about 300 dwelling-houses, a great number of which ware large and elegant, besides 150 or 200 other buildings, are almost all laid in ashes by the barbarity and wanton cruelty of that infernal villain Thomas Gage.

Oh, the goodness of God in preserving my life althoe thay fell on my right hand and my left! O, may this act of deliverance of thine, Oh God, lead me never to distrust the[e]; but may I ever trust in the[e] and put confodence in no arm of flesh! I was in great pane the first night with my wound.

Another farmer-turned-soldier, Colonel William Prescott of Pepperell, *who commanded at Bunker Hill and was to be the grandfather of the historian of* The Conquest of Mexico *and* The Conquest of Peru *reported:*

About an hour after the enemy landed, they began to march to the attack in three columns. I commanded my Lieutenant-Col Robinson and Major Woods, each with a detachment, to flank the enemy, who I have reason to think, behaved with prudence and courage. I was now left with perhaps one hundred and fifty men in the fort. The enemy advanced and fired very hotly on the fort, and meeting with a warm reception, there was a very smart firing on both sides. After a considerable time, finding our ammunition was almost spent I commanded a cessation till the enemy advanced within thirty yards, when we gave them such a hot fire that they were obliged to retire nearly one hundred and fifty yards before they could rally and come up again to the attack.

Our ammunition being nearly exhausted, could keep up only a scattering fire. The enemy, being numerous, surrounded our little fort with their bayonets. We was obliged to retreat through them, while they kept up as hot a fire as it was possible for them to make. We, having very few bayonets, could make no resistance. We kept the fort about one hour and twenty minutes after the attack with small arms . . .

General Howe's assessment was rightly the most worried:

I freely confess to you, when I look to the consequences of it, in the loss of so many brave officers, I do it with horror. The success is too dearly bought. Our killed, serjeants and rank and file, about 160; 300 wounded and in hospital, with as many more incapable of present duty. The Rebels left near 100 killed and 30 wounded, but I have this morning learnt from a deserter from them that they had 300 killed and a great number wounded.

We took five pieces of cannon, and their numbers are said to have been near 6000, but I do not suppose they had more than between 4 and 5000 engaged . . .

Entre nous, I have heard a bird sing that we can do no more this campaign than endeavour to preserve the town of Boston, which it is supposed the Rebels mean to destroy by fire or sword or both – and it is my opinion, with the strength we shall have collected here upon the arrival of the 4 battalions last from Ireland (one of which, with Bailey of the 23rd, came in the day before yesterday), that we must not risk endangering the loss of Boston – tho' should anything offer in our favour, I should hope we may not let pass the opportunity.

The intentions of these wretches are to fortify every post in our way; wait to be attacked at every one, having their rear secure, destroying as many of us as they can before they set out to their next strong situation, and, in this defensive mode (the whole country coming into them upon every action), they must in the end get the better of our small numbers. We can not, (as the General tells us) muster more now than 3400 rank and file for duty, including the Marines, and the three last regiments from Ireland.

Burgoyne gave the most lyrical description, drawing on his skills as a playwright to embroider his prose.

And now ensued one of the greatest scenes of war that can be conceived: if we look to the height, Howe's corps, ascending the hill in the face of intrenchments, and in a very disadvantageous ground, was much engaged; to the left the enemy pouring in fresh troops by thousands, over the land; and in the arm of the sea our ships and floating batteries cannonading them; straight before us a large and noble town in one great blaze – the church-steeples, being timber, were great pyramids of fire above the rest; behind us, the church-steeples and heights of our own camp covered with spectators of the rest of our army which was engaged; the hills round the country covered with spectators; the enemy all in anxious suspense; the roar of cannon, mortars and musketry; the crash of churches, ships upon the stocks, and whole streets falling together, to fill the ear; the storm of the redoubts, with the objects above described, to fill the eye; and the reflection that, perhaps, a defeat was a final loss to the British Empire in America, to fill the mind – made the whole picture, and a complication of horror and importance, beyond any thing that ever came to my lot to be a witness to.

Bunker Hill was a British victory. But even a few like them would still leave America victorious, as the British commanders knew. As General Clinton admitted, 'It was a dear bought victory, another such would have ruined us.' It was a battle that should never have been fought on a hill that should never have been defended. The most vivid commentaries come from the Americans, less august, less disciplined, some of them only boys like drummer Robert Steele in Ephraim Doolittle's regiment from Cambridge:

I beat to 'Yankee Doodle' when we mustered for Bunker Hill that morning . . . the British . . . marched with rather a slow step nearly up to our entrenchment, and the battle began. The conflict was sharp, but the British soon retreated with a quicker step than they came up, leaving some of their killed and wounded in sight of us. They retreated towards where they landed and formed again . . . came up again and a second battle ensued which was harder and longer than the first, but being but a lad and this the first engagement I was ever in, I cannot remember much more . . . than great noise and confusion. One or two circumstances I can, however, distinctly remember . . .

About the time the British retreated the second time, I was standing side of Benjamin Ballard, a Boston boy about my age, who had a gun in his hands, when one of our sergeants came up to us and said, 'You are young and spry, run in a moment to some of the stores and bring some rum. Major Moore is badly wounded. Go as quick as possible.'

We threw down our implements of war and run as fast as we could and passed over the hill . . .

We went into a store, but see no one there. I stamped and called out to rally some person and a man answered us from the cellar below. I told him what we wanted, but he did not come up, nor did we see him at all. I again told him what we wanted and asked him why he stayed down in the cellar. He answered, 'To keep out of the way of the shot,' and then said, 'If you want anything in the store, take what you please.'

I seized a brown, two quart, earthen pitcher and drawed it partly full from a cask and found I had got wine. I threw that out and filled my pitcher with rum from another cask. Ben took a pail and filled with water, and we hastened back to the entrenchment on the hill, when we found our people in confusion and talking about retreating. The British were about advancing upon us a third time. Our rum and water went very quick. It was very hot, but I saved my pitcher and kept it for sometime afterwards.

And Lieutenant Samuel Webb from Wethersfield, Connecticut:

We covered their retreat till they came up with us by a brisk fire from our small arms. The dead and wounded lay on every side of me. Their groans were piercing indeed, though long before this time I believe the fear of death had quitted almost every breast. They now had possession of our fort and four fieldpieces, and by much the advantage of the ground; and, to tell you the truth, our reinforcements belonging to this province, very few of them came into the field, but lay skulking the opposite side of the hill. Our orders then came to make the best retreat we could. We set off almost gone with fatigue and ran very fast up [Bunker Hill], leaving some of our dead and wounded in the field.

The genteel Ann Hulton, sister of the Boston Commissioner of Customs and long confined to Boston, saw it all with high emotion.

... From the heights of this place we have a view of the whole town, the harbor and country round for a great extent, and last Saturday I was a spectator of a most awful scene my eyes ever beheld.

The troops advanced with great ardour towards the intrenchments, but were much galled in the assault, both from the artillery and the small arms, and many brave officers and men were killed and wounded. As soon as they got to the intrenchments, the rebels fled, and many of them were killed in the trenches and in their flight. The marines, in marching through part of Charlestown, were fired at from the houses, and there fell their brave commander Major Pitcairn. His son was

38

likewise wounded. Hearing his father was killed, he cried out, 'I have lost my father'; immediately the corps returned, 'We have lost our father.' How glorious to die with such an epitaph.

Upon the firing from the houses, the town was immediately set in flames, and at four o'clock we saw the fire and the sword, all the horrors of war raging. The town was burning all night; the rebels sheltered themselves in the adjacent hills and the neighbourhood of Cambridge and the army possessed themselves of Charlestown Neck. We were exulting in seeing the flight of our enemies, but in an hour or two we had occasion to mourn and lament. Dear was the purchase of our safety! In the evening the streets were filled with the wounded and the dying; the sight of which, with the lamentations of the women and children over their husbands and fathers, pierced one to the soul. We were now every moment hearing of some officer or other of our friends and acquaintance who had fallen in our defence and in supporting the honor of our country . . .

In this army are many of noble family, many very respectable, virtuous and amiable characters, and it grieves one that gentlemen, brave British soldiers, should fall by the hands of such despicable wretches as compose the banditti of the country; amongst whom there is not one that has the least pretension to be called a gentleman. They are a most rude, depraved, degenerate race, and it is a mortification to us that they speak English and can trace themselves from that stock.

Since Adams went to Philadelphia, one Warren, a rascally patriot and apothecary of this town, has had the lead in the Provincial Congress. He signed commissions and acted as President. This fellow was happily killed, in coming out of the trenches the other day, where he had commanded and spirited the people, etc., to defend the lines, which, he assured them were impregnable. You may judge what the herd must be when such a one is their leader.

All of Howe's staff officers were killed or wounded on Bunker Hill, among them Major Pitcairn of Lexington fame, after surviving two wounds. Dr Warren was killed in the final assault and Captain Harris of the 5th Regiment of Foot was carried off the field to be trepanned, but survived to win renown as Lord Harris of Seringopatam in India. The last words of the mortally wounded Colonel Abercrombie were to ask that if any rebels were to be hanged could his old comrade of earlier and happier campaigns, Israel Putnam, please be spared.

The shedding of blood was decisive. It altered the tone even of Ben Franklin's smooth prose, even if in the end – always the diplomat – he did not post his angry letter to his old printer friend William Strahan.

Philadelphia, 5 July 1775

MR STRAHAN,

You are a member of Parliament and one of that Majority which has doomed my Country to Destruction. You have begun to burn our Towns and murder our People. Look upon your Hands! They are stained with the Blood of your Relations! You and I were long Friends: You are now my Enemy,

and

I am

Yours,

B. FRANKLIN

And it led to a call for volunteers by the Continental Congress. On the Rappahannock River in Virginia, John Harrower, himself an indentured servant teaching at a plantation school, and a recent immigrant, watched a rifle captain select his men, since there were more volunteers than he could feed or supply, and to avoid offence, he organised a competition.

He took a board a foot square and with chalk drew the shape of a moderate nose in the center and nailed it up to a tree at one hundred and fifty yards distance, and those who came nighest the mark with a single ball was to go. But by the first forty or fifty that fired, the nose was blown out of the board, and by the time his company was up, the board shared the same fate.

The British post, Ticonderoga, at the southern end of Lake Champlain, had fallen in May to a strange and quarrelsome couple, Ethan Allen and Benedict Arnold. Arnold was a stocky and handsome braggart from Connecticut, whose language was as robust as its pronunciation was crude, and whose reputation in his native state was already suspect. He was to prove one of the ablest battle commanders on either side, but he was himself to be on both sides. Benedict Arnold's name is now a synonym for traitor in America. We shall meet him later.

Knowing that the Americans were short of cannon, and that heavy cannon lay rusting at Fort 'Ty', Arnold secured from the Massachusetts Committee of Safety a commission to raid it, only to find that a similarly colourful and equally unreliable figure from the Vermont country was raising his 'Green Mountain Boys' with the same intent. They became joint commanders in what proved an easy exercise.

Ethan Allen, who was later to make a name for himself as a rationalist and pseudo-philosopher, wrote up the account of the campaign four years later in a rich prose, conspicuous only for its scant references to his co-commander.

I harangued the officers and soldiers in the manner following:

'Friends and fellow soldiers, you have, for a number of years, past, been a scourge and terror to arbitrary power. Your valour has been famed abroad and acknowledged, as appears by the advice and orders to me (from the general assembly of Connecticut) to use surprise and take the garrison now before us. I now propose to advance before you and in person conduct you through the wicket-gate; for we must this morning either quit our pretensions to valour, or possess ourselves of this fort-ress in a few minutes; and in as much as it is a desperate attempt (which none but the bravest of men dare undertake), I do not urge it on any contrary to his will. You that will undertake voluntarily poise your firelocks!'

I ordered the commander (Capt. Delaplace) to come forth instantly, or I would sacrifice the whole garrison; at which the captain came immediately to the door with his breeches in his hand, when I ordered him to deliver to me the fort instantly, who asked me by what authority I demanded it, I answered, 'In the name of the great Jehovah and the Continental Congress.'

We were now masters of Lake Champlain and the garrisons depending thereon.

For Gage there could be none of this eloquence. The occupation of what was increasingly being seen as an enemy country posed difficult problems, and suggested dangerous courses, as his letters to Lord Barrington at the War Office reveal.

Boston, 13 May 1775

. . . It will be long before any thing can be got from Pensacola and St Augustine, 100 men of the 14th Regiment has been already ordered to Georgia, and the regiment is very weak in numbers. As for the 7th Regiment it has been some time ordered to Crown-Point, to give assist-ance to the colony of New York, in quelling some commotions on their frontiers, since which we have had very bad accounts from their metro-polis, where they seem to be as rebellious as in other parts. The friends of government, are passive friends, quietly wishing to promote peace and tranquility, the opposers active and violent, and overturn all moderate men.

Barrington promised 11,000 men but offered the uneasy comment that 'the true way to reduce America is by sea only'.

A month later (12 June) Gage wrote again.

41

. . . You will have heard of the boldness of the rebels, in surprizing Ticonderoga; and making excurtions to the frontiers of Montreal; but I hope such hostilities will justify General Carleton in raising all the Canadians and Indians in his power to attack them in his turn, I have wrote to him to that effect; and you will know that the 7th Regiment is left under his command; I hope soon to have news from him by return of the transports, which I sent to Canada for supplies. You may be tender of using Indians, but the rebels have shewn us the example, and brought all they could down upon us here. Things are now come to that crisis, that we must avail ourselves of every resource, even to raise the Negros, in our cause. People would not believe that the Americans would seriously resist if put to the test, but their rage and enthusiasm, appeared so plainly in the month of August last, that I am certain had I acted, as very many here, and with you, thought I ought to have acted, that with the small force I then had, I could not have stood my ground. Perhaps this will now be credited. I have long since given my opinion to your lordship, to employ sufficient force in the beginning . . .

Nothing is to be neglected of which we can avail ourselves. Hanoverians, Hessians, perhaps Russians may be hired, let foreigners act here to the eastward, perticularly Germans, as they will find none of their country in these parts to seduce them. Spare arms should also be sent out, as people may be found hereafter willing to side with government . . .

I can't wait longer for reinforcements, and have been forced to publish martial law, and must attempt [to seize] some of the rebels posts without more delay . . .

You must have large armies, making diversions on different sides to divide their force.

The loss we have sustained is greater than we can bear. Small armies can't afford such losses, especially when the advantage gained tends to little more than the gaining of a post – a material one indeed, as our own security depended on it. The troops were sent out too late, the Rebels were at least two months before-hand with us, and your Lordship would be astonished to see the tract of country they have entrenched and fortified; their number is great, so many hands have been employed.

We are here, to use a common expression, taking the bull by the horns, attacking the enemy in their strong parts. I wish this cursed place was burned. The only use is its harbour which may be said to be material, but in all other respects it is the worst place either to act offensively from, or defensively. I have before wrote to your Lordship my opinion that a large army must at length be employed to reduce these people, and mentioned the hiring of foreign troops. I fear it must come to that, or else to avoid a land war and make use only of your fleet.

Gage's recall in September and Howe's appointment as his successor brought no new vigour to Boston. The garrison was demoralised; desertion and disease took their toll as the Pennsylvania Journal *reported.*

MASSACHUSETTS A gentleman who came out of Boston today, says the inhabitants have been numbered, and amount to six thousand five hundred and seventy-three. The soldiers number, women and children, thirteen thousand six hundred. Three hundred Tories are chosen to patrol the streets; forty-nine at night. It is very sickly there; from ten to thirty funerals in a day, and no bells allowed to toll; Master Lovell has been taken up and put in jail, in consequence of some letters found in Dr Warren's pockets.

MASSACHUSETTS As to intelligence from Boston, it is seldom we are able to collect any that may be relied on; and to repeat the vague flying rumors would be endless. We heard yesterday by one Mr Rolston, a goldsmith, who got out from Boston in a fishing schooner, that the distress of the troops increases fast, their beef is spent, their malt and cider all gone; all the fresh provisions they can procure, they are obliged to give to the sick and wounded; that thirteen of the provincials who were in jail, and were wounded at Charlestown, are dead; that no man dared to be seen talking to his friend in the street; that they are obliged to be within every evening at ten o'clock according to martial law, nor can any inhabitant walk the streets after that time without a pass from Gage; that Gage has ordered all the molasses to be distilled into rum for the soldiers; that he has taken away all licenses for selling of liquors, and given them to his creatures; that he has issued an order that no one else shall sell under a penalty of ten pounds; that the spirit which prevails among the soldiers is that of malice and revenge; that there is no true courage to be observed among them; that their duty is hard, always holding themselves in readiness for an attack, which they are in continual fear of; that Doctor Eliot was not on board of a man-of-war as was reported; Mr Lovell, with many others, is certainly in jail; that last week a poor milch cow was killed in town and sold for a shilling sterling a pound; that the transports from Ireland and New York arrived last week, but every additional man adds to their distress.

In Virginia, the Governor, John, Earl of Dunmore, took refuge on board ship, and vowed vengeance against the ex-colony over which he had lost control. He offered liberty to all indentured servants and slaves who joined the king's service.

I have thought fit to issue this Proclamation, hereby declaring that until the aforesaid good purposes can be obtained, I do, in virtue of the power and authority to me given by His Majesty, determine to execute martial law, and cause the same to be executed throughout this Colony. And to the end that peace and good order may the sooner be restored, I do require every person capable of bearing arms to resort to His Majesty's standard, or be looked upon as traitors to His Majesty's crown and Government, and thereby become liable to the penalty the law inflicts upon such offences – such as forfeiture of life, confiscation of lands, etc, etc,: and I do hereby further declare all indented servants, Negroes or others (appertaining to Rebels) free, that are able and willing to bear arms, they joining His Majesty's Troops as soon as may be, for the more speedily reducing this Colony to a proper sense of their duty to His Majesty's crown and dignity.

This might have embarrassed patriots who spoke of liberty without including slaves. It certainly aroused the fury of southern planters, like Henry Laurens:

My Negroes there all to a Man are strongly attached to me, so are all of mine in this Country, hitherto not one of them has attempted to desert on the contrary those who are more exposed hold themselves always ready to fly from the Enemy in case of a sudden descent – many hundreds of that Colour have been stolen and decoyed by the Servants of King George the third – Captains of British Ships of War and Noble Lords have busied themselves in such inglorious pilferage to the disgrace of their Master and disgrace of the Cause – these Negroes were first enslaved by the English – Acts of Parliament have established the Slave Trade in favour of the home residing English & almost totally prohibited the Americans from reaping any share of it – men of War Forts Castles Governors Companies & Committees are employed and authorized by the English Parliament to protect regulate and extend the Slave Trade – Negroes are bought by English Men and sold as Slaves to Americans – Bristol Liverpoole Manchester Birminham etc., etc., live upon the Slave Trade – the British Parliament now employ their Men of War to steal those Negroes from the Americans to whom they had sold them, pretending to set the poor wretches free but basely trepan and sell them into tenfold worse Slavery in the West Indies, where probably they will become the property of English-Men again and of

44

some who sit in Parliament; what meanness! what complicated wickedness appears in this scene! O England, how changed! how fallen!

You know my Dear Sir. I abhor Slavery, I was born in a Country where Slavery had been established by British Kings and Parliaments as well as by the Laws of that Country Ages before my existence, I found the Christian Religion and Slavery growing under the same authority and cultivation — I nevertheless disliked it — in former days there was no combatting the prejudices of Men supported by interest, the day I hope is approaching when from principles of gratitude as well as justice every Man will strive to be foremost in shewing his readiness to comply with the Golden Rule; not less than £20000, Stg. would all my Negroes produce if sold at public auction tomorrow I am not the Man who enslaved them. They are indebted to English Men for that favour, nevertheless I am devising means for manumitting many of them and for cutting off the entail of Slavery — great powers oppose me, the Laws and Customs of my Country, my own and the avarice of my Country Men — What will my Children say if I deprive them of so much Estate? these are difficulties but not insuperable.

The midshipman on board the good ship Otter, *part of the fleet, took pride in destroying Norfolk:*

December 9th We marched up to their works with the intrepidity of lions. But alas! we retreated with much fewer brave fellows than we took out. Their fire was so heavy that had we not retreated as we did, we should every one have been cut off. Figure to yourself a strong breastwork built across a causeway, on which six men only could advance abreast; a large swamp almost surrounded them, at the back of which were two small creastworks to flank us in our attack on their intrenchments. Under these disadvantages it was impossible to succeed; yet our men were so enraged that all the entreaties and scarcely the threats of their officers could prevail on them to retreat, which at last they did . . .

January 9th The detested town of Norfolk is no more! Its destruction happened on New Year's Day. About four o'clock in the afternoon the signal was given from the *Liverpool*, when a dreadful cannonading began from the three ships, which lasted till it was too hot for the rebels to stand on their wharves. Our boats now landed, and set fire to the town in several places. It burned fiercely all night, and the next day; nor are the flames yet extinguished; but no more of Norfolk remains than about twelve houses which have escaped the flames.

Colonel Robert Howe of the North Carolina troops saw the flames differently:

Norfolk, 2 January 1776

The cannonade of the town began about a quarter after three yesterday, from upwards of one hundred pieces of cannon, and continued till near ten at night, without intermission; it then abated a little, and continued till two this morning. Under cover of their guns they landed and set fire to the town in several places near the water, though our men strove to prevent them all in their power; but the houses near the water being chiefly all of wood, they took fire immediately, and the fire spread with amazing rapidity. It is now become general, and the whole town will, I doubt not, be consumed in a day or two. Expecting that the fire would throw us into confusion, they frequently landed, and were every time repulsed, I imagine with loss, but with what loss I cannot tell; the burning of the town has made several avenues which yesterday they had not, so that they may now fire with greater effect; the tide is now rising and we expect at high water another cannonade.

I have only to wish it may be as ineffectual as the last; for we have not one man killed, and but a few wounded. I cannot enter into the melancholy consideration of the women and children running through a crowd of shot to get out of the town, some of them with children at their breasts; a few have, I hear, been killed. Does it not call for vengeance, both from God and man?

Lord Dunmore now regarded Virginia as hostile country and, from the William, *ordered its destruction. The* New York Gazette *of 4 December reported:*

Lord Dunmore has taken into his service the very scum of the country to assist him in his diabolical schemes against the good people of this government, all well attached to his majesty.

1776

Life, Liberty and the pursuit
of Happiness

Despite the battles, and the six-month-old siege of Boston, few in January 1776 would have predicted the total separation in July. One Virginian wrote to a friend in Scotland:

. . . Tears stand in my eyes when I think . . . of this once happy . . . land of liberty. All is anarchy and confusion . . . We are all in arms . . . The sound of war echoes from north to south. Every plain is full of armed men . . . May God put a speedy and happy end to this grand and important contest between the mother and her children. The colonies do not wish to be independent; they only deny the right of taxation in Parliament. They would freely grant the King whatever he pleases to request of their own Assemblies, provided the Parliament has no hand in the disposing of it.

And in Philadelphia, as everywhere, women grieved at what might happen. One lady, deeming it wise to sign her letter only 'C.S.', wrote to a British officer in Boston, whom she knew to be 'a friend to the liberties of America', telling him of America's reluctant 'determination to resist'.

My only brother I have sent to the camp with my prayers and blessings; I hope he will not disgrace me. I am confident he will behave with honor, and emulate the great examples he has before him; and had I twenty sons and brothers they should go. I have retrenched every superfluous expense in my table and family . . . and what I never did before, have learnt to knit and am now making stockings of American wool for my servants, and this way I do throw in my mite for the public good . . .

Washington, writing to his brother Lund, grieved for other reasons.

47

The people of this government have obtained a character which they by no means deserved; their officers generally speaking are the most indifferent kind of people I ever saw. I have already broke one colonel and five captains for cowardice and for drawing more pay and provisions than they had men in their companies. There is two more colonels now under arrest and to be tried for the same offenses. In short, they are by no means such troops, in any respect, as you are led to believe of them from the accounts which are published, but I need not make myself enemies among them by this declaration, although it is consistent with truth. I daresay the men would fight very well (if properly officered) although they are an exceedingly dirty and nasty people.

Even Rhode Island generals like Nathanael Greene, the kind and able Quaker, shared his worries over discipline.

His Excellency . . . has not had time to make himself acquainted with the genius of this people. They are naturally as brave and spirited as the peasantry of any other country, but you cannot expect veterans of a raw militia of only a few months' service. The common people are exceedingly avaricious; the genius of the people is commercial from their long intercourse with trade. The sentiment of honor, the true characteristic of a soldier, has not yet got the better of interest. His Excellency has been taught to believe the people here a superior race of mortals, and finding them of the same temper and disposition, passions and prejudices, virtues and vices of the common people of other governments, they sink in his esteem.

Deserters were numerous, and Moses Harvey had to advertise for their recovery.

Deserted from Colonel Brewer's regiment and Captain Harvey's company, one Simeon Smith, of Greenfield, a joiner by trade, a thin spared fellow about five feet, four inches high, had on a blue coat and black vest, a metal button on his hat, black long hair, black eyes, his voice in the hermaphrodite fashion, the masculine rather predominant. Likewise, one Mathias Smith, a small, smart fellow, gray-headed, has a younger look in his face, is apt to say, 'I swear! I swear!' and between his words will spit smart; had on an old red great coat; he is a right gamester, although he wears a sober look. Likewise one John Darby, a long, hump-shouldered fellow, drawls his words, and for 'comfortable' says 'comfabel', had on a green coat, thick leather breeches, slim legs, lost some of his fore teeth . . . Whoever will take up said deserters and

The Blockade of Boston Harbour

Bunker Hill, a battle that should never have been fought on a hill that should never have been defended

Sir William Howe replaced General Gage as
commander in chief in September 1775

Benedict Arnold, who fought for both sides

The death of Montgomery during the attack on Quebec

secure them or bring them into camp, shall have two dollars reward for each, and all necessary charges paid by me.

Throughout the war loyalties were elusive. At least one in five of all Americans remained loyal to George III — though not all of them showed it — and some 20,000 wore the king's colours. Spies and turncoats, agents and double agents abounded. When Sergeant Thomas Hickey of Washington's own guard in New York was court-martialled for treason and, on being found guilty, hanged, the commander-in-chief made a display of the occasion 'pour encourager les autres'. Eighty men acted as escort and as many as 20,000 may have witnessed the execution — in America as in contemporary Britain they were fashionable spectacles.

The unhappy fate of *Thomas Hickey*, executed this day for mutiny, sedition, and treachery, the General hopes will be a warning to every soldier in the Army to avoid those crimes and all others, so disgraceful to the character of a soldier, and pernicious to his country, whose pay he receives and bread he eats. And in order to avoid those crimes, the most certain method is to keep out of the temptation of them, and particularly to avoid lewd women, who by the dying confession of this poor criminal, first led him into practices which ended in an untimely and ignominious death.

Almost as if in reprisal, when Howe's forces captured Captain Nathan Hale in September 1776, plainly dressed as a Dutch schoolmaster, in a citizen's brown suit and round, broad-brimmed hat, and Hale admitted, after being spotted — it is said by his cousin Samuel who was a Tory — that he was an American officer in disguise, he was hanged without trial.

Head Qrs New York Island, Sept 1776 . . . A Spy fm the Enemy (by his own full Confession) Apprehended Last night, was this day Executed at 11 oClock in front of the Artillery Park.

This laconic British Army order was not enough for American legend. The statue to him on the Old Campus at Yale carries the line:

'I only regret that I have but one life to lose for my country',

which were said to be his dying words. They were, in fact, derived from a line in Addison's Cato, *in which, as a member of the Linonian Society as an undergraduate, he had performed. Captain Frederick Mackenzie's account does not use these words, though it is a tribute to Hale's bravery.*

49

September 22 A person named Nathaniel Hale, a lieutenant in the Rebel army and a native of Connecticut, was apprehended as a spy last night upon Long Island; and having this day made a full and free confession to the Commander in Chief of his being employed by Mr Washington in that capacity, he was hanged at 11 o'clock in front of the park of artillery. He was about 24 years of age, and had been educated at the College of Newhaven in Connecticut. He behaved with great composure and resolution, saying he thought it the duty of every good officer to obey any orders given by his Commander in Chief; and desired the spectators to be at all times prepared to meet death in whatever shape it might appear.

The Ballad of Nathan Hale

The faith of a martyr, the tragedy shewed,
    As he trod the last stage, as he trod the last stage,
And Britons will shudder at gallant Hale's blood
    As his words do presage; as his words do presage.

Thou pale king of terrors, thou life's gloomy foe,
    Go frighten the slave, go frighten the slave;
Tell tyrants, to you their allegiance they owe
    No fears for the brave; no fears for the brave.

They took him and bound him and bore him away
    Down the hill's grassy side, down the hill's grassy side;
'Twas there the base hirelings, in royal array,
    His cause did deride; his cause did deride.

Five minutes were given, short moments, no more,
    For him to repent, for him to repent;
He prayed for his mother, he asked not another.
    To Heaven he went; to Heaven he went.

Until March, 6000 British troops were bottled up in Boston, and they found it grim, even with its civilian population reduced to 7000. Jonathan Sewall, the usually jovial attorney-general, turned to reflection:

Death has so long stalked among us that he is become much less terrible to me than he once was. Habit has a great influence over that mystical substance, the human mind. Funerals are now so frequent that for a month past you met as many dead folks as live ones in Boston streets, and we pass them with much less emotion and attention than we used to pass dead sheep and oxen in days of yore when such sights were to be seen in our streets . . .

I sometimes scold, but I oftener laugh; and I assure you I have never from the beginning felt the least disposition to cry. Everything I see is laughable, cursable, and damnable; my pew in the church is converted into a pork tub; my house into a den of rebels, thieves, and lice; my farm in possession of the very worst of all God's creation; my few debts all gone to the devil with my debtors. I have just parted with my coach horses for £24 sterling, which cost me £40 last fall and £20 more in keeping, while the circuit of my riding ground has been confined to my own yard or little more. I parted with them because they were starving in the midst of British armies and British fleets in the most plentiful country in the world.

John Leach, held in the Stone Gaol for spying, recorded the treatment accorded the American wounded captured at Bunker Hill.

The poor sick and wounded prisoners fare very hard, are many days without the comforts of life. Dr Brown complained to Mr Lovell and me, that they had no bread all that day and the day before. He spoke to the Provost, as he had the charge of serving the bread; he replied they might 'eat the nail heads, and gnaw the planks and be damn'd'. The comforts that are sent us by our friends, we are obliged to impart to these poor suffering friends and fee the soldiers and others with rum to carry it them by stealth, when we are close confined and cannot get to them. They have no wood to burn many days together, to warm their drink, and dying men drink them cold. Some of the limbs which have been taken off, it was said, were in a state of putrefaction, not one survived amputation.

In Boston they still enjoyed concerts, balls and plays, but their entertainments were sometimes interrupted. Lieutenant (later General) Martin Hunter recalled the occasion when the British troops in Boston were watching a piece called, aptly, The Farce of Boston:

. . . the play was just ended, and the curtain going to be drawn up for the farce, when the actors heard from without that an attack was made on the heights of Charlestown, upon which one of them came in, dressed in the character of a Yankee serjeant (which character he was to play), desired silence, and then informed the audience that the alarm guns were fired; that the rebels had attacked the town; and that they were at it tooth and nail over at Charlestown. The audience thinking this was the opening of the new piece, clapped prodigiously; but soon finding their mistake, a general scene ensued, they immediately hurried out of the house to their alarm posts; some skipping over the orchestra, trampling on the fiddles, and, in short, everyone making his most speedy retreat, the actors (who were all officers) calling out for water to get the paint and smut off their faces; women fainting, etc . . . We expected a general attack that night but the rebels knew better, and in a few hours everything was quiet.

Yet for the most part it was a quiet winter – an anonymous British officer was contemptuous:

The country is very plentiful and all sorts of provisions cheaper than in London, tho' much risen from such a number of people being got together. The inhabitants of this province retain the religious and civil principles brought over by their forefathers, in the reign of King Charles I, and are at least an hundred years behind hand with the people of England in every refinement. With the most austere show of devotion, they are destitute of every principle of religion or common honesty, and are reckoned the most arrant cheats and hypocrites on the whole continent of America. The women are very handsome, but, like old mother Eve, very frail. Our camp has been well supplied in that way since we have been on Boston common, as if our tents were pitched on Blackheath.

As to what you hear of their taking up arms to resist the force of England, it is mere bullying, and will go no further than words: when ever it comes to blows, he that can run fastest will think himself best off. Believe me, any two regiments here ought to be decimated, if they did not beat in the field the whole force of the Massachusetts Province; for tho' they are numerous, they are but a mob without order or discipline, and very aukward at handling their arms. If you have ever seen a train-band colonel marching his regiment from Ludgate-hill to the Artillery-Ground, in them you have the epitome of the discipline of an American army.

We expect to pass the winter very quietly. The Saints here begin to relish the money we spend among them, and I believe, notwithstanding all their noise, would be very sorry to part with us.

An Irishman was scornful:

And what have you got now with all your designing,
But a town without victuals to sit down and dine in;
And to look on the ground like a parcel of noodles
And sing how the Yankees have beaten the Doodles.
I'm sure if you're wise you'll make peace for dinner,
For fighting and fasting will soon make ye thinner.

Conditions in the besieging forces only slowly improved. As the Reverend William Emerson wrote to his wife on 17 July 1775:

There is a great overturning in camp as to order and regularity. New lords new laws. The Generals Washington and Lee are upon the lines every day. New orders from his Excellency are read to the respective regiments every morning after prayers. The strictest government is taking place, and great distinction is made between officers and soldiers. Everyone is made to know his place and keep it, or be tied up and receive not 1000 but thirty or forty lashes according to his crime. Thousands are at work every day from four till eleven o'clock in the morning. It is surprising how much work has been done.

Benjamin Thompson was, by contrast, very worried at the conditions he found.

The army in general is not very badly accoutered, but most wretchedly clothed, and as dirty a set of mortals as ever disgraced the name of a soldier . . . They have no women in the camp to do washing for the men, and they in general not being used to doing things of this sort, and thinking it rather a disparagement to them, choose rather to let their linen, etc., rot upon their backs than to be at the trouble of cleaning 'em themselves. And to this nasty way of life, and to the change of their diet from milk, vegetables, etc., to living almost entirely upon flesh, must be attributed those putrid, malignant and infectious disorders which broke out among them soon after their taking the field, and which have prevailed with unabating fury during the whole summer . . . The leading men among them (with their usual art and cunning) have been indefatigable in their endeavors to conceal the real state of the army in this respect, and to convince the world that the soldiers were tolerably healthy . . . But the number of soldiers that have died in the camp is comparatively small to those vast numbers that have gone off in the interior parts of the country. For immediately upon being taken down with these disorders they have in general been carried back into the country to their own homes, where they have not only died themselves, but by spreading the infection among their relatives and friends have introduced such a general mortality throughout New England as was never known since its first planting . . . The soldiers in general are most heartily sick of the service, and I believe it would be with the utmost difficulty that they could be prevailed upon to serve another campaign . . . Notwithstanding the indefatigable endeavours of Mr Washington and the other generals, and particularly of Adjutant General Gates, to arrange and discipline the army, yet any tolerable degree of order and subordination is what they are totally unacquainted with in the rebel camp. And the doctrines of independence and levellism have been so effectively sown throughout the country, and so universally imbibed by all ranks of men, that I apprehend it will be with the greatest difficulty that the inferior officers and soldiers will be ever brought to any tolerable degree of subjection to the commands of their superiors . . . Many of their leading men are not insensible of this, and I have often heard them lament that the existence of that very spirit which induced the common people to take up arms and resist the authority of Great Britain, should induce them to resist the authority of their own officers, and by that means effectively prevent their ever making good soldiers.

Life was just as rough in the British Army. Francis, Lord Rawdon, a captain in the 63rd Regiment, found the winter of 1775–6 hard to endure. Until December he was outside Boston from whence he wrote to his uncle.

At our lines neither officer nor man have the smallest shelter against the inclemency of the weather, but stand to the works all night. Indeed in point of alertness and regularity our officers have great merit. I have not seen either drinking or gaming in this camp. If anything, there is too little society among us. In general, every man goes to his own tent very soon after sunset, where those who can amuse themselves in that manner, read; and the others probably sleep. I usually have a red herring, some onions, and some porter about eight o'clock, of which three or four grave sedate people partake. We chat about different topics and retire to our beds about nine. There is not quite so much enjoyment in this way of life as in what . . . the troops in Boston enjoy. For some days past it has not ceased raining; every tent is thoroughly wet, and every countenance thoroughly dull. A keen wind which has accompanied this rain, makes people talk upon the parade of the comforts of a chimney corner; and we hear with some envy, of several little balls and concerts which our brethren have had in Boston.

Discipline was even more severe for the British than among the Americans as General Orders for 3 January made clear.

Thomas MacMahan, private soldier in His Majesty's Forty-third Regiment of Foot, and Isabella MacMahan, his wife, tried by . . . court martial for receiving sundry stolen goods, knowing them to be such, are found guilty of the crime laid to their charge, and therefore adjudge the said Thomas MacMahan to receive a thousand lashes on his bare back with a cat-of-nine-tails . . . and the said Isabella MacMahan, to receive a hundred lashes on her bare back, at the cart's tail, in different portions and the most conspicuous parts of the town, and to be imprisoned three months.

In January, twenty-five-year-old Colonel Henry Knox, a fat and genial Boston bookseller-turned-colonel of artillery, dragged forty-three cannon, fourteen mortars and two howitzers on sleds over the snows from Fort Ticonderoga; and early in March he began to position and buttress them on Dorchester Heights.

Howe decided on St Patrick's Day, 17 March 1776, to sail away, accompanied by 1000 Loyalist refugees, including some famous Boston names — Brattle, Bradstreet, Boylston, Faneuil and Saltonstall. Selectman Timothy Newell of Boston summed it up.

[March] 17th Lord's day This morning at 3 o'clock, the troops began to move — guards, chevaux de freze, crow feet strewed in the streets to prevent being pursued. They all embarked at about 9 o'clock and the whole fleet came to sail. Every vessel which they did not carry off, they rendered unfit for use. Not even a boat left to cross the river.

Thus was this unhappy distressed town (through a manifest interposition of divine providence) relieved from a set of men whose unparalleled wickedness, profanity, debauchery, and cruelty is inexpressible, enduring a siege from the 19th April 1775 to the 17th March 1776. Immediately upon the fleet's sailing the Select Men set off through the lines to Roxbury to acquaint General Washington of the evacuation of the town. After sending a message Major Ward, aid to General Ward, came to us at the lines and soon after the General himself, who received us in the most polite and affectionate manner, and permitted us to pass to Watertown to acquaint the Council of this happy event. The General immediately ordered a detachment of 2000 troops to take possession of the town under the command of General Putnam who the next day began their works in fortifying Forthill etc, for the better security of the town. A number of loaded shells with trains of powder covered with straw were found in houses left by the Regulars near the fortifycation.

In the winter of 1775–6 Congress sent Benedict Arnold and Richard Montgomery on an expedition against Canada. The country was believed to be lightly held, and ready, in Washington's phrase, 'to run to the same goal' as the United Colonies, 'the only link wanting in the great continental chain of Union'. In August 1775 the dashing young Irishman Montgomery with 2000 men had moved north along the Champlain waterway and, in November, captured Montreal.

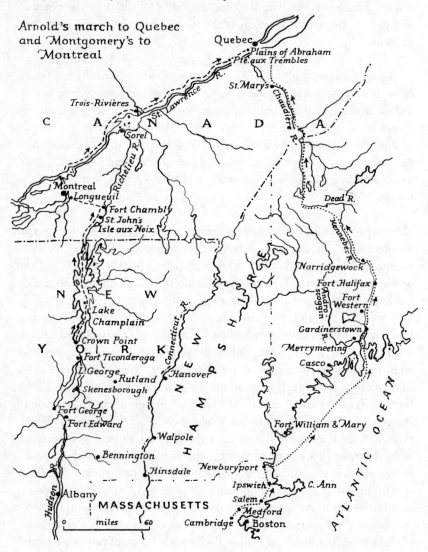

Arnold's march to Quebec and Montgomery's to Montreal

In September, Arnold and a force of 1000 men moved from Newburyport on the journey to Quebec. Arnold's maps told him it was only 185 miles, a distance he was sure he could cover in three weeks. In fact, it was nearly 500 miles through the Maine timberlands, up the Kennebec River over the Dead River portages and down the Chaudière to emerge facing Quebec itself.

John Joseph Henry, a Pennsylvania rifleman, noted some of the anguish of that march, which broke the spirit of James Warner. His wife, Jemima, who was

beautiful though coarse in manner, found him sitting at the foot of a tree, where he said he was determined to die. The tender-hearted woman, attending her ill-fated husband several days, urged his march forward; he again sat down. Finding all her solicitations could not induce him to rise, she left him, having placed all the bread in her possession, between his legs with a canteen of water. She bore his arms and ammunition to Quebec, where she recounted the story . . . Thus perished this unfortunate man.

Private Meigs' entry for 1 November confirmed the hardship:

This day I passed a number of soldiers who had no provisions and some that were sick, and not in my power to help or relieve them, except to encourage them. One or two dogs were killed which the distressed soldiers ate with good appetite, even the feet and skins . . . The travelling this day and yesterday very bad, over mountains and morasses.

The march took seven weeks and the men were reduced to living on boiled candles and roasted moccasin. Four hundred of their number were lost by death and desertion.

. . . Thus in about eight weeks we completed a march of near six hundred miles, not to be paralleled in history; the men having with the greatest fortitude and perseverence hauled their batteaux up rapid streams, being obliged to wade almost the whole way, near 180 miles, carried them on their shoulders near forty miles, over hills, swamps and bogs almost impenetrable, and to their knees in mire; being often obliged to cross three or four times with their baggage. Short of provisions, part of the detachment disheartened and gone back; famine staring us in the face; an enemy's country and uncertainty ahead. Notwithstanding all these obstacles, the officers and men, inspired and fired with the love of liberty and their country, pushed on with a fortitude superior to every obstacle, and most of them has not one day's provision for a week.

The expedition was in vain. When Montgomery joined Arnold in an attack on Quebec through four-foot snowdrifts, on New Year's Eve, an attack in which they were outnumbered two to one, Montgomery was killed, by the last shot fired by a drunken sailor; and Arnold was carried off the field with a ball through his leg.

I received a wound by a ball through my left leg at the time I had gained the first battery at the lower town, which, by the loss of blood, rendered me very weak. As soon as the main body came up, with some assistance I returned to the hospital, near a mile, on foot, being obliged to draw one leg after me, and a great part of the way under the continual fire of the enemy from the walls, at no greater distance than fifty yards. I providentially escaped, though several were shot down at my side.

Private John Henry left a fuller account of the attack:

It was not until the night of the thirty first of December, 1775, that such kind of weather ensued as was considered favorable for the assault. The forepart of the night was admirably enlightened by a luminous moon. Many of us, officers as well as privates, had dispersed in various directions among the farm and tippling houses of the vicinity. We well knew the signal for rallying. This was no other than a snow-storm. About twelve o'clock p.m. the heaven was overcast. We repaired to quarters. By two o'clock we were accoutered and began our march. The storm was outrageous, and the cold wind extremely biting. In this northern country the snow is blown horizontally into the faces of travelers on most occasions — this was our case . . .

We lost some brave men, when powerless to return the salutes we received, as the enemy was covered by his impregnable defences. They were even sightless to us; we could see nothing but the blaze from the muzzles of their muskets. A number of vessels of various sizes lay along the beach, moored by their hawsers or cables to the houses. Pacing after my leader, Lieutenant Steele, at a great rate, one of these ropes took me under the chin and cast me headlong down a declivity of at least fifteen feet. The place appeared to be either a dry dock or a sawpit. My descent was terrible; gun and all was involved in a great depth of snow. Most unluckily, however, one of my knees received a violent contusion on a piece of scraggy ice which was covered by the snow. On like occasions we can scarce expect, in the hurry of attack, that our intimates should attend to any other than their own concerns. Mine went from me, regardless of my fate. Scrabbling out of the cavity, without assistance, divesting my person and gun of the snow, and limping into the line, it was attempted to assume a station and preserve it. There were none of my friends – they knew me not. We had not gone twenty yards before I was thrown out and compelled to await the arrival of a chasm in the line, where a new place might be obtained.

Now we saw Colonel Arnold returning, wounded in the leg and supported by two gentlemen . . . Arnold called to the troops in a cheering voice as we passed, urging us forward, yet it was observable among the soldiery, with whom it was my misfortune to be now placed, that the colonel's retiring damped their spirits. A cant term, 'We are sold', was repeatedly heard in many parts throughout the line . . .

Hendricks, when aiming his rifle at some prominent person, died by a straggling ball through his heart. He staggered a few feet backwards and fell upon a bed, where he instantly expired. He was an ornament of our little society. The amiable Humphreys died by a like kind of wound, but it was in the street, before we entered the buildings. Many other brave men fell at this place; among these were Lieutenant Cooper, of Connecticut, and perhaps fifty or sixty non-commissioned officers and privates. The wounded were numerous, and many of them dangerously so. Captain Lamb, of the York artillerists had nearly half of his face carried away by the grape or canister shot. My friend Steele lost three of his fingers as he was presenting his gun to fire; Captain Hubbard and Lieutenant Fisdle were also among the wounded. When we reflect upon the force that came to annoy us, it is a matter of suprise that so many should escape death and wounding as did.

About nine o'clock a.m., it was apparent to all of us that we must surrender. It was done.

Thus – the words are those of Thomas Ainslie – the country round Quebec was freed from

a swarm of misguided people, led by designing men, enemies to the libertys of their country, under the specious title of the Assertors of American rights.

The British were shocked by their prisoners.

You can have no conception what kind of men composed their officers. Of those we took, one major was a blacksmith, another a hatter. Of their captains, there was a butcher . . . a tanner, a shoemaker, a tavern-keeper, etc. Yet they all pretended to be gentlemen.

The besieging army was wracked by hunger and decimated by smallpox, yet even in its slow, strategic retreat in the spring and summer of 1776 down the Richelieu and on Lake Champlain, Arnold delayed the British; he wrecked their navy on the lakes and emerged from a chronicle of desperation an unreluctant hero. But he won no plaudits except from Washington; his accounts were in disorder – and for a time he was under arrest. His bitterness grew. But as Admiral Mahan said later:

Never had any force, big or small, lived to better purpose, or died more gloriously . . . That the Americans were strong enough to impose the capitulation of Saratoga was due to the invaluable year of delay secured to them by their little navy on Lake Champlain.

If from Canada's point of view, the 1776 campaign was successful – and its invasion was never again attempted – the assault on Charleston was a total disaster. It unleashed – and it was to become a feature of the war – accusations and counter-accusations between the British land and naval forces. The fleet of ten ships sailed from Cork in February 1776 and was commanded by Admiral Sir Peter Parker; the army of 2500 men by moody and unsociable General Clinton.

They expected Loyalist support. Their first disappointment came at Moore's Creek in North Carolina, when Loyalists, mainly former Scottish Highlanders who had settled in the state (among them was the same Flora MacDonald who thirty years before had aided Bonnie Prince Charlie in Scotland) were defeated in a three-minute battle.

This morning, the North Carolina minute men and militia . . . had an engagement with the Tories at Widow Moore's Creek bridge. At the break of day an alarm gun was fired, immediately after which, scarcely leaving the Americans a moment to prepare, the Tory army with Captain [Donald] McLeod at their head made their attack on Colonels Caswell and Lillington, posted near the bridge, and finding a small entrenchment vacant concluded that the Americans had abandoned their post. With this supposition, they advanced in a most furious manner over the bridge. Colonel Caswell had very wisely ordered the planks to be taken up so that in passing they met with many difficulties. On reaching a point within thirty paces of the breastworks they were received with a very heavy fire, which did great execution. Captains McLeod and [Farquar] Campbell were instantly killed, the former having nine bullets and twenty-four swan shot through his body.

The insurgents retreated with the greatest precipitation, leaving behind them some of their wagons, etc. They cut their horses out of the wagons and mounted three upon a horse. Many of them fell into the creek and were drowned. Tom Rutherford ran like a lusty fellow: both he and Felix Keenan were in arms against the Carolinians, and they by this time are prisoners as is Lieutenant Colonel [James] Cotton, who ran at the first fire.

The battle lasted three minutes. Twenty-eight of the Tories besides the two captains are killed or mortally wounded, and between twenty and thirty taken prisoners, among whom is his Excellency General Donald MacDonald [the ageing commander-in-chief of the Tories who had remained in the Tory camp too ill to lead the assault]. This we think, will effectively put a stop to Toryism in North Carolina.

Flora MacDonald, riding a white horse, had addressed the Highlanders in Gaelic, before they moved away to battle, but her eloquence was in vain. Her husband, Allan, was taken prisoner, and as Loyalists their property was forfeit. She left two years later, then aged fifty-six, for her original home on Skye.

Fifty men were killed, wounded or drowned; 850 were taken prisoner; and they lost 1500 rifles, 350 muskets, much cash and even more prestige.

The channel into Charleston's splendid harbour was guarded by a log-and-earth fort on Sullivan's Island commanded by Colonel William Moultrie (whose brother John, as it happened, was a keen Tory). Clinton's troops failed to take the fort, either from a lack of boats, guts or intelligence. On 24 August the general wrote to Lord George Germain, who published the letter in the New York Gazette:

It appears by Lieutenant General Clinton's letter to Lord George Germain dated July 8, 1776, from the camp on Long Island, province of South Carolina, that Sir Peter Parker and the general, having received intelligence that the fortress erected by the rebels on Sullivan's Island (the key to Charleston harbour) was in an imperfect and unfinished state, resolved to attempt the reduction thereof by a *coup de main* and that in order that the army might co-operate with the fleet the general landed his troops on Long Island, which had been represented to him as communicating to Sullivan's Island by a ford passable at low water; but that he, to his very great mortification, found a channel, which was reported to have been eighteen inches deep at low water, to be seven feet deep, which circumstances rendered it impossible for the army to give that assistance to the fleet in the attack made upon the fortress that the general intended, and which he and the other troops under his command ardently wished to do . . . The cannonade of the fleet continued without any favourable appearances till night. Expecting, however, that it would be renewed in the morning, I made the best disposition I could of the small ordnance we could collect, to enable me if necessary whilst the tide suited, to have made one effort on Sullivan's Island, an attempt contrary, I must confess, to every military principle and justifiable only in the cases of the fleet's success or distress, to support the one or relieve the other. But at break of day, to our great concern, we found the fleet had retired, leaving a frigate aground, which was afterward, by order, set on fire. In this situation any feeble effort of ours could answer no good purpose, and finding the fleet had suffered considerably, and that the commodore had no intentions of renewing the attack, I proposed to him that as soon as possible I might proceed with the troops under my command to the north-ward.

The ships began a 'furious and incessant cannonade' but the fort's palmetto logs absorbed the shells — the palmetto is still appropriately the state's symbol. Moultrie's guns made a slaughter-house of the British ships, and the flagship Bristol *was hit seventy times. Sir Peter sailed away on 21 June, and* The Annual Register *for once was severe in its comments:*

To suppose that the Generals, and the Officers under their command should have been nineteen days in that small island, without ever examining until the very instant of action the nature of the only passage by which they could render service to their friends and fellows, fulfill the purpose of their landing and answer the ends for which they were embarked in the expedition would seem a great defect in military prudence and circumspection.

The Americans were properly jubilant.

A NEW WAR SONG
by Sir Peter Parker

(Tune: 'Well Met, Brother Tar')

My Lords, with your leave
An account I will give
That deserves to be written in meter;
For the Rebels and I
Have been pretty nigh —
Faith! almost too nigh for Sir Peter.

With much labour and toil
Unto Sullivan's Isle

62

I came fierce as Falstaff or Pistol,
But the Yankees (God rot 'em) —
I could not get at 'em —
Most terribly mauled my poor *Bristol*.

Bold Clinton by land
Did quietly stand
While I made a thundering clatter;
But the channel was deep
So he could only peep
And not venture over the water.

De'il take 'em; their shot
Came so swift and so hot
And the cowardly dogs stood so stiff sirs,
That I put ship about
And was glad to get out
Or they would have left me a skiff sirs!

Now bold as a Turk
I proceed to New York
Where with Clinton and Howe you may find me
I've the wind in my tail
And am hoisting my sail
To leave Sullivan's Island behind me.

But, my lords, do not fear,
For before the next year,
(Altho' a small island could fret us),
The Continent whole
We shall take, by my soul
If the cowardly Yankee will let us.

The last ship left on 2 August, the day the news reached Charleston that the Declaration of Independence had been signed.

On 12 April 1776 the Provincial Congress of North Carolina instructed its delegates to the Continental Congress 'to concur with the Delegates of the other Colonies in declaring Independence'. Virginia, a month later, instructed its representatives to 'propose' independence. It was thus in May 1776 that Richard Henry Lee of Virginia, his hand swathed in a black handkerchief to conceal the scars of an injury, put the rising temper of the country into words:

RESOLVED, That these United Colonies are, and of a right ought to be, free and independent States, that they are absolved from all allegiance to the British Crown, and that all political connections between them and the State of Great Britain is, and ought to be totally dissolved.

That it is expedient forthwith to take the most effectual measures for forming foreign Alliances.

That a plan of confederation be prepared and transmitted to the respective Colonies for their consideration and approbation.

Few had contemplated this resolution even three months before.
The Committee formed to draft the Declaration left the writing, for the most part, to Thomas Jefferson, for reasons Adams gives.

Though a silent member in Congress, he was so prompt, frank, explicit and decisive upon committees and in conversation — not even Samuel Adams was more so — that he soon seized upon my heart; and upon this occasion I gave him my vote, and did all in my power to procure the votes of others. I think he had one more vote than any others and that placed him at the head of the committee. I had the next highest number, and that placed me second. The committee met, discussed the subject, and then appointed Mr Jefferson and me to make the draught, I suppose because we were the first two on the list.

The sub-committee met. Jefferson proposed to me to make the draught.

I said 'I will not.'

'You should do it.'

'Oh! No.'

'Why will you not? You ought to do it.'

'I will not.'

'Why?'

'Reason enough.'

'What can be your reasons?'

'Reason first — you are a Virginian, and a Virginian ought to appear at the head of this business. Reason second — I am obnoxious, suspected and unpopular. You are very much otherwise. Reason third — you can write ten times better than I can.'

'Well,' said Jefferson, 'if you are decided, I will do as well as I can.'

'Very well. When you have drawn it up we will have a meeting.'

A meeting we accordingly had, and conned the paper over. I was delighted with its high tone and the flights of oratory with which it abounded, especially that concerning Negro slavery; though I knew his Southern brethren would never suffer it to pass in Congress, I certainly never would oppose [it]. There were other expressions which I would not have inserted, if I had drawn it up, particularly that which called the King tyrant. I thought this too personal; for I never believed George to be a tyrant in disposition or nature; I always believed him to be deceived by his courtiers on both sides of the Atlantic, and, in his official capacity only, cruel. I thought the expression too passionate, and too much like scolding, for so grave and solemn a document; but as Franklin and Sherman were to inspect it afterwards, I thought it would not become me to strike it out. I consented to report it, and do not now remember that I made or suggested a single alteration.

We reported to the committee of five. It was read, and I do not remember that Franklin or Sherman criticized any thing. We were all in haste. Congress was impatient, and the instrument was reported, as I believe, in Jefferson's handwriting, as he first drew it. Congress cut off about a quarter of it, as I expected they would; but they obliterated some of the best of it, and left all that was exceptionable, if anything in it was. I long wondered that the original draft has not been published, I suppose the reason is the vehement philippic against Negro slavery.

As you justly observe, there is not an idea in it but what had been hackneyed in Congress for two years before. The substance of it is contained in the declaration of rights and the violations of those rights, in the Journals of Congress, in 1774 . . .

Jefferson bridled at the criticism his draft received – the censure of the British people and of the slave trade were deleted – until Franklin counselled him:

I have made it a rule whenever in my power, to avoid becoming the draftsman of papers to be reviewed by a public body. I took my lesson from an incident which I will relate to you. When I was a journeyman printer one of my companions, an apprentice hatter, having served out his time was about to open a shop for himself. The first concern was to have a handsome signboard with a proper inscription. He composed it in these words: 'John Thompson, hatter, makes and sells hats for ready money.' – with the figure of a hat subjoined. But he thought he would submit it to his friends for their amendments. The first he showed it to thought the word 'hatter' tautologous, because followed by the words 'makes hats' which show he was a hatter. It was struck out. The next observed the customers would not care who made the hats. If good and to their mind, they would buy, by whomever made. He struck it out. A third said he thought the words 'for ready money' were useless, as it was not the custom of the place to sell on credit. Everyone who purchased expected to pay. They were parted with, and the inscription now stood: 'John Thompson sells hats.' 'Sells hats?' says his next friend. 'Why nobody will expect you to give them away. What then is the use of that word?' It was stricken out: and 'hats' followed it, the last rather as there was one painted on the board. So his inscription was reduced ultimately to 'John Thompson' with the figure of a hat subjoined.

The draft was presented to the Congress on 1 July. After nine hours of debate, still four Colonies were not in favour – Pennsylvania and South Carolina opposed it, Delaware was divided, the New York Delegation unable to vote because they awaited instruction from home. It was decided to postpone the final vote for one day. By the evening of 2 July, Delaware had voted in support – Caesar Rodney having ridden eighty miles on horseback, and in pain, from Dover to break the deadlock in his delegation.

When, in the Course of human events, it becomes necessary for one people to dissolve the political bands which have connected them with another, and to assume, among the Powers of the earth the separate and equal station to which the Laws of Nature and of Nature's God entitle them, a decent respect to the opinions of mankind requires that they should declare the causes which impel them to the separation.

We hold these truths to be self-evident, that all men are created equal, that they are endowed by their Creator with certain inalienable Rights, that among these, are Life, Liberty, and the pursuit of Happiness. That, to secure these rights, Governments are instituted among Men, deriving their just Powers from the consent of the governed. That, whenever any form of Government becomes destructive of these ends, it is the Right of the People to alter or to abolish it, and to institute new Government, laying its foundation on such Principles, and organizing its Powers in such form, as to them shall seem most likely to effect their Safety and Happiness. Prudence, indeed will dictate that Governments long established should not be changed for light and transient causes; and, accordingly, all experience hath shewn, that mankind are more disposed to suffer, while evils are sufferable, than to right themselves by abolishing the forms to which they are accustomed. But, when a long train of abuses and usurpations, pursuing invariably the same Object, evinces a design to reduce them under absolute Despotism, it is their right, it is their duty, to throw off such Government and to provide new Guards for their future Security. Such has been the patient sufferance of these Colonies; and such is now the necessity which constrains them to alter their former Systems of Government. The history of the present king of Great Britain is a history of repeated injuries and usurpations, all having in direct object the establishment of an absolute Tyranny over these States.

The second paragraph of the Declaration is the classic statement of the Jeffersonian case, even if the ambiguous phrase 'the pursuit of happiness' had replaced the original and more specific word 'property'.

The Gentleman's Magazine *moved from uncertainty in July —*

. . . there is no reasonable ground to conclude . . . that it is either the wish or the intention of the moderate and sensible part of the Americans to withdraw their obedience from the parent state. On the contrary, all America, by which we would be understood to mean a large majority of the industrious inhabitants of that continent, think it their greatest happiness to be considered as the free subjects of a Sovereign of the Brunswick line, by whom alone they can hope to be confirmed in their civil and religious rights, to have their complaints candidly considered, and their grievances redressed; . . . Why then, should we not hope that the King's troops will be received as friends, and that instead of the destroying sword, the Generals do carry with them the olive branch, and that the first news we receive may announce the preliminaries of peace.

— to a counterblast in September:

The declaration is without doubt of the most extraordinary nature both with regard to sentiment and language, and considering that the motive of it is to assign some justifiable reasons of their separating themselves from Great Britain, unless it had been fraught with more truth and sense, might well have been spared, as it reflects no honour upon either their erudition or honesty. We hold, they say, these truths to be self-evident: That all men are created equal. In what are they created equal? Is it in size, strength, understanding, figure, moral or civil accomplishments, or situation of life? Every plough-man knows that they are not created equal in any of these. All men, it is true, are equally created, but what is this to the purpose? It certainly is no reason why the Americans should turn rebels because the people of Great Britain are their fellow creatures, i.e. are created as well as themselves. It may be a reason why they should not rebel, but most indisputably is none why they should. They therefore have introduced their self-evident truths, either through ignorance, or by design, with a self-evident falsehood: since I will defy any American rebel, or any of their patriotic retainers here in England, to point out to me any two men, throughout the whole World, of whom it may with truth be said that they are created equal.

Most, though by no means all, Americans greeted the Declaration with jubilation. Jonathan Boucher preached his sermons with a revolver resting alongside his Bible in his pulpit, and soon sailed home.

Hence it follows, that we are free, or otherwise, as we are governed by law, or by the mere arbitrary will, or wills, of any individual, or any number of individuals. And liberty is not the setting at nought and despising established laws – much less the making our own wills the rule of our own actions, or the actions of others – and not bearing (whilst we dictate to others) the being dictated to, even by the laws of the land; but it is the being governed by law, and by law only. The Greeks described Eleutheria, or Liberty, as the daughter of Jupiter, the supreme fountain of power and law. And the Romans, in like manner, always drew her with the pretor's wand (the emblem of legal power and authority) as well as with the cap. Their idea, no doubt was, that liberty was the fair fruit of just authority, and that it consisted in men's being subjected to law. The more carefully well devised restraints of law are enacted, and the more rigorously they are executed in any country, the greater degree of civil liberty does that country enjoy. To pursue liberty then, in a manner not warranted by law, whatever the pretence may be, is clearly to be hostile to liberty: and those persons who thus promise you liberty are themselves the *servants of corruption* . . . True liberty, then, is a liberty to do every thing that is right, and the being restrained from doing any thing that is wrong. So far from our having a right to do every thing that we please, under a notion of liberty, liberty itself is limited and confined – but limited and confined only by laws which are at the same time both its foundation and its support . . .

On Broadway in New York, near the Battery, Isaac Bangs recounted the attack on the gilded equestrian statue of George III.

Last night the statue in the Bowling Green representing George

68

Gwelphs, alias George Rex, was pulled down by the populace. In it were 4,000 pounds of lead, and a man undertook to take 10 ozs of gold from the superfices, as both men and horse were covered with gold leaf. The lead, we hear, is to be run up into musket balls for the use of the Yankees, when it is hoped that the emanations from the leaden George will make as deep impressions in the bodies of some of his redcoated and Tory subjects, and that they will do the same execution in poisoning and destroying them as the superabundant emanations of the folly and pretended goodness of the real George, have made upon their minds, which have effectually poisoned and destroyed their souls, that they are not worthy to be ranked with any beings who have any pretensions to the principles of virtue and justice, but would to God that the unhappy contest might be ended, without putting us to the disagreeable necessity of sending them to dwell with those beings, for the company of whom alone their tempers and dispositions are now suitable.

It was estimated that 42,000 bullets could be manufactured from the statue, so that, in Ebenezer Hazard's words, 'the bloody-backs could have melted Majesty fired into them'.

In Virginia, royal Governor Lord Dunmore gave up the struggle to control his colony from the warship, HMS Fowey, *lying off battered Norfolk. With his men at the receiving end of General Andrew Lewis' cannon — the two men had fought together only two years before in 'Dunmore's War' against the Shawnee — and with the troops riddled with smallpox, he abandoned Gwyn's Island and sailed out of Chesapeake Bay.*

There was a last minute effort at a settlement, when a committee of the Congress, consisting of Franklin, Rutledge and John Adams, had a meeting on Staten Island with Admiral Lord Howe, Sir William's brother, on 11 September 1776. It proved unsatisfactory. On 20 July 1776, Franklin had written to Lord Howe making plain the extent of the gap between them. They had, just over a year before, held discussions in London, with the same purpose, also without result. The divide now was final. Franklin's letter, indeed, was his own personal declaration of independence.

Long did I endeavor, with unfeigned and unwearied zeal, to preserve from breaking that fine and noble china vase, the British empire; for I knew that, being once broken, the separate parts could not retain even their share of the strength or value that existed in the whole, and that a perfect reunion of those parts could scarce ever be hoped for. Your Lordship may possibly remember the tears of joy that wet my cheek, when, at your good sister's in London, you once gave me expectations that a reconciliation might soon take place. I had the misfortune to find those expectations disappointed, and to be treated as the cause of the mischief I was laboring to prevent. My consolation under that groundless and malevolent treatment was that I retained the friendship of many wise and good men in that country, and, among the rest, some share in the regard of Lord Howe.

I consider this war against us, therefore, as both unjust and unwise; and I am persuaded that cool, dispassionate posterity will condemn to infamy those who advised it; and that even success will not save from some degree of dishonor those who voluntarily engaged to conduct it. I know your great motive in coming hither was the hope of being instrumental in a reconciliation; and I believe, when you find *that* impossible on any terms given you to propose, you will relinquish so odious a command, and return to a more honorable private station.

In London, a triumvirate directed the war: North, Germain and Sandwich. Lord North, who was later to succeed to the family title as 2nd Earl of Guilford, was First Lord of the Treasury from 1770 until his resignation in March 1782. He had supported the tea tax but had no illusions of his own capacity in handling a war. 'On military matters', he said, 'I speak ignorantly and therefore without effect.' On several occasions he tried to resign, but the king overruled him. North was an expert at controlling the business of the House and at Treasury matters; he had a wry sense of humour, immense capacity for work and for self-deprecation, and he was much liked in the House.

Lord George Germain (Viscount Sackville from 1782) joined North's Cabinet in November 1775 and was responsible for colonial policy and for the conduct of the war. He behaved towards others with arrogance and scorn. He had served as a major-general in Europe during the Seven Years' War and had been court-martialled after the Battle of Minden and found guilty of disobeying orders, 'unfit to serve . . . in any military capacity whatever'. This verdict, it is now believed, was unduly harsh. His industry and expertise were never questioned but his personal judgements were often at fault, and he certainly put too much trust in Burgoyne. His real handicap, however, was probably less temperamental than meteorological: distance, climate and weather could — and usually did — wreck the best laid plans.

The Earl of Sandwich, First Lord of the Admiralty from 1771, was notorious for both private and public immorality. The Whig Opposition, and later (usually Whig) historians have denigrated him, but he was, in fact, shrewd and energetic. He guarded the Admiralty as a personal fief and admitted in a letter to Lord North, 'I could never understand the real state of the fleet.'

As Americans celebrated their Independence, the largest armada ever assembled in American waters was beginning to put men ashore on Staten Island. To oppose the disciplined British redcoats, some 20,000 strong, Washington had only 8500 ill-trained troops. They were subject, Colonel Baldwin wrote frankly to his wife, to the customary urban temptations.

The whores (by information) continue their employ, which is become very lucrative. Their unparalleled conduct is a sufficient antidote against any desires that a person can have that has one spark of modesty or virtue left in him . . . Perhaps you will call me censorious and exclaim too much upon bare reports when I say that I was never within the doors of nor exchanged a word with any of them except in the execution of my duty as officer of the day in going the grand round with my guard of escort, have broke up the knots of men and women fighting, pulling caps, swearing, crying, 'Murder!' etc, hurried them off to the Provost Dungeon by half dozens, there let them lay mixed till next day. Then some are punished and some get off clear – Hell's work . . .

Young Lord Rawdon found a different situation when his jaded troops were brought back from the abortive Charleston expedition.

The fair nymphs of this isle are in wonderful tribulation, as the fresh meat our men have got here has made them as riotous as satyrs. A girl cannot step into the bushes to pluck a rose without running the most imminent risk of being ravished, and they are so little accustomed to these vigorous methods that they don't bear them with the proper resignation, and of consequence we have the most entertaining courts-martial every day.

To the southward they behave much better in these cases, if I may judge from a woman who having been forced by seven of our men, made complaint to me, not of their usage, she said, No, thank God, she despised that, but one of them having taken an old prayer book for which she had a particular affection . . .

Despite the European rules against summer campaigning, and despite the thirteen-pounder musket and heavy clothing, Howe's men moved with briskness and efficiency. On 22 August – by which time he had 30,000 troops, and after a night of 'thunder, lightning and prodigious heavy rain' – between eight o'clock in the morning and noon, Howe put 15,000 men, forty cannon and the horses for his dragoons on the Long Island beaches. The British forces then moved from Long Island to Manhattan, and at each stage drove back Washington's forces ignominiously.

71

The fact however was that their want of judgement had shone equally conspicuous during the whole of this affair. They had imagined (which to say the truth our former method of beginning always at the wrong end had given them some reason to suppose) that we should land directly in front of their works, march up and attack them without further precaution in their strongest points. They had accordingly fortified those points with their utmost strength, and totally neglected the left flank, which was certainly incapable of defence. It was by marching round to this quarter that we had so totally surprised them on the 27th, so that the possibility of our taking that route seems never to have entered into their imaginations. If we could by any means have known their intentions that night, 7 or 8,000 or whatever number there were of them must have been destroyed.

A rifleman who had resisted the 57th Foot in the morning finished his account of the day's adventure:

. . . the main body of British, by a route we never dreamed of, had surrounded us, and driven within the lines or scattered in the woods, all our men except the Delaware and Maryland battalions, who were standing at bay with double their number. Thus situated we were ordered to attempt a retreat by fighting our way through the enemy, who had posted themselves and nearly filled every road and field between us and our lines. We had not retreated a quarter of a mile, before we were fired on by an advanced party of the enemy, and those in the rear playing their artillery on us. Our men fought with more than Roman valour. We forced the advanced party which first attacked us to give way, through which opening we got a passage sown to the side of a marsh, seldom before waded over, which we passed, and then swam a narrow river, all the while exposed to the enemy's fire . . . The whole of the right wing of our battalion, thinking it impossible to march through the marsh, attempted to force their way through the woods, where they, almost to a man, were killed or taken . . .

Most of our generals on a high hill in the lines, viewed us with glasses, as we were retreating, and saw the enemy we had to pass through, though we could not. Many thought we would surrender in a body without firing. When we began the attack General Washington wrung his hands, and cried out, 'Good God! what brave fellows I must this day lose!'

Although Sir William won the Order of the Bath, not all his fellow-officers

72

approved. Sir George Collier, in his cabin on the Rainbow *was sarcastic:*

Washington's army amounted to 11,000 men; ours was at least double that number. They, having to deal with a generous, merciful *forbearing* enemy, who would take no unfair *advantages*, must surely have been highly satisfactory to General Washington, and he was certainly very deficient in not expressing his gratitude to General Howe for his *kind* behaviour towards him. Far from taking the rash resolution of hastily passing over the East River after Gates and *crushing at once* a frightened, trembling enemy, he generously gave them time to recover from their panic, to throw up *fresh works*, to make new arrangements, and to recover from the torpid state the rebellion appeared in from its late shock.

Sir William was within half an hour of capturing Washington before he crossed the Hudson from Fort Washington to the Jersey shore. Perhaps he missed him deliberately, since the Howe brothers were peace commissioners as well as commanders, and wanted a surrender not an execution.

Discipline, Washington found, was hard to maintain. Lewis Morris of Morrisania in Westchester reported to his father, then serving in the Continental Congress.

As for the militia of Connecticut, Brigadier [Oliver] Wolcott and his whole brigade have got the cannon fever and very prudently skulked home. Such people are only a nuisance and had better be in the chimney corner than in the field of Mars. We have men enough without them who will fight and whose glory is the defense of their country – Colonel Hand's regiment plunder everybody in Westchester County indiscriminately, even yourself has not escaped. Montresor's island they plundered and committed the most unwarrantable destruction upon it, fifty dozens of bottles were broke in the cellar, the paper tore from the rooms and every pane of glass broke to pieces. His furniture and clothes were brought over to Morrisania and sold at public auction. Jimmy DeLancey, Oliver, and John, after giving their parole, are gone off to the enemy and their house is plundered. Mrs Wilkins is upon Long Island with her husband and her house is plundered, and hers and Mrs Moncrief's clothes were sold at vendue. Seabury has likewise eloped, and Mrs Wilkins has very industriously propagated that you had fled to France. Such brimstones will certainly meet their desert.

Washington was close to despair, as he told his brother Lund:

. . . Such is my situation that if I were to wish the bitterest curse to an

73

enemy on this side of the grave, I should put him in my stead with my feelings; and yet I do not know what plan of conduct to pursue. I see the impossibility of serving with reputation, or doing any essential service to the cause by continuing in command, and yet I am told that if I quit the command, inevitable ruin will follow from the distraction that will ensue.

But he was warmed by the reports of camaraderie across the enemy lines:

. . . and they were so civil to each other, on their posts, that one day, at a part of the creek where it was practicable, the British sentinel asked the American, who was nearly opposite to him, if he could give him a chew of tobacco: the latter, having in his pocket a piece of a thick twisted roll, sent it across the creek, to the British sentinel, who after taking off his bite, sent the remainder back again.

Whether by chance or design part of New York was destroyed by fire as Howe's secretary, Ambrose Serle, reported:

Some rebels who lurked about the town, set it on fire, and some of them were caught with matches and fire-balls about them. One man, detected in the act, was knocked down by a grenadier and thrown into the flames for his reward. Another who was found cutting off the handles of the water buckets to prevent their use, was first hung up by the neck till he was dead and afterwards by the heels upon a sign post by the sailors. Many others were seized on account of combustibles found upon them, and secured and, but for the officers, most of them would have been killed by the enraged populace and soldiery. The New England people are maintained to be at the bottom of this plot, which they have long since threatened to put into execution.

I walked on shore about noon, surveyed the devastation, which has taken in, 'tis supposed, about one fifth of the city . . .

There was now, as from Washington's Adjutant-General Joseph Reed, even some criticism of the commander-in-chief. He was given the name of 'the old fox', at first in disparagement; in the end as tribute to his shrewdness.

When I look around and see how few of the numbers who talked so largely of death and honour [are] around me, and those who are here are those from whom it could least be expected, I am lost in wonder and surprise. Your noisy Sons of Liberty I find are the quietest on the field . . .

Finding how things were going, I went over to the General to get some support for the brave fellows, who had behaved so well. By the time I got to him, the enemy appeared in open view, and in the most insulting manner sounded their bugle horns as is usual after a fox chase. I never felt such a sensation before. It seemed to crown our disgrace.

Oh! General – an indecisive mind is one of the greatest misfortunes that can befall an army. How often have I lamented it this campaign.

Reed was echoed even by his second-in-command, the erratic ex-British regular Charles Lee, though he was neither reliable nor trustworthy.

The ingenious manoeuvre of Fort Washington had unhinged the goodly fabrick we had been building. There never was so damned a stroke. *Entre nous*, a certain great man is most damnably deficient. He has thrown me into a situation where I have my choice of difficulties. If I stay in this Province I risk myself and army, and if I do not stay the Province is lost forever. I have neither guides, cavalry, medicines, money, shoes or stockings. I must act with the greatest circumspection. Tories are in my front, rear and on my flanks. The mass of the people is strangely contaminated.

Washington himself, always conservative, saw the need for a permanent army, the Continental Line, hierarchical, disciplined, and paid on time, and said so to his superiors.

It becomes evidently clear then, that as this Contest is not likely to be the Work of a day; as the War must be carried on systematically, and to do it, you must have good Officers, there are, in my Judgement, no other possible means to obtain them but by establishing your Army upon a permanent footing; and giving your Officers good pay; this will induce Gentlemen, and Men of Character to engage; and till the bulk of your Officers are composed of such persons as are actuated by Principles of honour, and a spirit of enterprise, you will have little to expect from them. – They ought to have such allowances as will enable them to live like, and support the Characters of Gentlemen; and not be driven by a scanty pittance to the low, and dirty arts which many of them practise, to filch the Publick of more than the difference of pau would amount to upon an ample allowance. Besides something is due to the Man who puts his life in his hand, hazards his health, and foresakes the Sweets of domestick enjoyments. Why a Captn. in the Continental Service should receive no more than 5/- Curry per day, for performing the same duties that an officer of the same Rank in the British Army receives 10/– Sterlg. for, I never could conceive; especially when the latter is provided with every necessity he requires, upon the best terms, and the former can scarce procure them, at any Rate. There is nothing that gives a Man consequence, and renders him fit for Command, like a support that renders him Independent of every body but the State he Serves.

In fact Congress had anticipated Washington. On 16 September 1776 it overcame its 'jealousy of a standing army' and agreed to establish a Continental Line. Surgeon James Thacher set it out:

To encourage enlistments, each soldier is to receive a bounty of twenty dollars, besides his wages and rations, and one hundred acres of land, if he serve during the war. The officers are to receive land in proportion to their respective ranks, from two hundred and five hundred acres. Their monthly pay is to be as follows:

Colonel, a month	$75.00	Lieutenant	$27.00
Lieutenant Colonel	60.00	Ensign	20.00
Major	50.00	Serjeant Major	9.00
Chaplain	33.33	Quarter-Master Serjeant	9.00
Surgeon	33.33	Drum-Major	8.00
Surgeon's-mate	18.00	Fife-Major	8.33
Adjutant	40.00	Serjeant	8.00
Quarter-Master	27.50	Corporal	7.33
Regimental Pay-master	26.67	Drummer and fifer	7.33
Captain	40.00	Privates	6.67

At the same time, they decided on the army's rations, but the amounts were, in fact, honoured more in theory than in observance.

One pound of beef or three-quarters of a pound of pork, or one pound of salt fish, per day; one pound of bread or flour per day; three pints of peas or beans per week, or vegetables equivalent, at six Shillings per bushel for peas or beans; one pint of milk per day, or at the rate of one Penny per pint; one half pint of rice, or one pint of Indian meal, per man per week; one quart of spruce beer or cider per man, per day, or nine gallons of molasses per Company of one hundred men, per week; three pounds of candles to one hundred men, per week, for squads; twenty-four pounds of soft, or eight pounds of hard soap, for one hundred men, per week.

Meanwhile, the Loyalist Thomas Hutchinson, in what was to become permanent exile in London, saw the harshness of the city for those who had guessed wrongly about the duration of the struggle. It was proving to be a long war.

It is certain that a prodigeous armament is preparing, and will be very soon sailing in one large body after another, until the whole is gone for America. The destination of the several parts, I am not able to tell you. As the command will be in the two brothers, one by sea, the other by land, people are less inquisitive than otherwise they would be. I do not think a choice of men could have been made more generally satisfactory to the kingdom, and under Providence, I think we may found a reasonable hope for a more favourable summer than the last. We Americans are plenty here, and very cheap. Some of us at first coming, are apt to think ourselves of importance, but other people do not think so, and few, if any of us are much consulted, or enquired after.

Washington did not rest easy until he had retreated across the Jerseys, and the Delaware flowed between the two armies. A British officer described the rebels' retreat:

As we go forward into the country, the rebels flee before us, and when we come back they always follow us, 'tis almost impossible to catch them. They will neither fight, nor totally run away, but they keep at such distance that we are always above a day's march from them. They seem to be playing at Bo Peep.

But even when he lost his militia – the Long Faces, who insisted on returning to their own firesides by the end of the year – Washington held on. He told Reed in December 1776:

My neck does not feel as though it was made for a halter. We must retire to Augusta County in Virginia, and . . . if overpowered, we must pass the Allegheny Mountains.

Both sides lived off the country in more senses than one. The Pennsylvania Council of Safety described the British depredations:

I have had an opportunity of hearing a number of the horrid depredations committed by that part of the British army which was stationed near Pennytown, under the command of Lord Cornwallis. Besides the

77

sixteen young women who had fled to the woods to avoid their brutality, and were there seized and carried off, one man had the mortification to have his wife and only daughter (a child of ten years of age) ravished; this he himself, almost choked with grief, uttered in lamentations to his friend, who told me of it, and also informed me that another girl of thirteen years of age was taken from her father's house, carried to a barn about a mile [away], there ravished, and afterwards made use of by five more of these brutes.

Furniture of every kind destroyed or burnt, windows and doors broke to pieces; in short, the houses left uninhabitable, and the people left without provisions, for every horse, cow, ox, hogs and poultry carried off, a blind old gentleman near Pennytown plundered of everything, and on his door wrote, 'Capt. Wills of the Royal Irish did this.'

The Americans not only assaulted women – especially those they suspected of being Tory – but they ransacked cellars too. At Brunswick, according to Lieutenant James McMichael:

Here our soldiers drank of spiritous liquors. They have chiefly got a disorder, which at camp is called the Barrel Fever, which differs in its effects from any other fever – its concomitants are black eyes and bloody noses.

Tom Paine, the British-born author of Common Sense, *was now with Washington's army, and, in the first of the series entitled* The American Crisis, *caught its spirit. His stirring tract was read to the troops.*

These are the times that try men's souls. The summer soldier and the sunshine patriot will, in this crisis, shrink from the services of his country; but he that stands it now, deserves the love and thanks of man and woman. Tyranny, like Hell, is not easily conquered; yet we have this consolation with us, that the harder the conflict the more glorious the triumph.

By 14 December, Howe saw the 1776 campaign as over, and distributed his 14,000 troops in a long line of posts from Staten Island to the Delaware. He settled in New York with the wife of his commissary, Mrs Loring, and was reported to be happy.

Then, suddenly, on Christmas night, before all his militia had departed and before the river froze, Washington crossed the ice-choked Delaware with 2400 men, the *snow cutting like a knife, and surprised Colonel Rall and his still festive Hessians* at Trenton. Rall was killed and nearly 1000 of his men captured.*

The Hessians were just ready to open fire with two of their cannon when Captain [William] Washington and Lieutenant [James] Monroe, with their men rushed forward and captured them. We saw Rall riding up the street from his headquarters, which were at Stacy Pott's house. We could hear him shouting in Dutch, 'My brave soldiers, advance.' His men were frightened and confused, for our men were firing upon them from fences and houses and they were falling fast. Instead of advancing they ran into an apple orchard. The officers tried to rally them, but our men kept advancing and picking off the officers.

Elisha Bostwick recalled the difficulties not only of the crossing, but of the re-crossing of the Delaware.

When crossing the Delaware with the prisoners in flat bottom boats the ice continually stuck to the boats, driving them down stream; the boatmen endevering to clear off the ice pounded the boat, and stamping with their feet, beconed to the prisoners to do the same, and they all set to jumping at once with their cues flying up and down, soon shook off the ice from the boats, and the next day re-crossed the Delaware again and returned back to Trenton, and there on the first of January 1777 our yeers service expired, and then by the pressing solicitations of his Excellency a part of those whose time was out consented on a ten dollar bounty to stay six weeks longer, and altho desirious as others to return home, I engaged to stay that time and made every exertion in my power to make as many of the soldiers stay with me as I could, and quite a number did engage with me who otherwise would have went home . . .

Washington did not lose a single man in the action; however, Lieutenant (and future President) James Monroe was wounded, and two men froze to death.

* The Hessians (from the area known as Hesse-Cassel) were German mercenaries recruited by the British mainly, but not exclusively, to fight in America. The British government had at its command a large navy but only a small army and it was common for Britain — and indeed for most nations at war — to recruit mercenaries. In this instance, Russia was approached first, but Queen Catherine, preoccupied with fighting the Turks, refused the British application. So the British government turned to Germany, and 30,000 Germans eventually fought for the king. Colonel Rall, there-fore, would have shouted in German; 'Dutch' being a well-known colonial mis-translation of 'Deutsche'.

1777

Oh fatal ambition!
Poor General Burgoyne!

With Cornwallis in pursuit, twelve days later the 'old fox' left fires burning to deceive the enemy and, after a night's march, struck at Princeton, inflicting heavy casualties – some three hundred British killed or wounded. His image restored, Washington settled into winter quarters at Morristown.

His numbers by this time were little more than 3000, and of these the militia started melting away on completion of their engagements at the end of the year. A determined British drive could have destroyed him, but it did not come. According to the rule-book, winter was for hibernating, not for warring. Howe was in New York, Cornwallis at Brunswick, General John Vaughan at Amboy.

Martha Washington joined her husband in camp at Morristown, and so did Martha Dangerfield Bland, wife of Colonel Theodorick Bland of Virginia. Mrs Bland wrote to her sister-in-law, Fanny Randolph, describing how the resting military spent their days.

I found Morris a very clever little village . . . in a most beautiful valley at the foot of five mountains. It has three houses with steeples which give it a consequential look . . . It has two families, refugees from New York, in it, otherwise it is inhabited by the errantist rustics you ever beheld . . . There are some exceeding pretty girls, but they appear to have souls formed for the distaff, rather than the tender passions, and really I never met with such pleasant-looking creatures. And the most inhospitable mortals breathing. You can get nothing from them but, 'dreadful good water', as they term everything that is good. Desperate and dreadful are their favourite words. You'd laugh to hear them talk . . .

Now let me speak of our noble and agreeable commander (for he commands both sexes, one by his excellent skill in military matters, the other by his ability, politeness, and attention). We visit them twice or three times a week by particular invitation. Every day frequently from inclination. He is generally busy in the forenoon, but from dinner till night he is free for all company. His worthy lady seems to be in perfect felicity, while she is by the side of her 'Old Man', as she calls him. We often make parties on horseback, the General, his Lady, Miss Livingston, and his aides-de-camp, who are Colonel [John] Fitzgerald, an agreeable broad-shouldered Irishman; Colonel [George] Johnston . . . who is exceedingly witty at everybody's expense, but can't allow other people to be so at his own, though they often take the liberty; Colonel [Alexander] Hamilton, a sensible, genteel, polite young fellow, a West Indian; Colonel [Richard Kidder] Meade; Colonel [Tench] Tilghman, a modest, worthy man who from his attachment to the General voluntarily lives in his family and acts in any capacity that is uppermost without fee or reward; Colonel [Robert Hanson] Harrison, brother of Billy Harrison that kept store in Petersburg and as much like him as possible, a worthy man; Captain [Caleb] Gibbs of the General's Guard, a good-natured Yankee who makes a thousand blunders in the Yankee style and keeps the dinner table in constant laugh. These are the General's family, all polite, sociable gentlemen, who make the day pass with a great deal of satisfaction to the visitors. But I had forgot my subject almost, this is our riding party, generally at which time General Washington throws off the hero and takes on the chatty agreeable companion. He can be downright impudent sometimes, such impudence, Fanny, as you and I like, and really, I have wished for you often.

Nicholas Cresswell, the British traveller, noted the tonic effect of Washington's success on American morale:

Volunteer companies are collecting in every county on the continent and in a few months the rascals will be stronger than ever. Even the parsons, some of them, have turned out as volunteers and pulpit drums or thunder, which you please to call it, summoning all to arms in this cursed babel. Damn them all.

There was now anguished soul-searching in the British ranks. Cornwallis had his promised home-leave sharply cancelled, and cursed that this unlucky affair 'of Rall's brigade' had 'given me a winter campaign'. Lieutenant-Colonel Allan Maclean thought that the fault lay higher up, as he wrote to Alexander Cummings from New York on 19 February.

Indeed, I find our mistakes in the campaign were many and some very capital ones; but I know I am writing to a friend who has some prudence and will not expose me, tho' I write real truths . . .

After what I said it would be unjust not to say that General Howe is a very honest man, and I believe a very disinterested one. Brave he certainly is and would make a very good executive officer under another's command, but he is not by any means equal to a C in C. I do not know any employment that requires so many great qualifications either natural or acquired as the Commander in Chief of an Army. He has moreover, got none but very silly fellows about him – a great parcel of old women – most of them improper for American service. I could be very ludicrous on this occasion, but it is truly too serious a matter that brave men's lives should be sacrificed to be commanded by such generals.

For excepting Earl Percy, Lord Cornwallis, both Lt Generals, and the Brigadier Generals Leslie and Sir William Erskine, the rest are useless. Lord Percy is greatly distinguished with Gen. Howe; Lord Cornwallis is, I believe, a brave man, but he allowed himself to be fairly out-generalled by Washington, the 4th January last at Trenton, and missed a glorious opportunity when he let Washington slip away in the night.

Loyalist Justice Jones felt even more strongly and when, in March, Howe was awarded the Order of the Bath, he exploded in anger.

This month was remarkable for the investiture of General Howe with the Order of the Bath, a reward for *evacuating* Boston, for *lying indolent* upon Staten Island for near two months, for suffering the whole rebel army to escape him upon Long Island and again at the White Plains, for *not putting an end to rebellion* in 1776 when so often in his power, for making such *injudicious cantonments* of his troops in Jersey as he did, and for *suffering* ten thousand veterans under experienced generals to be cooped up in Brunswick and Amboy for nearly six months by about six thousand militia under the command of an inexperienced general.

By the middle of May Washington had increased his forces to nearly 9000 men. Nicholas Cresswell, who had visited Mount Vernon before the outbreak of war, was impressed:

Washington is certainly a most surprising man, one of Nature's geniuses, a Heaven-born general, if there is any of that sort. That a Negro driver should with a ragged banditti of undisciplined people, the scum and refuse of all nations on earth, so long keep a British general at bay, nay, even oblige him, with as fine an army of veteran soldiers as ever England had on the American continent, to retreat, it is astonishing . . .

General Howe, a man brought up to war from his youth, to be puzzled and plagued for two years together with a Virginia tobacco-planter. O! Britain, how thy laurels tarnish in the hands of such a lubber! . . .

[Washington] undoubtedly pants for military fame and, considering the little military knowledge and experience he had before he was made a general, he has performed wonders. He was generally unfortunate (indeed I may with propriety say always) in every action where he was immediately concerned until the affair at Trenton in the Jerseys. Since that unlucky period (for us) he has only been too successful. His education is not very great nor his parts shining, his disposition is rather heavy than volatile, much given to silence. In short, he is but a poor speaker and but shines in the epistolary way. His person is tall and genteel, age betwixt forty and fifty, his behaviour and deportment is easy, genteel, and obliging, with a certain something about him which pleases everyone who has anything to do with him. There cannot be a greater proof of his particular address and good conduct than his keeping such a number of refractory, headstrong people together in any tolerable degree of decorum . . .

From my personal acquaintance with him, and from everything that I have been able to learn of him, I believe him to be a worthy honest man, guilty of no bad vice, except we reckon ambition amongst the number, and here we ought to reckon charitably. The temptation was very great to a mind naturally ambitious. Nature made him too weak to resist it.

As an officer he is quite popular, almost idolized by the southern provinces, but I think he is not so great a favorite with the northern ones. The ignorant and deluded part of the people look up to him as the Savior and Protector of their country, and have implicit confidence in everything he does. The artful and designing part of the people, that is, the Congress, and those at the head of affairs, look upon him as a necessary tool to compass their diabolical purposes.

He certainly deserves some merit as a general, that he with his banditti, can keep General Howe dancing from one town to another for two years together, with such an army as he has. Confound the great Chucklehead, he will not unmuzzle the mastiffs, or they would eat him and his ragged crew in a little time were they properly conducted with a man of resolution and spirit. Washington, my enemy as he is, I should be sorry if he should be brought to an ignominious death.

Howe realised he had to take the initiative: Washington's tactics, if not his temperament, required delay. On 23 July he sailed away from New York with 15,000 men, and headed for Philadelphia. But instead of sailing up the Delaware, Howe thought the river too hazardous and sailed around Cape Charles and up the Chesapeake, baffling Washington and his army, who found themselves 'compelled to wander about the country like Arabs in search of corn'. Howe's men landed at Head of Elk in Maryland, fifty-five miles away from Philadelphia, while Washington marched his army across country and positioned it between the city and the enemy.

Every man was to wear a green sprig in his hat as an 'emblem of hope', and not only were they to carry their arms well, but the drums and fifes were cautioned to play a quickstep, 'but with such moderation, that the men may step to it with ease, and without dancing along, or totally disregarding the music'. John Adams, who had earlier worried about the weather, 'which will spoil our show and wet the army', described the parade of Sunday, 24 August, to Abigail.

Four grand divisions of the army, and the artillery with the matrosses. They marched twelve deep, and yet took above two hours in passing by, General Washington and the other general officers with their aides on horseback. The Colonels and other field officers on horseback. We have now an army well appointed between us and Mr Howe and this army will be immediately joined by ten thousand militia, so that I feel as secure as if I were at Braintree, but not so happy. My happiness is nowhere to be found but there . . .

The army, upon an accurate inspection of it, I find to be extremely well armed, pretty well clothed, and tolerably disciplined . . . There is

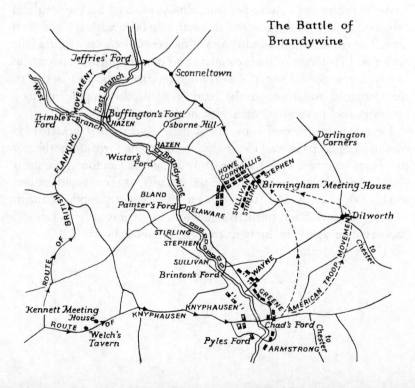

The Battle of Brandywine

such a mixture of the sublime and the beautiful together with the useful in military discipline, that I wonder every officer we have is not charmed with it. Much remains to be done. Our soldiers have not quite the air of soldiers. They don't step exactly in time. They don't hold up their heads quite erect, nor turn out their toes so exactly as they ought. They don't all of them cock their hats, and such as do, don't all wear the same way.

Washington stationed his men on the Brandywine Creek, which runs parallel to the Schuylkill River (Philadelphia's south-western boundary) and some fifteen to twenty miles to the west of that stream. There were seven or eight fords, one or more of which the British would have to use to reach Philadelphia; of these, Chad's Ford seemed the most likely. General Sullivan guarded the fords upstream.

Howe repeated his Long Island operation turning the American right flank. It all went according to plan, as Major John André recorded.

The design, it seemed was that General Knyphausen, taking post at Chad's Ford, should begin early to cannonade the enemy on the opposite side, thereby to take up his attention and make him presume an attack was then intended with the whole army, whilst the other column should be performing the *detour*. Lord Cornwallis's wing being engaged was to be the signal for the troops under General Knyphausen to cross the ford when they were to push their advantage.

Washington was totally deceived by this manoeuvre, as Colonel Timothy Pickering's journal attests:

September 11th This morning a cannonade took place, the enemy having advanced to the heights opposite to those occupied by us, on the other side of the ford . . . The enemy made no attempt to cross at this place.

The enemy remaining paraded on the distant heights, and continuing the cannonade, induced me to think they did not intend to cross at Chad's Ford, but only to amuse us while their main army crossed at some other place. The event proved the conjecture right. The enemy's main body crossed the Brandywine six or eight miles above, on our right. The General had intelligence of this by some messenger; but it was contradicted by others; and, the information remaining a long time surprisingly uncertain, it was late before a disposition was made to receive the enemy on that quarter.

The whole army this night retired to Chester. It was fortunate for us that the night came on, for under its cover the fatigued stragglers and some wounded made their escape.

The Americans lost over 1000 men, the British 500, so the diary of Joseph Clark of Princeton made gloomy reading.

The sun was set when I left the hill from whence I saw the fate of the day. His Excellency I saw within 200 yards of the enemy, with but a small party about him, and they drawing off from their station, our army broke at the right, and night coming on, adding a gloom to our misfortunes, amidst the noise of cannon, the hurry of people, and wagons driving in confusion from the field, I came off with a heart full of distress. In painful anxiety I took with hasty step the gloomy path from the field, and travelled 15 miles to Chester, where I slept two hours upon a couple of chairs . . .

Sergeant Major John Hawkins of Congress' Own Regiment found his predicament very confusing.

I lost my knapsack, which contained the following articles, viz: 1 uniform coat, brown faced with white; 1 shirt; 1 pair of stockings; 1 sergeant's sash; 1 pair knee buckles; $\frac{1}{2}$ lb soap; 1 orderly book; 1 memo book of journal and state of my company; 1 quire paper; 2 vials ink; 1 brass inkhorn; 40 morning returns, printed blanks; 1 tin gill cup; a letter, and a book . . . I likewise lost my hat, but recovered it again.

The weather was very warm and though my knapsack was very light, was very cumbersome, as it swung about when walking or running and in crossing fences was in the way, so I cast it away from me, and had I not done so would have been grabbed by one of the ill-looking Highlanders, a number of whom were firing and advancing very brisk towards our rear. The smoke was so very thick that about the close of the day, I lost sight of our regiment and just at dark I fell in with the North Carolina troops and about two o'clock in the morning arrived at Chester . . .

Joseph Townshaw, a young Quaker, gazed with near-panic at the battlefield after it was all over.

Some of the doors of the meeting-house were torn off and the wounded carried thereon into the house to be occupied for an hospital . . .

The wounded officers were first attended to. After assisting in carrying two of them into the house I was disposed to see an operation performed by one of the surgeons, who was preparing to amputate a limb by having a brass clamp or screw fitted thereon a little above the knee joint. He had his knife in his hand, the blade of which was . . . circular . . . and was about to make the incision, when he recollected that it might be necessary for the wounded man to take something to support him during the operation. He mentioned to some of his attendants to give him a little wine or brandy . . . to which he replied, 'No doctor it is not necessary, my spirits are up enough without it.'

Thomas Burke of North Carolina, a newly elected and irascible member of Congress — and yet another recent immigrant — was forthright in his views. He had no doubt that the disaster was General Sullivan's fault. Indeed, he wrote and told him so.

I was present at the action of Brandywine and saw and heard enough to convince me that the fortune of the day was injured by miscarriages where you commanded.

I understood you were several days posted with the command on the right wing, that you were cautioned by the Commander in Chief early in the day to be particularly attentive to the enemy's motions who he supposed would attempt to cross higher up the creek and attack your flank, that you were furnished with proper troops for reconnoitring, and yet you were so ill informed of the enemy's motions that they came up at a time and by a rout which you did not expect. That you conveyed intelligence to the Commander in Chief which occasioned his countermanding the dispositions he had made for encountering them on the rout by which it afterwards appeared they were actually advancing. That when at length the mistake was discovered you brought up your own division by an unnecessary circuit of two miles, and in the greatest disorder, from which they never recovered, but fled from the fire of the enemy without resistance. That the miscarriages on that wing made it necessary to draw off a great part of the strength from the center which exposed General Wayne to the superiority of the enemy.

I concluded that the troops under your command had no confidence in your conduct, and from the many accounts I had officially received of your miscarriages, I conceived, and am still possessed of an opinion, that you have not sufficient talents for your rank and office, tho I believe you have strong dispositions to discharge your duty well. I consider it as your misfortune, no fault. It is my duty, as far as I can, to prevent its being the misfortune of my country.

Brandywine saw an example of the old-fashioned rules of war. Among the screen of scouts of the German veteran Knyphausen's force was an ex-dragoon, Captain (later Major) Patrick Ferguson. He was the inventor of a breech-loading, rapid-fire rifle capable of loosing off six aimed shots each minute, and was given command of a small corps of picked sharpshooters — of which until then the British had been conspicuously short. Ferguson was scouting ahead of his men when the sound of horses' hoof-beats drove him to take cover. He had the chance, in fact, of ending the life of the enemy commander, or perhaps of the war. In the battle itself, Ferguson's right elbow was to be shattered.

We had not lain long . . . when a rebel officer, remarkable by a hussar dress, passed towards our army within a hundred yards of my right flank, not perceiving us. He was followed by another dressed in dark green or blue, mounted on a bay horse, with a remarkably large cocked hat.

I ordered three good shots to steal near . . . and fire at them, but the idea disgusted me. I recalled the order. The hussar in returning made a circuit, but the other passed again within a hundred yards of us, upon which I advanced from the woods towards him.

On my calling, he stopped, but after looking at me, proceeded. I again drew his attention and made signs to stop but he slowly continued his way. As I was within that distance at which in the quickest firing I could have lodged half-a-dozen of balls in or about him before he was out of my reach, I had only to determine. But it was not pleasant to fire at the back of an unoffending individual, who was acquitting himself very coolly of his duty, so I let him alone.

The day after, I had been telling this story to some wounded officers who lay in the same room with me, when one of our surgeons, who had been dressing the wounded rebel officers, came in and told us they had been informing him that General Washington was all the morning with the light troops and only attended by a French Officer in a hussar dress, he himself dressed and mounted in every point as above described. I am not sorry that I did not know at the time who it was.

Further up-river and twenty-three miles west of Philadelphia, near Paoli, 1500 men under Anthony Wayne were attacked by Major-General Grey's forces with unloaded rifles. British and Hessian bayonets inflicted three hundred casualties and not a shot was fired. Grey was henceforth known as 'No Flint Grey'.
Captain John André testified to the scale of British success:

On approaching the right of the camp we perceived the line of fires, and the Light Infantry being ordered to form the front, rushed along the line putting to the bayonet all they came up with, and overtaking the main herd of the fugitives, stabbed great numbers and pressed on their rear till it was thought prudent to order them to desist.

Near 200 must have been killed, and a great number wounded. Seventy-one prisoners were brought off; forty of them badly wounded were left at different houses on the road. A major, a captain and two lieutenants were amongst the prisoners. We lost Captain Wolfe killed and one or two private men; four or five were wounded, one an officer, Lieut. Hunter of the 52d Light Company.

Major Samuel Hay of the Continental Army wrote to Colonel William Irvine about the attack:

We lay the 18th and 19th undisturbed, but, on the 20th, at 12 o'clock at night, the enemy marched out, and so unguarded was our camp that they were amongst us before we either formed in any manner for our safety, or attempted to retreat, notwithstanding the General had full intelligence of their designs two hours before they came out. The enemy rushed on with fixed bayonets and made the use of them they intended. So you may figure to yourself what followed. The party lost 300 privates in killed, wounded and missing, besides commissioned and non-commissioned officers. Our loss is Col Grier, Captain Wilson and Lieutenant Irvine wounded (but none of them dangerously) and 61 non-commissioned and privates killed and wounded, which was just half the men we had on the ground fit for duty.

The 22d, I went to the ground to see the wounded. The scene was shocking – the poor men groaning under their wounds, which were all by stabs of bayonets and cuts of Light-Horsemen's swords. Col Grier is wounded in the side by a bayonet, superficially slanting to the breast bone. Captain Wilson's stabbed in the side, but not dangerous, and it did not take the guts or belly. He got also a bad stroke on the head with the cock nail of the locks of a musket. Andrew Irvine was run through the fleshy part of the thigh with a bayonet. They are all lying near David Jones' tavern. I left Captain McDowell with them to dress and take care of them, and they all are in a fair way of recovery. Major La Mar, of the 4th Regiment, was killed, and some other inferior officers.

Congress fled, first to Lancaster, and then to York, Pennsylvania, after conferring dictatorial powers on Washington. On 27 September, Cornwallis led his men into

Philadelphia with bands playing. They would stay nine months. Franklin, in Paris, was one of the few Americans not to be disheartened. When told that Howe had taken Philadelphia, he replied:

'No! Philadelphia captured Howe!'

Howe's main force was at Germantown, five miles outside the city, so that they could protect supply routes until the Delaware forts could be taken.

Washington, who had withdrawn steadily before him, decided on a surprise attack, on the same lines as at Trenton, but with four columns. His plans went adrift when, on Knox's urging, he decided to destroy rather than by-pass 'the Chew House'. Colonel Timothy Pickering confided the event to his journal:

This house of Chew's was a strong stone building and exceedingly commodious, having windows on every side, so that you could not approach it without being exposed to a severe fire; which, in fact, was well directed and killed and wounded a great many of our officers and men. Several of our pieces, six-pounders, were brought up within musket-shot of it, and fired round balls at it, but in vain: the enemy, I imagine, were very little hurt; they still kept possession.

It was proposed to send a flag to summon the enemy posted there to surrender, Lieutenant-Colonel Smith, Deputy Adjutant General, offering himself to carry it.

I did not expect to see him return alive. I imagined they would pay no respect to the flag, they being well posted, and the battle far enough from being decided. The event justified my apprehensions: in a few minutes Mr Smith was brought back with his leg broken and shattered by a musket-ball fired from the house.

American casualties exceeded British — 700 to 530. Adam Stephen, a gallant Virginian, was convicted of 'unofficerlike behaviour' and drunkenness and dismissed the service — his troops had panicked and their firing was confused. A French officer serving with the Americans drew significant lessons from the campaign thus far.

If General Howe does not take care, he may find himself made very uneasy, even in his camp at Germantown, by the Americans; and if one of their divisions . . . gone astray in the woods . . . had not been two hours late, the English would have been repulsed as far as Philadelphia and perhaps farther.

But the principal advantage of General Howe's army over General Washington's in the two battles fought by them, must be ascribed to their being more trained to the use of the bayonet. The American army know their superior dexterity in firing well, and rely entirely upon it. The British army know it likewise, and dread it. Hence in all engagements the British soldiers rush on with the bayonet after one fire, and seldom fail of throwing the Americans into confusion. Habit, which forms men to do anything, I am persuaded would soon render these brave people as firm at the approaches of a bayonet, as the whistling of a musket ball. General [Charles] Lee, I am told, took great pains to eradicate the universal prejudice he found among the Americans, in favor of terminating the war with fire arms alone. 'We must learn to face our enemies,' said he, 'man to man in the open field, or we shall never beat them.' The late General Montgomery, who served his apprenticeship in the British Army, knew so well that nothing but the bayonet would ever rout troops that had been trained to it, that he once proposed in the Convention of New York, of which he was a member, that directions should be given, both in Europe and in this country, to make all muskets intended for the American soldiers two inches longer than the muskets now in use in the British Army, in order that they may have an advantage of their enemy, in a charge with bayonets, for, he said, 'Britain will never yield but to the push of the bayonet.'

The west, the Indian country, was by 1777, in a state of near-anarchy, uncertain over sovereignty, boundaries and allegiance. Each frontier community had to look after itself. Some frontier companies disguised themselves as Indians and fought with savagery.

George Roush of Hampshire County, Virginia, for example, served as an Indian scout for three years. In the evidence he gave when, sixty years later, he claimed a pension, he said that he was then stationed at Fort Pitt.

Declarant states that in obedience to the order of his said Captain Brady, he proceeded to tan his thighs and legs with wild cherry and white oak bark and to equip himself after the following manner, to wit, a breechcloth, leather leggins, moccasins, and a cap made out of a raccoon skin, with the feathers of a hawk, painted red, fastened to the top of the cap. Declarant was then painted after the manner of an Indian warrior. His face was painted red, with three black stripes across his cheeks, which was a signification of war. Declarant states that Captain Brady's company was about sixty-four in number, all painted after the manner aforesaid.

A party of Indians was espied by declarant and those who were with him, to wit, Captain Brady and fifteen of his soldiers. It was late in the evening. The Indians encamped in an old hunting camp which had been built by the Indians. Declarant is of opinion that the Indians had come for the purpose of hunting. There were six in number, five men and [an] old squaw. When it was ascertained that the Indians intended to remain in the camp all night, Captain Brady ordered his men to encamp not far distant from the Indians, and at the hour of twelve in the night Captain Brady marched his men within about thirty paces of the Indian camp, and we lay behind a log until it began to get light, at which time we were discovered by the dogs which the Indians had brought with them for the purpose, as we suppose, of hunting. The barking of the dogs alarmed the Indians, and one of them woke and knocked the priming out of his gun and primed it fresh and walked the way we were laying and encouraged the dogs, which continued fiercely barking, during which time the other four Indians were yet asleep in the camp. Declarant thinks that the Indian discovered Captain Brady, who lay behind the log. Captain Brady had on a French capa coat made of fine sky blue cloth, which declarant thinks the Indian discovered above the [log]. We lay behind the log.

The Indian wheeled and walked carelessly back towards the camp, keeping his eye on the spot where we lay. We did not let him take but a few paces toward the camp before Captain Brady gave the signal agreed on, which was an alternate hunch of the elbow. Declarant and a man by the name of Applegate fired, and the Indian fell dead to the ground. The report of our guns awaked those in the camp, and they got up and stood by the fire. We fired and killed three, one of which was a squaw, and then approached the camp, and an Indian sprung out of the camp and ran up the hill. Captain Brady gave orders for us not to shoot running, as of the fifty Indians that we had seen on the evening before.

Whilst we were examining their guns, an Indian boy, which we supposed to be of the age of fifteen or sixteen years, came near and halloed to us and said, 'Unhee, what did you shoot at?'

And a man by the name of Fulks answered in the Indian language and said, 'A raccoon.' The Indian came across the creek, and when he come in shooting distance one of our company shot him. On our return to the fort on Yellow Creek, we were retarded by a party of Indians. From intelligence afterwards, about forty-four in number in all were engaged. [A skirmish] took place. Six or seven rounds were fired. The result was that one of our men was killed by the name of Rickantaua [?], two wounded. We were soon overpowered by number, that we were compelled to retreat. The number of the Indians killed we at that time could [not] ascertain, but from intelligence after received by James Whiticar, who was a prisoner amongst the Indians at that time, the Indians lost twenty-four killed on the first of action, and six wounded which reached the Sandusky towns, and four of the six wounded died.

Meanwhile, the north would bring a drama of its own. General John Burgoyne arrived in Canada on 6 May 1777. He had been to London and had — as he thought it — concerted plans with Lord George Germain, the Secretary for War. He would march south from Canada and, by mastering the Hudson Valley, would cut off rebellious New England from the other, less militant, states. Howe would drive north to assist him.

Burgoyne hoped to supplement his 7213 men (three brigades of British regulars and three of Hessians) with Canadian Loyalists, and 'one thousand or more savages'. However, only about 250 Tories and 400 Indians joined the expedition. A massive artillery train of 138 guns was to be manhandled along forest trails, succeeded by large numbers of women and children, who followed their men to war in the wilderness.

On 27 June Burgoyne arrived at Crown Point. Three days later he issued his orders for the attack on Ticonderoga. He thought the issuing of a Proclamation would strike the right note. His style was always grandiloquent — he was, in Horace Walpole's phrase, to be 'Julius Caesar Burgonius'.

By John Burgoyne, Esq., Lieutenant-General of his Majesty's armies in America, Colonel of the Queen's regiment of light dragoons, Governor of Fort William, in North Britain, one of the Representatives of the Commons of Great Britain in Parliament, and commanding an army and fleet employed on an expedition from Canada, etc., etc., etc.,

The forces entrusted to my command are designed to act in concert, and upon a common principle, with the numerous armies and fleets which already display in every quarter of America, the power, the justice, and, when properly sought, the mercy of the King.

The cause in which the British arms are thus exerted, applies to the most affecting interests of the human hearts; and the military servants of the crown, at first called forth for the sole purpose of restoring the rights of the constitution, now combine with love of their country, and duty to their sovereign, the other extensive incitements which spring from a due sense of the general privileges of mankind. To the eyes and ears of the temperate part of the public, and to the breasts of suffering

93

thousands in the provinces, be the melancholy appeal, whether the present unnatural rebellion has not been made a foundation for the completest system of tyranny that ever God, in his displeasure, suffered for a time to be exercised over a forward and stubborn generation.

Arbitrary imprisonment, confiscation of property, persecution and torture, unprecedented in the inquisitions of the Romish church, are among the palpable enormities that verify the affirmative. These are inflicted by assemblies and committees, who dare to profess themselves friends to liberty, upon the most quiet subjects, without distinction of age or sex, for the sole crime, often for the sole suspicion, of having adhered in principle to the government under which they were born, and to which, by every tie, divine and human, they owe allegiance. To consummate these shocking proceedings, the profanation of religion is added to the most profligate prostitution of common reason; the consciences of men are set at naught; and multitudes are compelled not only to bear arms, but also to swear subjection to an usurpation they abhor.

Animated by these considerations; at the head of troops in the full powers of health, discipline, and valor; determined to strike where necessary, and anxious to spare where possible, I, by these presents, invite and exhort all persons, in all places where the progress of this army may point, and by the blessing of God I will extend it far, to maintain such a conduct as may justify me in protecting their lands, habitations, and families . . .

If, notwithstanding these endeavors, and sincere inclinations to affect them, the frenzy of hostility should remain, I trust I shall stand acquitted in the eyes of God and men in denouncing and executing the vengeance of the State against the wilful outcasts. The messengers of justice and of wrath await them in the field; and devastation, famine and every concomitant horror that a reluctant but indispensable prosecution of military duty must occasion, will bear the way to their return.

He continued to reinforce fire with flame.

During our progress occasions may occur, in which neither difficulty nor labor nor life are to be regarded. THIS ARMY MUST NOT RETREAT.

Such exuberance invited ridicule. Francis Hopkinson, formerly a member of the Continental Congress from New Jersey made proper — or improper — fun of him.

94

MOST HIGH, MOST MIGHTY, MOST PUISSANT, AND SUBLIME GENERAL

When the forces under your command arrived at Quebec, in order to act in concert and upon a common principle with the numerous fleets and armies which already display in every quarter of America the justice and mercy of your King, we, the reptiles of America, were struck with unusual trepidation and astonishment. But what words can express the plenitude of our horror when the Colonel of the Queen's regiment of light dragoons advanced towards Ticonderoga. The mountains shook before thee, and the trees of the forest bowed their lofty heads; the vast lakes of the north were chilled at thy presence, and the mighty cataracts stopped their tremendous career, and were suspended in awe at thy approach. Judge, then, oh ineffable Governor of Fort William in North Britain, what must have been the terror, dismay, and despair that overspread this paltry continent of America, and us its wretched inhabitants. Dark and dreary, indeed, was the prospect before us, till, like the sun in the horizon, your most gracious, sublime, and irresistible proclamation opened the doors of mercy, and snatched us, as it were, from the jaws of annihilation.

We foolishly thought, blind as we were, that your gracious master's fleets and armies were come to destroy us and our liberties; but we are happy in hearing from you (and who can doubt what you assert?) that they were called forth for the sole purpose of restoring the rights of the constitution to a forward and stubborn generation.

And is it for this, oh sublime lieutenant-general, that you have given yourself the trouble to cross the wide Atlantic, and with incredible fatigue traverse uncultivated wilds? And we ungratefully refuse the proffered blessing? To restore the rights of the constitution you have called together an amiable host of savages, and turned them loose to scalp our women and children, and lay our country waste — this they have performed with their usual skill and clemency, and we yet remain insensible of the benefit, and unthankful for so much goodness!

We submit, we submit, most puissant Colonel of the Queen's regiment of light dragoons, and Governor of Fort William in North Britain! We offer our heads to the scalping knife and our bellies to the bayonet. Who can resist the force of your eloquence? Who can withstand the terror of your arms? The invitation you have made in the consciousness of Christianity, your royal master's clemency, and the honor of soldiership, we thankfully accept. The blood of the slain, the cries of injured virgins and innocent children, and the never ceasing sighs and groans of starving wretches now languishing in the jails and prison ships of New York, call on us in vain, whilst your sublime proclamation is sounded in our ears. Forgive us, oh our country! Forgive us, dear posterity! Forgive us, all ye foreign powers who are anxiously watching our conduct in this important struggle, if we yield implicitly to the persuasive tongue of the most elegant Colonel of her Majesty's regiment of light dragoons.

A New Jerseyman, assumed to be Francis Hopkinson, wrote in the New York Journal *on 8 September 1777:*

> By John Burgoyne and Burgoyne, John, Esq.,
> And graced with titles still more higher
> For I'm Lieutenant-general, too,
> Of George's troops both red and blue,
> On this extensive continent;
> And of Queen Charlotte's regiment
> Of light dragoons the Colonel;
> And Governor eke of Castle Wil-
> and furthermore, when I am there,
> In House of Commons I appear
> (Hoping ere long to be a Peer),
> Being a member of that virtuous band
> Who always vote at North's command;
> Directing too the fleet and troops
> From Canada as thick as hops;
> And all my titles to display,
> I'll end with thrice et cetera.
>   The troops consigned to my command
> Like Hercules to purge the land
> Intend to act in combination
> With th' other forces of the nation,
> Displaying wide thro' every quarter
> What Britain's justice would be after . . .
> Your ears and eyes have heard and seen
> How causeless this revolt has been;
> And what a dust your leaders kick up
> In this rebellious civil hiccup,
> And how, upon this cursed foundation,
> Was reared a system of vexation
> Over a stubborn generation.

General John Burgoyne, or
'Julius Caesar Burgonius'

Major John André

General John Burgoyne addressing the Indians

Joseph Brant, the Mohawk chief

Burgoyne moved south with agonising slowness. On 4 July, however, Ticonderoga became untenable as Lieutenant William Digby of the Shropshire Regiment describes.

About noon we took possession of Sugar Loaf hill, on which a battery was immediately ordered to be raised. It was a post of great consequence, as it commanded a great part of the works of Ticonderoga, all their vessels, and likewise afforded us the means of cutting off their communication with Fort Independent, a place also of great strength and the works very extensive. But here the commanding officer was reckoned guilty of a great oversight in lighting fires on that post tho' I am informed it was done by the Indians, the smoke of which was soon perceived by the enemy in the fort; as he should have remained undiscovered till night, when he was to have got two 12-pounders up, tho' their getting there was almost a perpendicular ascent, and drawn up by most of the cattle belonging to the army.

They no sooner perceived us in possession of a post, which they thought quite impossible to bring cannon up to, than all their pretended boastings of holding out to the last, and choosing rather to die in their works than give them up, failed them, and on the night of the 5th, they set fire to several parts of the garrison, kept a constant fire of great guns the whole night, and under the protection of that fire and clouds of smoke, they evacuated the garrison, leaving all their cannon, ammunition and a great quantity of stores.

Dr James Thacher, serving with the Continental Line, confirms how quickly American resistance collapsed, in his diary of 14 July:

By reason of an extraordinary and unexpected event, the course of my Journal had been interrupted for several days. At about 12 o'clock, in the night of the 5th instant, I was urgently called from sleep, and informed that our army was in motion, and was instantly to abandon Ticonderoga and Mount Independence. I could scarcely believe that my informant was in earnest, but the confusion and bustle soon convinced me that it was really true, and that the short time allowed demanded my utmost industry. It was enjoined on me immediately to collect the sick and wounded, and as much of the hospital stores as possible, and assist in embarking them on board the batteaux and boats at the shore.

Having with all possible despatch completed our embarkation, at 3 o'clock in the morning of the 6th, we commenced our voyage up the South bay to Skeenesborough, about 30 miles. Our fleet consisted of five armed gallies and two hundred batteaux and boats deeply laden with cannon, tents, provisions, invalids and women. We were accompanied by a guard of six hundred men, commanded by Colonel Long, of New Hampshire. The night was moon light and pleasant, the sun burst forth in the morning with uncommon lustre, the day was fine, the water's surface serene and unruffled. The shore on each side exhibited a variegated view of huge rocks, caverns and clifts, and the whole was bounded by a thick, impenetrable wilderness. My pen would fail in the attempt to describe a scene so enchantingly sublime. The occasion was peculiarly interesting, and we could but look back with regret, and forward with apprehension. We availed ourselves, however, of the means of enlivening our spirits. The drum and fife afforded us a favorite music; among the hospital stores we found many dozens of choice wine, and we cheered our hearts with the nectareous contents.

At 3 o'clock in the afternoon, we reached our destined port at Skeenesborough, being the head of navigation for our gallies. Here we were unsuspicious of danger, but behold! Burgoyne himself was at our heels. In less than two hours we were struck with surprise and consternation by a discharge of cannon from the enemy's fleet on our gallies and batteaux lying at the wharf. By uncommon efforts and industry they had broken through the bridge, boom and chain, which cost our people such immense labor, and had almost overtaken us on the lake, and horridly disastrous indeed would have been our fate. It was not long before it was perceived that a number of their troops and savages had landed and were rapidly advancing towards our little party.

The officers of our guard now attempted to rally the men and form them in battle array; but this was found impossible, every effort proved unavailing and in the utmost panic they were seen to fly in every direction for personal safety. In this desperate condition, I perceived our officers scampering for their baggage; I ran to the batteau, seized my chest, carried it a short distance, took from it a few articles, and instantly followed in the train of our retreating party. We took the route to Fort Ann through a narrow defile in the woods, and were so closely pressed by the pursuing enemy that we frequently heard calls from the rear to 'march on, the Indians are at our heels'. Having marched all night, we reached Fort Ann at 5 o'clock in the morning, where we found provisions for our refreshment. A small rivulet called Wood Creek is navigable from Skeenesborough to Fort Ann, by which means some of our invalids and baggage made their escape; but all our cannon [and] provisions and the bulk of our baggage, with several invalids, fell into the enemy's hands.

Fort Ann being a small picket fort of no importance, orders were given to set it on fire, and on the 8th we departed for Fort Edward, situated about 30 miles southward on the banks on the Hudson River.

Sergeant Roger Lamb, who became the 9th Regiment's most famous sergeant, recounts the events at Fort Anne.

Early next morning, 9th July, an American soldier came from the fort. He said that he had deserted, though it was afterwards discovered that he was a spy. He stated that there were one thousand men in the fort, and that they were in the greatest consternation, under an apprehension of the British attacking and storming them. Upon this intelligence Colonel Hill dispatched a message to General Burgoyne, stating his situation and how far he had advanced, which was eight or ten miles from the main army.

Not many minutes after this message was sent off, the pretended deserter disappeared. He had viewed the situation and seen the strength of the British, which did not amount to above one hundred and ninety men including officers. It was soon found that he had made a faithful report to his friends, for in less than half an hour they came out of the fort with great fury. The British outline of sentries received them with the greatest bravery and steadiness, and obliged them to retreat. They then formed again, and came on with redoubled violence. The officers could be heard encouraging them on to the attack, though their numbers could not be seen, the woods being so thick, but it was soon found that they not only outflanked, but were endeavoring to surround the British. When the troops arrived at the summit of the hill, they formed in Indian file, and kept up a well directed fire till all the ammunition was expended. The enemy observing that the firing ceased, were encouraged to press forward with redoubled vigor, and endeavored to surround them in order to cut them off. Just at this critical moment a war whoop was heard, which resounded through the woods. This sound, which was so obnoxious at that time to the Americans, threw them into the utmost consternation.

The war whoop was sounded by Captain Money, deputy quartermaster general. He had been detached by General Burgoyne early in the morning from Skeenesborough, with a party of Indians, in order to join this detachment. When they came within four miles of Fort Anne, they heard the firing, Captain Money ordered them to advance as fast as possible to assist, but they refused to obey him, and either stood still or advanced very slow. Being anxious to join the party at all events, he ran

99

forward by himself with all his might, and came to the bottom of the hill where, just as all the ammunition was expended, he gave the war whoop . . .

By the end of July, Burgoyne was at Fort Edward at the head of the Hudson. This was an obvious success for him, but the going now was rough. Bridges were gone, cattle also; crops were blackened. It had taken Burgoyne twenty-four days to cover the last twenty-three miles. The physical difficulties of ravines and rocky gorges made impassable by heavy rain, felled trees and strategically placed boulders, terrain thick with mosquitoes and wild game, made this easy country to defend. But even more hazardous were the British troops' own allies, the Indians, who were unreliable and ruthless, as Lieutenant Anburey recorded in the case of Jane McCrea, a Loyalist engaged to one of Burgoyne's officers.

Some Indians, who were out on a scout, by chance met with her in the woods. They first treated her with every mark of civility they are capable of, and were conducting her into camp when, within a mile of it, a dispute arose between the two Indians, whose prisoner of war she was, and the words growing very high, one of them, who was fearful of losing the reward for bringing her safe into camp, most inhumanely struck his tomahawk into her skull and she instantly expired.

The situation of the General [Burgoyne], whose humanity was much shocked at such an instance of barbarity, was very distressing and critical, for however inclined he might be to punish the offender, still it was hazarding the revenge of the savages, whose friendship he had to court, rather than seek their enmity . . .

The chief of the tribe to which the Indian belonged readily consented to his being delivered up to the General, to act with him as he thought proper, but at the same time said, it was the rules of their war, that if two of them at the same instant seized a prisoner, and seemed to have equal claim, in case any dispute arose between them, they soon decided the contest, for the unhappy cause was sure to become a victim to their contention.

Burgoyne exacerbated feelings by pardoning Wyandot Panther, her supposed murderer, lest other Indians desert. He had already offered rewards to Indians for American scalps. This all made superb and disturbingly well-buttressed American frontier propaganda.

Nor were the Hessian allies of much value. Colonel Baum, who spoke no English, was at the head of a motley group of some 800 men in quest of horses for his unhorsed Hessian Dragoons, when they were defeated in a torrential rainstorm at Bennington on 16 August, by Colonel John Stark's weather-beaten New Hampshire Militia. There was much confusion over who was friend or enemy, with heavy losses on both sides. Stark claimed to have killed 200 Germans and to have 700 prisoners — a very high number. The Germans, on the other hand, admitted the loss of 590 men.

    Lieutenant Glich, one of the Hessian officers, left a vivid account.

For a few seconds, the scene which ensued defies all power of language to describe. The bayonet, the butt of the rifle, the saber, the pike were in full play; and men fell, as they rarely fall in modern war, under the direct blows of their enemies. But such a struggle could not . . . be of long continuance. Outnumbered, broken . . . our people wavered and fell back, or fought singly and unconnectedly, till they were either cut down at their posts . . . or compelled to surrender.

By contrast, Peter Clark, a Lyndboro farmer, told a gleeful tale, in a letter to his wife.

We do not know how many we have killed. Our scouts daily find them dead in the woods. One of our scouts found, the beginning of this week twenty-six of the enemy lying dead in the woods. They stank so they could not bury them . . . The wounded Hessians die three or four in a day. They are all in Bennington Meeting House which smells so it is enough to kill anyone to be in it.

    It was a defeat of professionals by amateurs. The professionals were appallingly over-equipped for a wilderness in mid-summer: their jackboots reached the mid-thigh and weighed twelve pounds a pair, and they wore elbow-length leather gauntlets in forest trails. By contrast their opponents looked like a collection of Rip Van Winkles, as Frederick Kidder remembered.

To a man, they wore small-clothes, coming down and fastening just below the knee, and long stockings with cowhide shoes ornamental by large buckles, while not a pair of boots graced the company. The coats and waistcoats were loose and of huge dimensions, with colors as various as the barks of oak, sumach and other trees of our hills and swamps could make them, and their shirts were all made of flax and, like every other part of the dress, were homespun. On their heads was worn a large round-top and broad-brimmed hat. Their arms were as various as their costume. Here an old soldier carried a heavy Queen's Arm, with which he had done service at the conquest of Canada twenty years previous while by his side walked a stripling boy, with a Spanish fusee not half its weight or calibre which his grandfather may have taken at the Havana, while not a few had old French pieces that dated back to the reduction of Louisburg. Instead of the cartridge box, a large powder horn was slung under the arm, and occasionally a bayonet might be seen bristling in the ranks. Some of the swords of the officers had been made by our Province blacksmiths, perhaps from some farming utensil; they looked serviceable, but heavy and uncouth.

From Fort Oswego on Lake Ontario, another column of some 400 British, Hessian and Loyalist troops, led by Brigadier Barry St Leger, was pushing eastwards along the Mohawk Valley to rendezvous with Burgoyne at Albany. They were accompanied by 1000 Iroquois Indians led by Joseph Brant, a Mohawk chief, otherwise known as Thayenadenega. While besieging Fort Stanwix and within 100 miles of Albany, St Leger was checked at Oriskany by a group of frontier Germans under tough, middle-aged, square-shaped Nicholas Herkimer. As news reached him of the approach of an American relief force led by Benedict Arnold, the Indians deserted, and St Leger retreated to Oswego — and Montreal. Burgoyne was left now to fend for himself.

By early September, with small prospect now of aid from east or west, Burgoyne — two months, but only forty miles out from Fort 'Ty' — was sending increasingly urgent calls for help to Clinton in New York. His messengers did not get through, or were unlucky. According to a captain of the Connecticut Line, one of them

fell in with a small scouting party of ours under the command of a sergeant of Webb's regiment, who with his men were dressed in British uniform which had been captured in a transport ship. Their speech and appearance being the same, and our sergeant managing with the utmost address, proposed themselves to General Clinton, who, our sergeant said, was out from the fort and not far off.

On seeing the American general [George] Clinton, he instantly discovered that he was deceived and swallowed something hastily, which being noticed, the general ordered the regimental surgeon to administer a strong emetic, which in its powerful operation occasioned his throwing up a silver ball of the size of a pistol bullet, which on being cleansed and opened was found to contain the note. He was tried the next day and the proof being full and complete was condemned and executed as a spy.

It is a good story. It is also told of Sir Henry Clinton's messenger to Burgoyne, and by no less an authority than Surgeon Thacher.

After the capture of Fort Montgomery, Sir Henry Clinton dispatched a messenger by the name of Daniel Taylor, to Burgoyne, with intelligence. Unfortunately he was taken on his way as a spy, and finding himself in danger was seen to turn aside and take something from his pocket and swallow it. General George Clinton, into whose hands he had fallen, ordered a severe dose of emetic tartar to be administered. This produced the happiest effect as respects the prescriber, but it proved fatal to the patient. He discharged a small silver bullet, which after being unscrewed was found to enclose a letter from Sir Henry Clinton to Burgoyne. 'Out of thine own mouth thou shalt be condemned.' The spy was tried, convicted and executed. The following is an exact copy of the letter enclosed.

Fort Montgomery, 8 October 1777

Nous voici — and nothing between us but Gates. I sincerely hope this little success of ours may facilitate your operations. In answer to your letter of the 28th September by C. C. I shall only say, I cannot presume to order, or even advise, for reasons obvious. I heartily wish you success.

Faithfully yours

H. CLINTON

Couriers seemed to have brief lives and violent ends.

General Horatio Gates had taken over command of the American forces at Albany on 19 August. He was an ex-British regular, competent, popular, cautious — Burgoyne called him 'the old midwife'.

Gates had moved forward to occupy a strong point, Bemis Heights, named after the man who kept a pub there. As Gates' numbers grew steadily, Burgoyne's fell from disease and desertion. His horses were dying of starvation; uniforms and boots were in tatters; the salt pork and flour essential to the men's rations, were running out.

However, in two columns, one of which he led himself, Burgoyne attacked Freeman's Farm* on 19 September. Although remaining in occupation of the field, British losses were heavier than American, thanks to Daniel Morgan's sharpshooters, and to the dash of Benedict Arnold. Captain Wakefield had vivid memories of the attack.

I shall never never forget the opening scene of the first day's conflict. The riflemen and light infantry were ordered to clear the woods of the Indians. Arnold rode up, and with his sword pointing to the enemy

---

*Saratoga witnessed two battles, each known by the names Freeman's Farm, Bemis Heights and Saratoga. The three references are interchangeable.

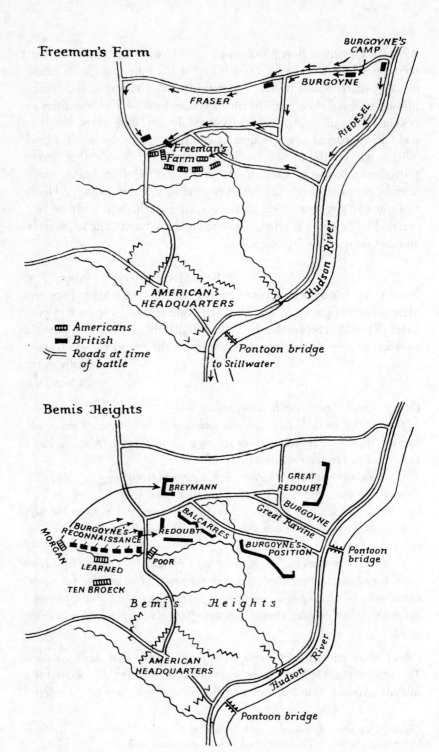

Freeman's Farm

BURGOYNE'S CAMP

BURGOYNE

FRASER

RIEDESEL

Freeman's Farm

Hudson River

AMERICAN HEADQUARTERS

Americans
British
Roads at time of battle

Pontoon bridge
to Stillwater

Bemis Heights

BREYMANN

GREAT REDOUBT

BURGOYNE

Great Ravine

BALCARRES

BURGOYNE'S RECONNAISSANCE

MORGAN

REDOUBT

BURGOYNE'S POSITION

Pontoon bridge

POOR

LEARNED

TEN BROECK

Bemis Heights

AMERICAN HEADQUARTERS

Hudson River

Pontoon bridge

emerging from the woods into an opening partially cleared, covered with stumps and fallen timber, addressing Morgan, he said, 'Colonel Morgan, you and I have seen too many redskins to be deceived by that garb of paint and feathers; they are asses in lions' skins, Canadians and Tories; let your riflemen cure them of their borrowed plumes.'

And so they did; for in less than fifteen minutes the 'Wagon Boy', with his Virginia riflemen, sent the painted devils with a howl back to the British lines. Morgan was in his glory, catching the inspiration of Arnold, as he thrilled his men; when he hurled them against the enemy, he astonished the English and Germans with the deadly fire of his rifles.

Nothing could exceed the bravery of Arnold on this day; he seemed the very genius of war. Infuriated by the conflict and maddened by Gates' refusal to send reinforcements, which he repeatedly called for, and knowing he was meeting the brunt of the battle, he seemed inspired with the fury of a demon.

Almost from the start, Lieutenant Anburey became aware that Burgoyne's forces lost some of their manpower.

The Indians were running from wood to wood, and just as soon as our regiment had formed in the skirts of one, several of them came up, and by their signs were conversing about the severe fire on our right. Soon after the enemy attacked us, and at the very first fire the Indians run off through the woods.

From the situation of the ground, and their being perfectly acquainted with it, the whole of our troops could not be brought to engage together, which was a very material disadvantage, though everything possible was tried to remedy that inconvenience, but to no effect. Such an explosion of fire I never had any idea of before, and the heavy artillery joining in concert like great peals of thunder, assisted by the echoes of the woods, almost deafened us with the noise. To an unconcerned spectator, it must have had the most awful and glorious appearance, the different battalions moving to relieve each other, some being pressed and almost broke by their superior numbers. The crash of cannon and musketry never ceased till darkness parted us, when they retired to their camp, leaving us masters of the field; but it was a dear-bought victory if I can give it that name as we lost many brave men. The 62nd had scarce 10 men a company left, and other regiments suffered much, and no very great advantage, honor excepted, was gained by the day.

Anburey was also given the grisly task of burying the dead. He saw fifteen, sixteen and twenty buried in one hole . . . heads, legs and arms above ground. No other distinction is paid to officer or private, than the officers are put in a hole by themselves. Our army abounded with young officers, in the subaltern line, and in the course of this unpleasant duty, three of the 20th Regiment were interred together, the age of the eldest not exceeding seventeen. This friendly office to the dead, though it greatly affects the feeling, was nothing to the scenes in bringing in the wounded; the one were past all pain, the other in the most excruciating torments, sending forth dreadful groans. They had remained out all night, and from the loss of blood and want of nourishment, were upon the point of expiring. Some of them begged they might lay and die, others again were insensible, some upon the least movement were put in the most horrid tortures, and all had near a mile to be conveyed to the hospitals; others at their last gasp, who for want of our timely assistance must have inevitably expired. These poor creatures, perishing with cold and weltering in their blood, displayed such a scene, it must be a heart of adamant that could not be affected by it, even to a degree of weakness.

In the course of the late action, Lieutenant Harvey of the 62nd, a youth of sixteen and a nephew of the Adjutant General of the same name, received several wounds and was repeatedly ordered off the field by Colonel Anstruther. But his heroic ardor would not allow him to quit the battle, while he could stand and see his brave lads fighting beside him. A ball striking one of his legs, his removal became absolutely necessary, and while they were conveying him away, another wounded him mortally. In this situation the Surgeon recommended him to take a powerful dose of opium, to avoid a seven or eight hours of most exquisite torture. This he immediately consented to, and when the Colonel entered the tent with Major Harnage, who were both wounded, they asked whether he had any affairs they could settle for him? His reply was, 'That being a minor, everything was already adjusted.' But he had one request, which he had just life enough to utter, 'Tell my uncle I died like a soldier!'

Still hoping for support from Clinton in New York, Burgoyne hesitated about his next move. 'At no time did the Jews await the coming of the Messiah with greater expectations than we awaited the coming of General Clinton.' The saviour never came, though he did move up the Hudson to seize two forts — Clinton and Montgomery. Clinton did not learn the grimness of Burgoyne's plight until 5 October. He got within forty miles of Albany by mid-October; Saratoga was thirty miles to its north.

On 7 October, Burgoyne tried a flanking movement, which failed. The Ameri-
cans — Arnold again conspicuous — attacked frontally in the second battle of Sara-
toga. The British line held, but their losses were heavy (600 out of 1500 engaged).
Burgoyne withdrew to open ground around Saratoga; Gates did not give battle but
bombed ceaselessly. 'It rained incessantly; the roads were bad; the cattle were nearly
starved for want of forage and the bridge over the Fish Kill had been destroyed by the
enemy.' Half-starved horses could no longer pull bogged-down guns and wagons
through thick mud, and were abandoned. The men were exhausted and dispirited,
hungry and soaked. And, now, they were in retreat.

   Burgoyne surrendered, insisting that it was 'a convention not a capitulation'. The
two generals dined together.

General Gates, advised of Burgoyne's approach, met him at the head of
his camp, Burgoyne in a rich royal uniform and Gates in a plain blue
frock. When they had approached nearly within sword's length, they
reined up, and halted. I then named the gentleman, and General Burgoyne, raising his hat most gracefully, said, 'The fortune of war, General Gates, has made me your prisoner,' to which the conqueror, returning a courtly salute, promptly replied, 'I shall always be ready to bear
testimony, that it has not been through any fault of your excellency.'
Major General Phillips then advanced and he and General Gates saluted,
.and shook hands with the familiarity of old acquaintances. The Baron
Riedesel and the other officers were introduced in their turn . . .

A Boston newspaper added verisimilitude.

General Gates invited General Burgoyne and the other principal officers
to dine with him. The table was only two planks laid across two empty
beef barrels. There were only four plates for the whole company. There
was no cloth, and the dinner consisted of a ham, a goose, some beef and
some boiled mutton. The liquor was New England rum, mixed with
water, without sugar; and only two glasses, which were for the two
Commanders-in-Chief; the rest of the company drank out of basins.
The officer remarks, 'The men that can live thus, may be brought to
beat all the world.'

   After dinner, General Gates called upon General Burgoyne for his
toast which embarrassed General Burgoyne a good deal; at length, he
gave General Washington; General Gates, in return, gave the King.

   General Gates wrote to his wife from Albany, three days after Burgoyne's
surrender:

The voice of fame, ere this reaches you, will tell how greatly fortunate we have been in this department. Burgoyne and his whole army have laid down their arms, and surrendered themselves to me and my Yankees. Thanks to the Giver of all victory for this triumphant success. I got here the night before last, and the army are now encamped upon the heights to the southward of this city. Major-General Phillips, who wrote me that saucy note last year from St John's is now my prisoner, with Lord Petersham, Major Ackland, son of Sir Thomas, and his lady, daughter of Lord Ilchester, sister to the famous Lady Susan, and about a dozen members of Parliament, Scotch lords, &c. I wrote to T Boone by Mr Fluck, an engineer, whom I permitted to pass Canada, and who goes immediately from thence to England. I could not help, in a modest manner, putting him in mind of the fete champetre that I three years ago told him General Burgoyne would meet with if he came to America. If Old England is not by this lesson taught humility, then she is an obstinate old slut, bent upon her ruin.

The Baroness Riedesel, the wife of the commander of the Hessians accompanying Burgoyne, had been with the column throughout — as nurse, housekeeper and always optimist — and had observed that:

It is very true that General Burgoyne liked to make himself easy and that he spent half his nights in singing and drinking and diverting himself with . . . his mistress . . . who was as fond of champagne as himself.

Her housekeeping duties were somewhat out of the ordinary:

On the following morning the cannonade again began, but from a different side. I advised all to go out of the cellar for a little while, during which time I would have it cleaned, as otherwise we would all be sick. They followed my suggestion and I at once set many hands to work, which was in the highest degree necessary; for the women and children being afraid to venture forth had soiled the whole cellar . . .

I had just given the cellars a good sweeping and had fumigated them by sprinkling vinegar on burning coals and each one had found his place prepared for him, when a fresh and terrible cannonade threw us all once more into alarm. Many persons, who had no right to come in, threw themselves against the door. My children were already under the cellar steps and we would all have been crushed if God had not given me strength to place myself before the door and with extended arms prevent all from coming in . . .

And her nursing experience was considerably broadened by the horrors of war.

About three o'clock in the afternoon . . . they brought in to me upon a litter poor General Fraser . . . Our dining table which was already spread was taken away and in its place they fixed up a bed for the general . . .

The general said to the surgeon, 'Do not conceal anything from me. Must I die?'

The ball had gone through his bowels . . . Unfortunately, however, the general had eaten a hearty breakfast, by reason of which the intestines were distended and the ball, so the surgeon said, had not gone . . . between the intestines but through them. I heard him often amidst his groans exclaim, 'Oh, fatal ambition! Poor General Burgoyne! My poor wife!'

Prayers were read to him. He then sent a message to General Burgoyne begging that he would have him buried the following day at six o'clock in the evening on the top of a hill which was a sort of redoubt.

Fraser died the next morning at eight o'clock.

Colonel Louis du Portail, serving as Washington's engineer-in-chief, blamed Germain and Howe for the British disaster.

It is not due to the good conduct of the Americans that the campaign in general has been terminated so happily, but by the faults of the English. It was a capital fault of the British government in wishing General Burgoyne to traverse more than 200 leagues of country almost a desert to join forces with Generals Howe and Clinton. This plan might have seemed to be a good one in the cabinet in London, but appears miserable in the eyes of those who had an exact knowledge of the nature of the country.

However, neither did he give much credit to the Americans.

They move without spring or energy, without vigor and without passion for the cause in which they are engaged . . . There is an hundred times more enthusiasm for that revolution in any one coffee house at Paris than in all the Thirteen Provinces united.

But, whatever Burgoyne's braggadocio, he was dashing, personally courageous, and humane to his men at a time when it was unusual. The surrender at Saratoga, as Sergeant Lamb confirmed, was chiefly a consequence of the terrain.

Taking all the results of this battle, if we had reason to boast of it, our advantages from it were very few indeed. In fact, difficulty and danger appeared to grow out of it. The intricacy of the ground before us increased at every step. Our scouting, reconnoitring and foraging parties encountered perils uncalculated and unseen before. Our enemy, being at home, was well used to the places, and thus possessed of every local advantage that favours an army.

To procure provisions, and forage, without sending out large parties or bodies of soldiers, became impossible, and, therefore, the Indians themselves, who were attached to march with and reinforce us, began to desert. Plunder and freebooting was greatly their object, and to be debarred from that, as they found themselves, they turned away from privations and regular warfare, which they were disused to maintain. Of this we had evidence, for as a party of our troops posted near a wood were severely galled on the right of our line by the fire of the enemy, the Indians who accompanied us seemed to hold a consultation among themselves, precipitately retreated, and abandoned the army altogether.

In this circumstance of our military affairs, the Canadians and Colonists reinforcing us afforded no effectual assistance; they evidently betrayed their wishes of withdrawing from our forces, not being previously made up in mind for the severity and hardships of war, in the inveterate and wasting progress of its continuance, which, instead of favouring them with comfortable prospects of a returning tranquility, assumed day by day a more ferocious and unpromising aspect. Such then being the gloomy face of affairs in the great cause at issue, and the Colonial armies becoming daily stronger and more formidable opponents to us, it was not surprising that the tribes of Indians and the corps of loyal Colonists along with us should feel disheartened and relax their efforts in his Majesty's service.

Perhaps the real explanation of the British defeat at Saratoga is contained in an extract in the Pennsylvania Packet, *5 September 1778, which reported a conversation between Generals Burgoyne and Fraser on the morning of the final battle. When Fraser said that he would soon be in Albany,*

'Hold,' said General Burgoyne, 'the *owners of the land* (meaning the militia) are come out against us. We cannot proceed any farther so fast as we have done.' The same day the second battle at Stillwater was fought, in which the militia acquitted themselves like veterans, and the whole British army was routed. The consequence of this defeat is the glorious Convention of Saratoga, which was signed yesterday. A French officer who has served under General Gates during the campaign says: 'When dere be no more militia in dis country, I be one very great Tory.'

When the news of Burgoyne's capitulation reached London, the coffee-houses found it rich material for satire.

> Burgoyne, alas, unknowing future fates,
> Could force his way through woods but not through Gates

And the London Evening Post *summed up the campaign.*

> Gage did nothing and went to pot;
> Howe lost one town, another got;
> Guy★ nothing lost and nothing won
> Dunmore was homeward forced to run;
> Clinton was beat, but got a Garter;†
> And bouncing Burgoyne caught a Tartar;
> Thus all we gain from millions spent
> Is to be laughed at, and repent.

But for the Loyalists it was now a story of disaster, persecution and exile. John Peters had lived with his wife and seven children in the disputed country known as the New York Grants. He left a vivid account of the family's experiences.

March 1777. Two deserters from the Rebel Country arrived at Montreal and informed that my property had been seiz'd, Confiscated, and myself outlawed, and that Mrs Peters and the Children had been turned out of my House in the Month of January, 1777, that she and her Children had been sent of[f] in a Slay with one Bed by *Deacon* Bailey to Ticonderoga 140 Miles thro' the Woods, Snow, Storm, and bad Roads. That Mrs Peters, a small and delicate Woman, had been compelled to travel with her young Children in her Arms in deep Snow and Rain and were almost dead when they arrived at Ticonderoga, where the Rebel General Wayne received them with humanity and used them kindly till

★Carleton, Governor-General of Canada.
†This is incorrect. Clinton was knighted, but did not receive the Garter.

April, when he sent her and her Children thirty Miles on their way to Canada and left them with three Weeks provisions in a deserted House near fifty Miles from any Inhabitants between them and Canada. Here she stayed Eighteen Days with her Children only (the oldest but fourteen Years), her Servant having been detained by Deacon Bailey (for which General Wayne said he ought to be damn'd). At length a British Boat discovered and carried them to a Vessel and thence to Saint Johns [St Jean on the Richelieu River], where they all arrived on the 4th of May, 1777, well but naked and dirty.

May 6th, 1777, I met my Wife and Children at Saint Johns . . . with Cloathing and other necessarys and I carried them to Montreal by Water, over the Rapids at Chamblee. I had a French pilot and four Men (Sailors) in a Batteaux . . . Descending these Rapids we struck a Rock and the Stern of the Batteaux broke and open'd. We was near the trough of a Mill; the Sailors were in the water in a moment. It was lucky we was so nigh shore. I was but up to my middle in water to take Mrs Peters on my Shoulders and landed her safe. In the meantime the Sailors had haul'd the broken boat so near shore as my eldest Son John (he was fourteen Years old) took the Youngest, my Seventh, in his Arms, and the sailors the rest. The French Pilot ran of[f] very fast. The sailors were for following and beating him, but I stopped them. They said he told them he knew every Rock. I told them it was true, for we had struck every one above where we were wreck'd. I put them in good humour & give them some Grogg. We lost a loaf of Sugar in the Water. Got another Batteaux from the Commanding Officer at Chamblee and went down the River Sorrel 40 Miles . . . Mr McCummings . . . provided Lodgings and in the morning gave us a breakfast and we went up the River to Montreal. The reason we went by water was the roads were so bad. We could not by land get from St Johns to Montreal . . .

August 16th, 1777, I commanded the Loyalists at Bennington, where I had 291 Men of my Regiment with me, and I lost above half of them in that Engagement. The action commenced about nine o'Clock in the Morning and continued till near four o'Clock afternoon, when we retired in much confusion. A little before the Royalists gave way, the Rebels pushed with a Strong party on the Front of the Loyalists where I commanded. As they were coming up I observed a Man fire at me, which I returned. He loaded again as he came up and discharged again at me, and, crying out: 'Peters, you Damned Tory, I have got you,' he rushed on me with his Bayonet, which entered just below my left Breast, but was turned by the Bone. By this time I was loaded and I saw that it was a Rebel Captain, and old Schoolfellow & Playmate, and a

Couzin of my Wife's. Tho' his Bayonet was in my Body, I felt regret at being obliged to destroy him . . .

The report of the defeat of the Royal Troops at Bennington reaching Montreal, Gen McLean, Colonel of the 84th Regiment, went to Mrs Peters and told her bad news had come from General Burgoynes Camp and that she must expect to hear of many being killed and wounded, but if Colonel Peters or her son were among them she must hold up with good courage and not despond, as he would see to care being taken of her and her Family that they should never want.

After some conversation in like manner, Gen McLean thought proper to let her know that there was a report that Col Peters and his Son were both wounded and since Dead. Mrs Peters said 'my calamities are very great, but, thank God, they died doing their duty to their King and Country. I have Six Sons left, who, as soon as they shall be able to bear Arms, I will send against the Rebels, while I and my Daughter will mourn for the Dead and pray for the living.'

The significance of Burgoyne's capitulation was not lost on the government of Louis XVI, which began to plan for open intervention on the American side. It had little effect on Sir William Howe in Philadelphia, except for a campaign in words to blame Clinton for failing to go to Burgoyne's help. His own army in Philadelphia had a relaxed time of it, as Francis Hopkinson attested.

Sir William he, snug as a flea,
Lay all this time a snoring
Nor dream'd of harm as he lay warm
In bed with Mrs Loring

Now in a fright, he starts upright
Awak'd by such a clatter;
He rubs both eyes, and boldly cries,
For God's sake, what's the matter?

At his bed-side he then espied
Sir Erskine at command, sir,
Upon one foot, he had one boot,
and th' other in his hand, sir.

'Arise, arise' Sir Erskine cries,
'The rebels — more's the pity,
Without a boat are all afloat,
And Rang'd before the city.

113

'The motley crew, in vessels new,
With Satan for their guide, sir,
Pack'd up in bags, or wooden kegs,
Come driving down the tide, sir.

'Therefore prepare for bloody war,
These kegs must all be routed,
Or surely we despised shall be,
And British courage doubted.'

*The kegs were simply barrels of explosives designed to damage any British ships they
might meet, and they did little damage — except to British 'face'. Trade in Philadelphia was brisk — French brandy was 19/— a quart, West India rum 15/— and
gin 9/—. It was said that there were 122 new stores, of which one was kept by an
Englishman, one by an American and 120 by 'Scotsmen or Tories from Virginia'.
The stage was popular and the ladies, notably Peggy Chew, Peggy Shippen and Polly
Redman had a gay time.*

I will now, my dear, suppose you anxious for an account of our last
winter. You have no doubt, heard that 'twas a gay one, as likewise the
censure thrown on many of the poor girls for not scorning the pleasures
that courted them. You, my friend, I am certain, have liberality of
sentiment, and can make proper allowances for young people in the
bloom of life and spirits, after being so long deprived of the gaieties and
amusements of life, which their ages and spirits called for. How hard a
task it must then be to resist temptation of that nature! Plays, concerts,
balls, assemblies in rotation courted their presence. Politics were never
introduced. The known Whig ladies were treated with equal politeness
and attention with the Tory ladies. I myself, though a noted one, was at
last prevailed on to partake of some of the amusements, though nothing
could have made me believe, at the beginning of the winter, that such a
thing was possible. I am generally styled, in raillery, with several other
ladies, 'rebel', but I had always effrontery enough to declare that I
gloried in the name, and thought it virtuous to rebel in some cases as in
the present. They never failed collecting the Whig news for me, and
from them I received the glorious news of Burgoyne's defeat . . . which
lengthened faces amazingly.

The press, as always, was alarmist.

We hear from London, that a treaty is to be concluded with Russia for
taking thirty-six thousand Russians into pay; and with the King of

114

Prussia, but the contents are not known. It is not for a body of his troops; but twelve thousand more Hessians, Wurtemburgers, Palatines, and Mecklenburgers, are agreed for. Four and twenty new regiments are to be raised in England and Ireland of five hundred men each, so that the army in America, next campaign, will not be short of eighty thousand men.   *New-Jersey Gazette, 5 December*

It is observable that at the opening of every campaign in the spring, the British plunderers, and their Tory emmissaries, announce the total reduction of America before the winter. In the fall they find themselves as remote from their purpose as they were in the spring; and then we are threatened with innumerable hosts from Russia and Germany, who will utterly extirpate us the ensuing summer, or reduce us to the most abject submission. They have so beat this beaten track, that for mere sake of variety, I would advise them to explore a new road; and not compel us to nauseate a falsehood, not only because we know it to be one, but for its perpetual repetition without the least variation of alternity. According to custom, therefore, the new lie (that is the old lie reiterated) for next summer is, that we are to be devoured, bones and all, by thirty-six thousand Russians; besides something or other that is to be done to us by the King of Prussia. What this is to be, is still a profound secret; but as it will be doubtless something very extraordinary, and it being impossible to conceive what else he can do to us, after we are swallowed by the Russians, he is probably, by some political emitic or other, to bring us up again. I should think, in common complaisance to human reason, that absurdities so gross, and figments so destitute of probability, could only deceive those who choose to be deceived. The Empress of Russia, though a sovereign in petticoats, knows too well that the true riches of a nation consist in the number of its inhabitants, to suffer such a number of her inhabitants to be knocked in the head in America, for the sake of facilitating the frantic project of a more southern potentate in breeches, deluded by a blundering ministry, and the universal derision of Europe. It is her interest (and I shall wonder if ever princes proceed upon any other principle, before the commencement of the millennium) to have America dismembered from Great Britain, which must of necessity reduce the naval power of the latter, and make Russia a full match for her on the ocean. And as for the King of Prussia, considering that there never was any love lost between him and the family of Brunswick, and that he has long been jealous of the maritime strength of Britain, these artifices of fraud might, with equal plausibility, have introduced the Emperor of Japan as entering into leagues and alliances with our late master at St James. It is nothing but an impudent forgery from first to last, and merely fabricated to restore to their natural shape and features, the crest fallen countenances of the Tories, and if possible, to intimidate the genuine sons of America.

The utmost they can do, they have already done; and are this moment as far from any prospect of subjecting us to the dominion of Britain, as they were in the ridiculous hour in which General Gage first arrived in Boston. This is no secret with those who have the management of their armies in America, how greatly so-ever the nation itself it may be deluded by the pompous accounts of their progress. But whatever becomes of Old England at last, these gentlemen are sure of accumulating immense wealth during the war; and are therefore determined to keep up the delusion as long as possible. Burgoyne is the only one of any distinction, who has virtue enough to own the truth; and I am credibly informed, that he has frankly declared, that he was most egregiously deceived in the Americans, that he has been led to believe they would never come to bayoneting, that they behaved with the greatest intrepidity in attacking intrenchments, that although a regiment of his grenadiers and light infantry displayed in an engagement with Colonel Morgan's battalion of riflemen, the most astonishing gallantry, Morgan exceeded them in dexterity and generalship, and that it was utterly impossible ever to conquer America.

'Hortentius' (Governor William Livingstone)
New-Jersey Gazette, 24 December

A week before Christmas 1777, Washington took his men into winter camp twenty miles away from Philadelphia, at Valley Forge, on the west side of the Schuylkill — 'a dreary kind of place', he said, 'and uncomfortably provided.' While for the British, the winter brought good beef and rich butter, the American officers, said Sullivan, were 'so naked they were ashamed to be seen'. The diary of the sickly doctor, twenty-seven-year-old surgeon Albigence Waldo of Connecticut, is vivid reading.

Dec 12th We are ordered to march over the river — it snows — I'm sick — eat nothing — no whiskey — no baggage — Lord — Lord — Lord. The army were till sunrise crosssing the river — some at the wagon bridge and some at the raft bridge below. Cold and uncomfortable . . .

Dec 14th Poor food — hard lodging — cold weather — fatigue — nasty clothes — nasty cookery — vomit half my time — smoked out of my senses — the Devil's in it — I can't endure it — why are we sent here to starve and freeze – what sweet felicities have I left at home – a charming wife – pretty children – good food – good cookery – all agreeable – all harmonious. Here, all confusion – smoke and cold – hunger and filthiness – a pox on my bad luck. Here comes a bowl of beef soup – full of burnt leaves and dirt, sickish enough to make a Hector spew – away with it Boys – I'll live like the chameleon upon air.

Dec 15th Quiet. Eat persimmons, found myself better for their lenient operation . . .

What have you for dinner boys? 'Nothing but fire cake & water, Sir.' – 'Gentlemen, the supper is ready.' What is your supper lads? 'Fire cake & water, Sir.'

What have you got for breakfast, lads? 'Fire cake and water, Sir.' The Lord send that our Commissary of Purchases may live on fire cake and water, till their glutted guts are turned to pasteboard . . .

Dec 25th, Christmas We are still in tents – when we ought to be in huts – the poor sick, suffer much in tents this cold weather –

Dec 28th Yesterday, upwards of fifty officers in General Greene's Division resigned their commission, six or seven of our regiment are doing the like today. All this is occasion'd by officers' families being so much neglected at home on account of provisions. Their wages will not by considerable purchase a few trifling comfortables here in camp, and maintain their families at home, while such extravagant prices are demanded for the common necessaries of life . . . When the officer has been fatiguing through the wet and cold and returns to his tent where he finds a letter directed to him from his wife, fill'd with the most heart-aching, tender complaints a woman is capable of writing, acquainting him with the incredible difficulty with which she procures a little bread for herself and children, and finally concluding with expressions bordering on despair of procuring a sufficiency of food to keep soul & body together through the winter – that the money is of little consequence to her – that she begs him to consider that charity begins at home, and not suffer his family to perish with want, in the midst of plenty . . .

Dr Benjamin Rush, an Edinburgh-educated doctor, was appalled at what he saw.

The encampment dirty and stinking, no forage for 7 days – 1500 horses died from ye want of it. 3 Ounces of meal and 3 pounds of flour in 7 days. The Commander-in-Chief and all ye Major Generals live in houses out of ye camp.

He admitted that the commander-in-chief was 'the idol of America' but he thought

*that he was 'under the baneful influence of Generals Greene and Knox and Col.
Hamilton, one of his aids, a young man of 21 years of age.' As to Major Generals
Greene, Sullivan, Stirling, and Adam Stephen:*

'The 1st a sycophant to the general, timid, speculative, without enterprise; the 2nd, weak, vain, without dignity, fond of scribbling, in the
field, a madman. The 3rd, a proud, vain, lazy, ignorant, drunkard. The
4th a sordid, boasting, cowardly sot.'

*His judgment was correct in the case of Adam Stephen, court-martialed and
cashiered in disgrace for drunkenness. The state of the army was not impressive:*

'The troops dirty, undisciplined and ragged; guns fired 100 a day;
pickets left 5 days and sentries 24 hours, without relief; bad bread; no
order; universal disgust.'

1778

You cannot conquer America

The spring brought hope to the Americans. The German officer Baron Friedrich von Steuben, who claimed to have been a lieutenant-general on the staff of Frederick the Great, but who was in fact originally a captain – Wilhelm Steube – became drill-master. His methods were unorthodox but effective.

On arriving, the only English word he knew was 'Goddamn'. To make his instructions clear he called on his aide, Ben Walker, even to do his swearing. He spoke French on the parade ground to interpreters who translated his commands for him. He made himself understood and respected, and his polyglot capacity to swear won him the soldiers' affection.

Viens, Walker, mon ami, mon bon ami! Sacré! Goddamn de gaucheries of dese badouts! Je ne puis plus. I can curse dem no more!

He had only a few months to turn out fighting men, whereas European training had required two or three years to produce the complex manoeuvres of linear tactics. He cut down the motions for loading, introduced a step and cadence suited to rough country, and taught his men to march in a column of four. He was a martinet but only a martinet could make an army out of a rabble. And behind the bluster there was a sharp intelligence, as his instructions to his company officers indicated.

At six o'clock in the morning the division is ordered to general parade, and the soldiers in the squads of always eight, are drilled in ordinary marching. A non-commissioned officer marches at their right, a little in advance, to give the time and the step, and he drills them in marching with and without music or drums. This drill lasts two hours. At nine o'clock is the parade; the soldiers are then taught the few movements in which they are to be instructed after the use of arms. At noon, particular instruction is given to the non-commissioned officers. At three o'clock, drilling in divisions as in the morning; at six o'clock PM meeting of the adjutants in my quarters for instructions in theoretic manoeuvering and the emphasis to be used in giving the word of command.

A captain cannot be too careful of the company the state has committed to his charge. He must pay the greatest attention to the health of his men, their discipline, arms, accoutrements, ammunition, clothes and necessaries. His first object should be to gain the love of his men by treating them with every possible kindness and humanity, inquiring into their complaints and when well founded, seeing them redressed. He should know every man of his company by name and character. He should often visit those who are sick, speak tenderly to them, see that the public provision, whether of medicine or diet, is duly administered, and procure them besides such comforts and medicines as are in his power.

He realised the absence of that bedrock of the European army — the sergeant-major — and tried to inculcate in officers a genuine concern for their men. There were too many servants — one half of the camp, he said, seemed to be waiting on the other.

He transformed the character of Washington's army; concern with sanitation and garbage reduced sick lists; refusal to permit three-month recruits returning home to take their equipment with them as a perquisite of service drastically reduced losses; and training in tactics and manoeuvre became a feature of the army. At last a professionalism was born, as the careers of Greene, Knox and Wayne all indicated. The young Hessian, Johann Ewald, who later wrote a study of guerilla war based on his experiences in America, wrote:

I was sometimes astonished when American baggage fell into our hands . . . to see how every wretched knapsack, in which were only a few shirts and a pair of torn breeches, would be filled with such military works as *The Instructions of the King of Prussia to his Generals*, Theilke's *Field Engineer*, the partisans Jenny and Grandmaison . . . This was a true indication that the officers of this army studied the art of war while in camp, which was not the case with the opponents of the Americans, whose portmanteaux were rather filled with bags of hair powder, boxes of sweet-smelling pomatum, cards (instead of maps), and then often, on top of all, novels or stage plays.

Washington had to deceive the British by exaggerating his numbers; the deception worked on local people also. There was mounting impatience. Dr Waldo assessed the scene shrewdly.

The enemy have been some days [on] the west [of] Schuylkill, from opposite the city to Derby. Their intentions not yet known. The city is at present pretty clear of them. Why don't his Excellency rush in and retake the city . . .? Because he knows better than to leave his post and be catched like a d——d fool cooped up in the city. He has always acted wisely hitherto. His conduct when closely scrutinized is uncensurable. Were his inferior generals as skillful as himself, we should have the grandest choir of officers ever God made.

Many country gentlemen in the interior parts of the states who get wrong information of the affairs and state of our camp are very much surprised at General Washington's delay to drive off the enemy, being falsely informed that his army consists of double the number of the enemy's. Such wrong information serves not to keep up the spirit of the people, as they must be by-and-by undeceived to their no small disappointment. It brings blame on his Excellency, who is deserving of the greatest encomiums. It brings disgrace on the Continental troops who have never evidenced the least backwardness in doing their duty, but on the contrary have cheerfully endured a long and very fatiguing campaign . . . Impartial truth in future history will clear up these points and reflect lasting honor on the wisdom and prudence of General Washington . . .

Reinforcements steadily came in; the troops were innoculated against smallpox; the dogwood bloomed. On 1 May Washington heard the news that in February France had signed a treaty of alliance. So now the Americans had an ally with men, ships and money. They held a feu de joie.

On firing the third signal gun, the feu de joye commenced. It was conducted with great judgement and regularity. The gradual progression of the sound from the discharge of the cannon and the musketry, swelling and rebounding from the neighbouring hills, and gently sweeping along the Schuylkill; with the intermingled huzzas – to 'Long live the King of France', 'Long live the friendly European powers', and 'Long live the American States', composed a military music more agreeable to the soldier's ear than the most finished pieces of your favorite, Handel.

Some republicans, like Major Samuel Shaw, were not happy.

By Heavens! If our rulers had any modesty, they would blush at the idea of calling in foreign aid! 'tis really abominable, that we should send to France for soldiers, when there are so many sons of America idle.

Such a step ought not (had these great men any sensibility) to have been taken until the strength of the country had been nearly exhausted, and our freedom tottering on the brink of ruin. Let us be indebted to France, Spain or even the Devil himself, if he could furnish it, for a navy, because we cannot get one seasonably among ourselves. But do let us, unless we are contented to be transmitted to posterity with disgrace, make an exertion of our own strength by land, and not owe our independence entirely to our allies.

General Conway, an Irish-born officer who was in the employ of France and serving with the Americans, and General James Wilkinson, voiced criticisms of Washington. A letter by Conway to Horatio Gates was the substance of what has gone down in history as 'the Conway Cabal'. There is no hard evidence of an organised movement to replace Washington by Gates, who would no doubt willingly have accepted the call had it come, but Conway was challenged (and badly wounded in the mouth) to a duel — with pistols at ten paces — by General John Cadwalader, and returned to France.

Washington's position was strengthened, not weakened, by the affair. Sheer survival was more important even than success in battle in ensuring ultimate victory.

Conway was not only, in Washington's eyes, 'an incendiary', but a foreigner. Washington was plagued with such volunteers, who came over with letters of introduction from Silas Deane or Benjamin Franklin, the American ambassadors in Paris. Of one, the nineteen-year-old Marquis de Lafayette, Washington became fond; others — du Portail as an engineer, Steuben as drill-master, Pulaski as an organiser of cavalry — rendered great service. But there were too many; they all demanded seniority in rank and they all found the ways of the natives very strange, as did the Chevalier de Pontgibaud, aide-de-camp to Lafayette.

I was astonished to find what peculiar ideas our host, the Americans of New England, had of the French. One day I dismounted from my horse at the house of a farmer upon whom I had been billeted. I had hardly entered the good man's house when he said to me.

'I am very glad to have a Frenchman in the house.'

I politely enquired the reason for this preference.

'Well,' he said, 'you see the barber lives a long way off, so you will be able to shave me.'

'But I cannot even shave myself,' I replied. 'My servant shaves me, and he will shave you also if you like.'

'That's very odd,' said he. 'I was told that all Frenchmen were barbers and fiddlers.'

I think I never laughed so heartily. A few minutes later my rations arrived, and my host seeing a large piece of beef amongst them said,

'You are lucky to be able to come over to America and get some beef to eat.'

I assured him that we had beef in France, and excellent beef too.

'That is impossible,' he replied, 'or you wouldn't be so thin.'

Such was – when liberty was dawning over the land – the ignorance shown by the inhabitants of the United States Republic in regard to the French.

The entry of France, however, transformed the war. It led the British to withdraw from Philadelphia, and Ambrose Serle revealed the alarm that spread among the British commanders, including Quarter-Master General Sir William Erskine.

Friday 22nd. A confirmation of the sad intelligence of yesterday was communicated to Mr Galloway by Sir Wm Erskine from Sir Wm Howe and Sir H Clinton. It filled my poor friend, as might be expected, with horror and melancholy on the view of his deplorable situation: exposed to the rage of his bitter enemies, deprived of a fortune of about £70,000, and now left to wander like Cain upon the earth without home and without property. Many others are involved in the like dismal case for the same reason – attachment to their King and country, and opposition to a set of daring Rebels who might soon be crushed by spirited exertions. I now look upon the contest as at an end. No man can be expected to declare for us when he cannot be assured of a fortnight's protection. Every man, on the contrary, whatever might have been his primary inclinations, will find it his interest to oppose and drive us out of the country. I endeavored to console, as well as to advise my friend. I felt for him and with him. Nothing remains for him but to attempt reconciliation with (what I may now venture to call) the United States of America; which probably may not succeed, as they have attainted him in body and goods by an Act of the Legislature of Pennsylvania. O thou righteous God, where will all this villainy end!

But on 8 May Howe received the news that Sir Henry Clinton was to be his successor. He had requested to be replaced and was pleased by the news. His troops gave him a farewell involving a water parade of barges and galleys, a tournament and a ball – an English feu de joie. The fireworks of this 'mischiana' was the only gunpowder Howe had smelt for nine months.

Many residents, and indeed many officers, thought the celebrations in deplorable taste. Much more outraged was Mrs Henry Drinker, whose husband had been punished for Loyalism.

'This day', she said, 'may be remembered by many for the scenes of folly and vanity . . . How insensible do these people appear, while our land is so greatly desolated, and death and sore destruction has overtaken and impends over so many.'

On 17 June, Clinton withdrew his 11,000 men overland by way of New Brunswick, on the Raritan, to Amboy and Staten Island, thence by boat to New York. They moved slowly, hampered by 1500 military and refugee baggage wagons, which stretched out along twelve miles of the road.

Charles Lee had been ordered to attack the British rearguard, but hesitated, with devastating consequences. Washington's Council of War acted, said Alexander Hamilton, Washington's young aide-de-camp, as 'a body of midwives'.

General Lee's conduct with respect to the command of this corps was truly childish. According to the incorrect notions of our army, his seniority would entitle him to command of the advanced corps, but he in the first instance declined it in favor of the Marquis.

Some of his friends having blamed him for doing it, and Lord Stirling having shown a disposition to interpose his claim, General Lee very inconsistently reasserted his pretensions. The matter was a second time accommodated; General Lee and Lord Stirling agreed to let the Marquis command. General Lee, a little time after, recanted again, and became very importunate. The General, who all along had observed the greatest candor in this matter, grew tired of such fickle behavior, and ordered the Marquis to proceed.

The enemy, in marching from Allentown had changed their disposition, and thrown all their best troops in the rear. This made it necessary, to strike a blow with propriety, to reinforce the advanced corps. Two brigades were detached for this purpose, and the General, willing to accommodate General Lee, sent him with them to take command of the whole advanced corps, which rendezvoused the forenoon of the 27th at English Town, consisting of at least 5000 rank and file, most of them select troops. General Lee's orders were, the moment he received intelligence of the enemy's march, to pursue them and to attack their rear.

This intelligence was received about five o'clock in the morning of the 28th, and General Lee put his troops in motion accordingly. The main body did the same. The advanced corps came up with the enemy's rear a mile or two beyond the [Monmouth] Courthouse. I saw the enemy drawn up, and am persuaded there were not a thousand men — their front from different accounts was then ten miles off. However favorable this situation may seem for attack, it was not made.

The Marquis de Lafayette also recorded the event, writing in the third person as always.

The army of the United States, which was of nearly equal force, directed itself from Valley Forge to Coryell's Ferry, and from thence to King's Town, within a march of the enemy; it was thus left at the option of the Americans, either to follow on their track or to repair to White Plains.

In a council held on this subject, Lee very eloquently endeavoured to prove that it was necessary to erect a bridge of gold for the enemy; that while on the very point of forming an alliance with them, every thing ought not to be placed at hazard; that the English army had never been so excellent and so well disciplined he declared himself to be for White Plains: his speech influenced the opinion of Lord Stirling and of the brigadiers-general.

M. de Lafayette, placed on the other side spoke late, and asserted that it would be disgraceful for the chiefs, and humiliating for the troops, to allow the enemy to traverse the Jerseys tranquilly; that, without running any improper risk, the rear guard might be attacked; that it was necessary to follow the English, manoeuvre with prudence, take advantage of a temporary separation, and, in short, seize the most favourable opportunities and situations. This advice was approved by many of the council, and above all by M. du Portail, chief of the engineers, and a very distinguished officer. The Majority were, however, in favour of Lee; but M. de Lafayette spoke again to the general on this subject in the evening, and was seconded by Hamilton, and by Greene.

When contact was eventually made at Monmouth Courthouse, Lee withdrew his men. Private Joseph Martin was among those ordered to retreat.

We had not retreated far before we came to a defile, a muddy sloughy brook; while the artillery were passing this place, we sat down by the road side; – in a few minutes the Commander-in-chief and suit crossed the road just where we were sitting. I heard him ask our officers, 'by whose order the troops were retreating,' and being answered, 'by Gen. Lee's,' he said something, but as he was moving forward all the time this was passing, he was too far off for me to hear it distinctly; those that were nearer to him said that his words were – 'D——n him'; whether he did thus express himself or not I do not know; it was certainly very unlike him, but he seemed at the instant to be in a great passion his looks if not his words seemed to indicate as much.

The same observer noticed other details.

One little incident happened during the heat of the cannonade, which I was eye-witness to, and which I think would be unpardonable not to mention. A woman whose husband belonged to the Artillery, and who was then attached to a piece in the engagement, attended with her husband at the piece the whole time. While in the act of reaching a cartridge and having one of her feet as far before the other as she could step, a cannon shot from the enemy passed directly between her legs without doing any other damage than carrying away all the lower part of her petticoat. Looking at it with apparent unconcern, she observed that it was lucky it did not pass a little higher, for in that case it might have carried away something else, and continued her occupation.

At the famous confrontation about this episode between Washington and Lee, Washington, according to General Charles Scott of Virginia,

swore on that day till the leaves shook on the trees, charming, delightful. Never have I enjoyed such swearing before or since. Sir, on that ever-memorable day, he swore like an angel from Heaven . . .

(How Scott was present, and not with his own command, is not clear, and his account is probably invented. It should be added that, in profanity, he was an expert in his own right.)

There was another observer, a Maryland captain, however, who confirmed the story.

General Washington rode up and upbraided General Lee for his dastardly conduct. General Washington demanded of General Lee the reason for the retreat, to which General Lee replied: 'Sir, these troops are not able to meet British grenadiers.'

'Sir,' said General Washington, much excited, 'they are able, and by God they shall do it,' and immediately gave orders to countermarch the column.

Lee was court-martialled, and suspended from the service. He defended himself thus:

By all that's sacred, General Washington had scarcely any more to do in it than to strip the dead. By want of proper intelligence we were ordered to attack the covering party supposed to consist only of fifteen hundred men. Our intelligence, as usual, was false – it proved to be the whole flower of the British army, grenadiers, light infantry, cavalry and artillery, amounting in the whole to seven thousand men. By the temerity, folly and contempt of orders of General Wayne, we found ourselves engaged in the most extensive plain in America, separated from our main body the distance of eight miles . . .

The General has the madness to charge me with making a shameful retreat – I never retreated, in fact (for 'till I joined him, it was not a retreat but a necessary, and I may say in my own defence, masterly maneuver). I say I never retreated but by his positive order who invidiously sent me out of the field when the victory was assur'd. Such is my recompense for having sacrificed my friends, my connections, and perhaps my fortune for having twice extricated this man and his whole army out of perdition, and now having given him the only victory he ever tasted.

Lee was not restored to any position, and died four years later in Philadelphia, at 'The Sign of the Conestoga Wagon', in poverty and disgrace, attended at the last only by two of his faithful dogs. His will was as bizarre as his life.

I desire most earnestly that I may not be buried in any church, or church yard, or within a mile of any Presbyterian or Anabaptist meeting house; for since I have resided in this country, I have had so much bad company while living, that I do not choose to continue it when dead.

I recommend my soul to the Creator of all worlds and of all creatures, who must, from his visible attributes, be indifferent to their modes of worship or creeds, whether Christian, Mohammedans, or Jews; whether instilled by education, or taken up by reflection; whether more or less absurd; as a weak mortal can no more be answerable for his persuasions, notions, or even skepticism in religion, than for the color of his skin.

Monmouth Courthouse was one of the longest battles of the war, and the hottest – the temperature was over 100° F – and Washington's huge new white horse, a gift from the Governor of New Jersey, died of exhaustion. Each side lost some 350 officers and men, of which sixty of the British died from sunstroke. General Simcoe reported proudly that the Queen's Rangers lost none from desertion; he was right to emphasise what was unusual – at least 500 British (most of them Hessians) deserted. Indeed, of the 30,000 Hessian mercenaries in the war as a whole, some 12,000 never returned to Europe, and most of these were deserters, not casualties.

Monmouth Courthouse was to be the last major military engagement in the north. Anthony Wayne, one of nature's optimists, saluted a great victory.

Tell the Philadelphia ladies that the heavenly sweet, pretty redcoats, the accomplished gentlemen of the Guards and Grenadiers on the plains of Monmouth, 'The Knights of the Blended Rose' and 'Burning Mount' have resigned their laurels to Rebel officers, who will lay them at the feet of those virtuous daughters of America who cheerfully gave up ease and affluence in a city for liberty and peace of mind in a cottage . . .

The American forces returned to Philadelphia, led by thirty-eight-year-old Benedict Arnold — recovering from his second leg wound in the war, which he had received at Bemis Heights — at the head of the American Light Horse, with so many 'drawn swords in their hands' that they alarmed the peaceful citizenry. General Knox and his wife, Lucy, came over from Valley Forge but the city 'stank so abominably that it was impossible to stay there'. Arnold stayed to meet, and within the year to marry, the aristocratic nineteen-year-old Peggy Shippen, to buy a mansion — Mount Pleasant — on the Schuylkill, and to enjoy the good life, which for him now meant liveried servants and a coach-and-four.

Was there any permanent legacy of the nine-month British occupation of Philadelphia? One exile's comments on his return were bitter:

Upon getting into the city, I was surprised to find that it had suffered so little. I question whether it would have fared better had our own troops had possession of it, that is, as to the buildings, but the morals of the inhabitants have suffered vastly. The enemy introduced new fashions and made old vices more common; the former are the most absurd, ridiculous and preposterous you can conceive. I can give no description that will convey an adequate idea of them. So far as they concern the gentlemen, they appear to be principally confined to the hat, which is now amazingly broad-rimmed and cocked very sharp; were they flapped after the manner of the people called Quakers, these brims would be useful in this hot weather, because they would afford an agreeable shade to the face, but in the present mode, they serve only as an encumbrance to the blocks they cover.

The females who stayed in the city while it was in possession of the enemy cut a curious figure. Their hats, which are of the flat round kind, are of the size of a large japanned tea-waiter; their caps exceed any of the fantastic prints you have seen, and their hair is dressed with the assistance of wool, &c., in such a manner as to appear too heavy to be supported by their necks. If the caps would not blow off, a north-

Benjamin Franklin, American ambassador in Paris

Silas Deane, Franklin's fellow ambassador

The Marquis de Lafayette

wester would certainly throw these belles off their center, as Yorick did the milliner — by accident.

I cannot yet learn whether the cork rumps have been introduced here, but some artificial rumps or other are necessary to counter-balance the extraordinary natural weight which some of the ladies carry before them. You will probably be surprised at this, but you may rely upon it as a fact. Indeed, many people do not hesitate in supposing that most of the young ladies who were in the city with the enemy, and wear the present fashionable dresses, have purchased them at the expence of their virtue. It is agreed on all hands, that the British officers played the devil with the girls; the privates, I suppose, were satisfied with the common prostitutes.

Last Saturday an imitation of the mischianza, with which General Howe was honor'd was humbly attempted. A noted strumpet was paraded through the streets with her head dressed in the modern British taste, to the no small amusement of a vast crowd of spectators. She acted her part well — to complete the farce, there ought to have been another lady of the same character (as General Howe had two), and somebody to represent a British officer.

If the news of Saratoga sent a shock-wave through Philadelphia, its effect on London was volcanic. Lord Chatham thundered in the Lords:

No man thinks more highly than I of the virtue and valour of British troops; I know they can achieve anything except impossibilities; and the conquest of English America is an impossibility. You cannot, I venture to say it, *you cannot conquer America* . . . What is your present situation there? We do not know the worst, but we know that in three campaigns we have done nothing, and suffered much . . . Conquest is impossible: you may swell every expense and every effort still more extravagantly; pile and accumulate every assistance you can buy or borrow; traffic and barter with every little pitiful German prince that sells his subjects to the shambles of a foreign power; your efforts are forever vain and impotent; doubly so from this mercenary aid on which you rely; for it irritates to an incurable resentment the minds of your enemies. To overrun them with the mercenary sons of rapine and plunder; devoting them and their possessions to the rapacity of hireling cruelty! If I were an American, as I am an Englishman, while a foreign troop was landed in my country, I never would lay down my arms, never — never — never!

Lord North's government, with an impressive intelligence network throughout Europe, knew all that was going on in Paris, and especially at Passy, where Benjamin Franklin had his headquarters. The Secretary of the American Embassy, Edward Bancroft, was throughout the war a British spy ('Edwards') and was not discovered for a century. Only George III was suspicious of him, not only because he was a double-spy, but also a notorious stock-jobber. In 1784 Bancroft gave a detailed account of his work to the Marquis of Carmarthen, the Foreign Secretary.

Duke Street, London, 17 September 1784
In the month of June 1776, Mr Silas Deane arrived in France, and pursuant to an instruction given him by the Secret Committee of Congress, wrote to me in London, requesting an interview in Paris, where I accordingly went early in July and was made acquainted with the purposes of his mission and with everything which passed between him and the French Ministry. After staying two or three weeks there, I returned to England, convinced that the Government of France would endeavour to promote an absolute separation of the then United Colonies from Great Britain, unless a speedy termination of the revolt, by reconciliation or conquest, should frustrate this project.

I had then resided near ten years, and expected to reside the rest of my life, in England; and all my views, interests and inclinations were adverse to the independancy of the Colonies, though I had advocated some of their claims from a persuasion of their being founded in justice. I therefore wished that the Government of this country might be informed of the danger of French interference, though I could not resolve to become the informant. But Mr Paul Wentworth having gained some general knowledge of my journey to France and of my intercourse with Mr Deane, and having induced me to believe that the British Ministry were likewise informed on this subject, I at length consented to meet the then Secretaries of State, Lords Weymouth and Suffolk, and give them all the information in my power; which I did with the most disinterested views, for I not only did not ask, but expressly rejected, every idea of any reward.

The Declaration of Independancy was not then known in Europe, and I hoped that Government, thus informed of the danger, would prevent it by some accomodation with the Colonies, or by other means. It had been my original intention to stop after this first communication; but having given the first notice of a beginning intercourse between France and the United Colonies, I was urged on to watch and disclose the progress of it; for which purpose I made several journeys to Paris and maintained a regular correspondence with Mr Deane through the couriers of the French Government. And in this way I became *entangled* and obliged to proceed in a kind of business as repugnant to my feelings as it had been to my original intentions.

Being thus devoted to the service of Government, I consented, like others, to accept such emoluments as my situation indeed required. And in Feb'y 1777, Lord Suffolk, to whom by Lord Weymouth's consent my communications were then made, formally promised me, in the King's name, a pension for life of £200 per annum, to commence from the Christmas preceeding. This was for services *then rendered;* and as an inducement for me to go over and reside in France and continue my services there until the revolt should terminate or an open rupture with that nation ensue, his Lordship farther promised that when either of these events should happen, my permanent pension of £200 per annum should be increased to £500 *at least*.

Confiding in this promise, I went to Paris, and during the first year resided in the same house with Dr Franklin, Mr Deane, etc., and regularly informed this Government of every transaction of the American Commissioners; of every step and vessel taken to supply the revolted Colonies with artillery, arms, etc.; of every part of their intercourse with the French and other European courts; of the powers and instructions given by Congress to the Commissioners, and their correspondence with the Secret Committees, etc.; and when the Government of France at length determined openly to support the revolted Colonies, I gave notice of this determination, and of the progress made in forming the two Treaties of Alliance and Commerce, and when these were signed, on the evening of the 6th of Feb'y, I at my own expence, by a special messenger and with unexampled dispatch conveyed this intelligence to this city, and to the King's Ministers, within 42 hours from the instant of their signature, a piece of information for which many individuals here would, for purposes of speculation, had given me more than all that I have received from Government. Afterwards, when that decisive measure of sending Count d'Estaing with the fleet from Toulon to commence hostilities at the Delaware and New York was adopted, I sent intelligence of the direct object and plan of the expedition.

The Treaty of Alliance between France and the United States came, then, as no surprise to Britain. It was the all but inevitable result of Saratoga — and of Germantown, a battle that impressed the Comte de Vergennes, the French Foreign Minister. The French had long intended to weaken Britain without, if it could be avoided, abetting social revolution, which might not stop at frontiers. Their methods so far had been by contributing indirect aid, without resorting to open warfare, mainly through a fictitious company, Hortalez et Cie., set up by the playwright, and adventurer, Caron de Beaumarchais, who was later to write The Marriage of Figaro. *In 1776 one million livres' worth ($200,000) of supplies was given; the sum was doubled in 1777.*

J'ai recu de Monsieur Du Vergier, – Conformément aux ordres de Monsieur le Comte de Vergennes en date du 5. courant que je lui ai remis. La somme d'un million, dont je rendrai compte à monditsieur Comte de Vergennes à Paris ce 10. juin 1776.

Signé: CARON DE BEAUMARCHAIS. Bon pour un million de livres tournois.

Pour copie conforme.

Le commissaire de relations Extérieures.

BUCHOT

(I have received from M. Du Vergier, in conformity with the instructions from the Count de Vergennes under date of the 5th current, which I have remitted to him. The sum of one million, for which I will give an accounting to the Count de Vergennes. At Paris the 10th June 1776.

Signed: CARON DE BEAUMARCHAIS. For one million livres, Tours currency. [Worth about 10 *d.*]

A true copy.

The commissioner of foreign affairs.)

Many of the weapons used at Saratoga were products of this French aid. In 1777 Beaumarchais had twelve vessels operating out of Nantes, Le Havre, Bordeaux and Marseilles; the number eventually increased to forty.

It was never clear whether these supplies were a gift, for which nominal payments in produce, especially tobacco and rice, were made to disguise them as commercial, or whether Congress was expected to repay. The accounting for this expenditure would blacken the reputation of Silas Deane, Franklin's fellow-ambassador, and cloud Beaumarchais' last years – he died bankrupt in 1799.

Beaumarchais addressed the American people in explanation:

Hamburg, 10 April 1795

Americans, I have served you with unwearied zeal; I have received during my life nothing but bitterness for my recompense, and I die your creditor. Suffer me, then, in dying, to bequeath to you my daughter to endow with a portion of what you owe me. Perhaps, after me, through the injustice of other persons, from which I shall no longer be able to defend myself, there will remain nothing in the world for her; and perhaps Providence has wished to procure for her, through your delay in paying me, a resource after my death against complete misfortune. Adopt her as a worthy child of the state!

The Alliance owed much to Franklin's standing as philosophe *and negotiator. Condorcet described a meeting of Franklin and Voltaire at the Academy of Sciences.*

They then went to a public meeting of the Academy of Sciences. The scene was a moving one: Placed side by side, these two men, born in different worlds, venerated for their years, their reputations, the things they had done with their lives, and both delighting in the influence they had exerted in their age.

They embraced each other amid shouts of approval. Some one said that Solon was embracing Sophocles. But the French Sophocles had demolished error and advanced the reign of reason, while the Solon from Philadelphia, resting the constitution of his country on the unshakable foundation of the rights of man, had no occasion to fear that he would see during his lifetime doubtful laws fashioning chains for his country and opening the door to tyranny.

His fellow-commissioner, John Adams, was similarly admiring.

After dinner we went to the Academy of Sciences and heard M. d'Alembert, as perpetual secretary, pronounce eulogies on several of their members, lately deceased. Voltaire and Franklin were both present, and there presently arose a general cry that M. Voltaire and M. Franklin should be introduced to each other. This was done, and they bowed and spoke to each other. This was no satisfaction; there must be something more. Neither of our philosophers seemed to divine what was wished or expected; they, however, took each other by the hand. But this was not enough; the clamor continued, until the explanation came out. 'Il faut s'embrasser, à la Française.' The two aged actors upon this great theatre of philosophy and frivolity then embraced each other, by hugging one another in their arms, kissing each other's cheeks, and then the tumult subsided. And the cry immediately spread through the whole kingdom, and, I suppose, over all Europe, 'Qu'il était charmant de voir embrasser Solon et Sophocle!'

And so indeed was Arthur Lee, then fellow-agent but later critic of Franklin.

Mons. Gérard, first secretary to Count Vergennes, met the commissioners at Passy. He said he came from the counts Maurepas and Vergennes, to congratulate the commissioners upon the news [of the American victory at Saratoga], to assure them of the great pleasure it gave at Versailles, and to desire on the part of the king any farther particulars they might have. He was informed that extracts were making from all the papers, which should be sent the moment it was finished; and Mr L. promised to send extracts from his brother's letter, which contained some farther particulars. Mr Gérard said they might depend on three millions of livres also from Spain, but he believed it would be through the Havannah and New-Orleans. He said as there now appeared no doubt of the ability and resolution of the states to maintain their independency, he could assure them it was wished they would reassume their former proposition of an alliance, or any new one they might have, and that it could not be done too soon; that the court of Spain must be consulted, that they might act in harmony, and prepare for war in a few months.

The Alliance was signed on 6 February 1778. The two countries were to be firm allies until independence was won, and would not make separate peace settlements without the consent of the other. France was to have no claim on the North American mainland but could have a free hand in the West Indies.

ART. V If the United States should think fit to attempt the reduction of the British power, remaining in the northern parts of America, or the islands of Bermudas, those countries or islands, in case of success, shall be confederated with or dependent upon the said United States.

ART. VI The Most Christian King renounces forever the possession of the islands of Bermudas, as well as of any part of the continent of North America, which before the treaty of Paris in 1763, or in virtue of that treaty, were acknowledged to belong to the Crown of Great Britain, or to the United States, heretofore called British Colonies, or which are at this time or have lately been under the power of the King and Crown of Great Britain.

ART. VII If His Most Christian Majesty shall think proper to attack any of the islands situated in the Gulph of Mexico, or near that Gulph, which are at present under the power of Great Britain, all the said isles, in case of success, shall appertain to the Crown of France.

ART. VIII Neither of the two parties shall conclude either truce or peace with Great Britain without the formal consent of the other first obtained; and they mutually engage not to lay down their arms until the independence of the United States shall have been formally or tacitly assured by the treaty or treaties that shall terminate the war.

ART. XI The two parties guarantee mutually from the present time and forever against all other powers, to wit: The United States to His Most Christian Majesty, the present possessions of the Crown of France in America, as well as those which it may acquire by the future treaty of peace: And His Most Christian Majesty guarantees on his part to the United States their liberty, sovereignty and independence, absolute and unlimited, as well in matters of government as commerce, and also their possessions, and the additions or conquests that their confederation may obtain during the war, from any of the dominions now, or heretofore possessed by Great Britain in North America, conformable to the 5th and 6th articles above written, the whole as their possessions shall be fixed and assured to the said States, at the moment of the cessation of their present war with England.

French intervention in 1778 represented a swing in Paris from a commercial and indirect war with Britain to a maritime struggle. Vergennes' policy was to engage the British fleet in the Channel, threaten an invasion, and detach a squadron to the West Indies. The primary French objective was the West Indian sugar islands. With two bases, Toulon and Brest, their ships could slip into the Atlantic with ease. The strengthening of the fleet owed much to Antoine de Sartine, Minister of Marines, who had made available sixty-three ships of the line of sixty-four guns and over (twenty-one of which were by 1778 in American waters) and 67,000 seamen.

By contrast, Britain, at the risk of invasion, had nevertheless to hold the Americas, West Indies and Mediterranean stations. The British Navy was run down, as the captain of HMS Viper on the American station complained:

I am very much disturbed for Petty Officers as well as Warrant [Officers]. My Carpenter infirm & past duty; my Gunner made from a livery servant – neither seaman nor gunner; my Master hardly a man in years, never an Officer before, made from a boy on one of the guardships, he then keeping a public house at Gosport. Petty Officers I have but one, who owns himself mad at times. A Master's Mate I have not, nor anything I can make a Boatswain's Mate. I have not one person I could trust with the charge of a vessel I might take, to bring her in.

A fleet is not built overnight, and it would take time to undo the years of neglect, notably under the 4th Earl of Sandwich:

135

Too infamous to have a friend
Too bad for bad men to commend.

By 1777 fears of war with France brought the situation to a head. The dockyard at Portsmouth had twice been attacked by arsonists, first by Mathurin Duct, and then by that eccentric agent of Silas Deane, James Aitken, or 'John the Painter', who was hanged for his crime. The fleet had obviously lost its American seamen — and its American pine for its masts. The Armed Neutrality of Europe would in 1780 even threaten its supplies of Stettin oak.

In 1778, however, with eleven of the line away on the North American station, Admiral Keppel could muster only thirty vessels for the defence of home waters, of which he said that 'only six ships were fit to meet a seaman's eye'. There were only some 20,000 seamen. Ports and coastal towns were raided by press gangs to find willing (or unwilling) sailors; homeward bound ships were boarded in the docks and their crews conscripted; an Act was hurriedly passed permitting merchant craft to sail with foreign seamen forming up to three-quarters of their crews; the East India Company loaned for the duration 6000 of their sea-going employees and three seventy-four-gun ships, the Ganga, *the* Bombay Castle, *and the* Carnatic.

Before the signing of the Treaty and in defiance of international law (and to some embarrassment on Vergennes' part) the French Government allowed American privateers to use French ports, to raise crews, sell prizes and to refit. Britain protested but it availed little.

Lord Stormont wrote from Paris to Lord Weymouth on 16 April 1977:

... I then, my Lord, went to a subject of more importance: I mean the French vessels that are to be manned by French soldiers and commanded by American captains. I told him [M. de Vergennes] that it was more necessary for me to repeat what I had said both to his Excellency and the Monsieur de Maurepas upon this very unpleasant subject, as I found that the number of those vessels increased and that instead of four ships, which my first intelligence mentioned, there would be eight or ten. I added, my Lord, that I did not indeed know the names of these ships nor the ports of France from which they were to sail, but that I did know there was such a design, and was certain that there were several American captains now at Paris who expected the command of those ships and were waiting here till they could be got ready. I likewise informed him, my Lord, that according to my last intelligence those ships are designed not only to cruise in our seas but to insult our coast (I have information which says one of the projects is an attack on Glasgow). I ended with saying that we had, to be sure, little to apprehend from such enterprises, but I begged him to consider what an impression the mere attempt must necessarily make – ships built in France for the use of the rebels, manned with French sailors and commanded by American captains, who sail from the ports of France to insult and attempt to ravage the coast of Great Britain.

I spoke to him, my Lord, very strongly but in the politest and most friendly manner, and went all along upon this supposition: that after the mutual assurances that had passed and the public proofs we meant to give of our pacific intentions, everything that had a contrary tendency must be as disagreeable to this Court as it could be to mine. He readily assented to this, said that if there was any such thing in agitation it should be prevented, *qu'on y mettroit ordre*, and that no such attempt ever should be made from the ports of France, and that they never would suffer their sailors to be so employed.

In a word, my Lord, his promises were as fair as I could wish; but I do not expect the performance to be complete. I see but too plainly that my best endeavours will not prevent these secret succours; but still, my Lord, I shall continue them, as they show we are upon the watch and tend to retard and lessen the evil they cannot remove.

What had begun as the adventures of privateers out of Marblehead and Gloucester had by 1778 become big business. One of the first prizes captured, the British storeship Nancy, *contained 2000 muskets, 100,000 feints, 30, 000 round shot and a thirteen-inch brass mortar, christened – with rum – the* Congress. *By the end of 1776, the raiders had captured over 250 West Indiamen, and insurance rates in London rose by twenty-eight per cent. Between May 1776 and January 1778, 700 vessels were taken in all. Congress commissioned some 1700 privateers, and individual states another 2000; they ranged from under 100 to 500 tons and the average crew was 100. They also took 2000 prizes and 16,000 prisoners.*

Under the command of Esek Hopkins, a Continental squadron raided Nassau in 1776, to capture 100 cannon. But the American Navy had few other successes, and by 1783 only two of the seventeen ships were still in service. Each state had also a ship or ships, and engaged in isolated raids. Thus American naval activity ranged spasmodically from operations on Lake Champlain and the Mississippi, in the Caribbean, along the Atlantic – and along the coast of Britain. Of them all, the privateers were certainly the most effective.

As many as 60,000 Americans fought the war in this way for booty, for rum, sugar, Irish linen and English woollens, and for glory. They far outnumbered the regular American Navy and their numbers weakened the striking power. Congress appropriated funds for a navy, under the pressing of George Wythe of Virginia.

Why should not America have a navy? No maritime power near the seacoast can be safe without it. It is no chimera. The Romans suddenly built one in their Carthaginian war. Why may not we lay a foundation for it? We abound with firs, iron ore, tar, pitch, turpentine; we have all the materials for the construction of a navy.

The privateers were a thorn in the flesh of Franklin, and to Vergennes — but both knew that they helped to weaken Britain.

The French Alliance thus drastically altered British strategy. It had held to a land invasion of North America by way of the Middle States via New York and Philadelphia — of which the sole legacy was in 1778 the occupation of New York City — or by way of the Hudson Valley (now a decisive failure). A land war as, at the outset, Barrington had advised Gage — and, after an interval, Gage had then told Barrington — would not be easy; with France (and possibly Spain) also in the war, it would be impossible. That land war would now have to be scaled down and the British bases would be a handful of coastal towns.

Clinton's evacuation of Philadelphia was designed to free 5000 men to attempt the seizure of St Lucia (after Martinique the major French base in the West Indies), and 3000 to St Augustine and West Florida. Indeed the directive had come from the king:

The paper delivered this day by the French Ambassador is certainly equivalent to a declaration, and therefore must entirely overturn every plan for strengthening the army under the command of Lieut-Gen Clinton with an intent of carrying on an active war in North America: what occurs now is to fix what numbers are necessary to defend New York, Rhode Island, Nova Scotia, and the Floridas: it is a joke to think of keeping Pennsilvania for we must from the army now in America form a corps sufficient to attack the French islands, and two or three thousand men ought to be employed with the fleet to destroy the ports and warfs of the rebels.

There were, without them, less than 2000 troops. If New York could not be held, the army would fall back on Rhode Island; if not that, then Halifax, the main supply headquarters of the war, and Quebec. Neither before nor after 1776 did Britain see the thirteen mainland colonies in isolation from the other seventeen colonies stretching in a great 2000-mile maritime arc from Newfoundland to Jamaica and Honduras. The islands depended on America for food, and on the British Navy for protection — now two opposed forces. As a last resort, by way of its inviting tidal rivers, there might still be an invasion of the south, the 'southern strategy'. Here there were said to be Loyalist numbers.

The major threat now was to the home islands; the North American, though not

138

*the West Indian, war became a side-show. Lord Effingham, Admiral Augustus
Keppel and that small group of generals and flag officers who would not fight against
Americans, were ready now to fight the auld enemy. The Dukes of Argyll, Hamilton
and Atholl, Lords Seaton and Macdonald, the towns of Glasgow, Edinburgh, Aber-
deen and Birmingham, all offered to raise additional regiments. But the forces,
however strong, had to be deployed over vast distances and problems of communication
and of control were now greatly magnified. What had begun as a half-hearted
colonial struggle had, by French (and in 1779 Spanish, and in 1780 Dutch and
Russian) intervention, become a world war.*

*To this new strategy there was a preliminary: a final peace effort. In November
1777, North presented these overtures to Parliament but, Christmas intervening,
they were not approved until 17 February 1778, eleven days after the Franco-
American treaty of alliance, and after bitter debate. Chatham vehemently opposed the
proposals and, during the debate, collapsed and was carried out of the Lords, a dying
man.*

*A few British leaders had been brought by this time to a public admission of
defeat. Thomas Pownall spoke for a stubborn Whig minority in Parliament when he
declared on 21 March 1778:*

We know that the Americans are and must be independent; and yet we
will not treat them as such. If government itself retains the least idea of
sovereignty, it has already gone too far for that; if it entertains the least
hope of peace, it has not gone far enough; and every step we shall take to
put the Americans back from independency, will convince them the
more of the necessity of going forward.

*The terms were taken to New York by a mission headed nominally by the Earl of
Carlisle, but directed in fact by William Eden (until then the effective head of
British Intelligence, and later Earl of Auckland). It was charged to offer anything,
and everything, except independence. The offer was too little, and too late. Henry
Laurens, speaking for Congress, wrote to the Earl of Carlisle on 17 June:*

I have received the letter from your excellencies of the 9th instant, with
the enclosures, and laid them before Congress. Nothing but an earnest
desire to spare the further effusion of human blood could have induced
them to read a paper containing expressions so disrespectful to his most
Christian majesty, the good and great ally of these states, or to consider
propositions so derogatory to the honor of an independent nation.
   The acts of the British parliament, the commission from your

sovereign, and your letter suppose the people of these states to be subjects of the crown of Great Britain, and are founded on the idea of dependence, which is utterly inadmissible.

I am further directed to inform your excellencies that Congress are inclined to peace, notwithstanding the unjust claims from which this war originated and the savage manner in which it hath been conducted. They will, therefore, be ready to enter upon the consideration of a treaty of peace and commerce not inconsistent with treaties already subsisting, when the king of Great Britain shall demonstrate a sincere disposition for that purpose. The only solid proof of this disposition will be an explicit acknowledgment of the independence of these states, or the withdrawing of his fleets and armies.

By this time, Clinton was evacuating Philadelphia and the treaty with France was signed. Congress refused to negotiate except on a basis of independence and a withdrawal of British forces. In fact, the cases of liquor the commission took as gifts were used by Congress to welcome Conrad Alexandre Gérard, the first French minister, to the new republic.

Long before the Treaty of Alliance, Franklin had been stretching the rules. He was helped by the presence in European waters of a motley group of captains: Lambert Wickes, in whose Reprisal *Franklin had sailed to Nantes in 1776, Gustavus Conyngham and, not least, John Paul Jones. Jones was a Scot who had left his native Solway (where a murder charge was pending) to go to North America where he changed his name, served on a slave ship and was commissioned a lieutenant in the Continental Navy in December 1775. He was hungry for fortune, for fame — indeed, there are striking similarities in his career to that of Benedict Arnold; though his seamanship was never up for sale.*

The American Commissioners in France — primarily, that is, Franklin — told the Committee of Foreign Affairs of the Continental Congress that they would go beyond privateering, and wrote thus in May 1777:

We have not the least doubt but that two or three of the Continental frigates sent into the German Ocean, with some lesser swift sailing cruisers, might intercept and seize a great part of the Baltic and Northern trade, could they be in those seas by the middle of August, at farthest; and the prizes will consist of articles of the utmost consequence to the States. One frigate would be sufficient to destroy the whole of the Greenland whale fishery, or take the Hudson Bay ships returning . . .

As early as April 1778, John Paul Jones had been instructed to raid the English coast. Commanding the Ranger *(eighteen six-pounder guns and 140 men), he struck at Whitehaven on the north-west coast. British newspapers reflected the growing alarm. Thus, the* London Morning Post *on 28 April 1778:*

Whitehaven, 28 April 1778

Late last night or early this morning a number of armed men (to the amount of 30) landed at this place by two boats from an American privateer, as appears from one of the people now in custody. Whether he was left through accident or escaped by design is yet uncertain.

This much has however been proved: that a little after 3 o'clock this morning he rapped at several doors in Marlborough Street (adjoining one of the piers) and informed them that fire had been set to one of the ships in the harbour; matches were laid in several others; the whole world would be soon in a blaze, and the town also destroyed; that he was one belonging to the privateer, but had escaped for the purpose of saving the town and shipping from further destruction.

and the Morning Chronicle and London Advertiser *on 23–26 May:*

This day arrived the mail from Flanders. Paris, May 17. An American privateer, said to be the same which lately made a descent in Scotland, hath brought into Brest an English frigate, the crew consisting of 160 men, which was taken after an engagement wherein the Captain of the frigate and 40 men were killed. M. de Sartine has been written to on this occasion and it is said he answered that the King could not properly detain the English as prisoners of war.

and the Gazetteer and New Daily Advertiser *on 15 June:*

We hear that since John Paul arrived at Brest, he has written to Lord Selkirk, informing that he had no personal enmity to his Lordship, but that it was his intention (when at St. Mary's Isle) to take him as an hostage, in order to bring about an exchange of prisoners. He also, it is said, gives a long and pompous account of his engagement with the *Drake*.

and again on 22 June:

Lord Selkirk has received a letter from John Paul Jones, of the *Ranger* privateer, directed to Lady Selkirk wherein he says Lord Selkirk's plate is to be sold for the benefit of his crew, and promises to buy it and return it or the value in a present to Lady Selkirk.

A twenty-eight-day voyage brought Jones seven prizes, many prisoners, much booty —
and fame.

Alongside Washington's war of manoeuvre in the east, and the vicious but episodic
local struggle against Loyalists, there was the ugliest war of all, along the unmapped
western frontier. That frontier stretched in a great arc from the Maine timberlands
to the Georgia swamps, through northern Vermont and upstate New York, across
western Pennsylvania to Ohio and Detroit, then south into Kentucky and along the
Appalachians. All of this territory was exposed to Indian attacks. Both sides tried to
enlist Indians, but the British, from their forts at Niagara or Detroit or Sandusky
and Michilimakinac, or strong in their grip on the Mohawks, were the more
successful. The Americans clearly were invading Indian hunting rights, and could be
seen as enemies.

But this was a war of sections and of attitudes that transcended the clash of Indian
and white, and which had begun before 1776: the Paxton Boys' march on Philadelphia
in 1764; the Regulation troubles in the Carolinas, occasioned by the illegal fees and
excessive taxes of dishonest sheriffs and court officials, which led to the 'Battle of the
Alamance' in May 1771, after which six of the ringleaders were hanged; the Indian
clashes of 1774 known as Dunmore's War. Those in the west felt under-represented
in eastern assemblies with inadequate defence against Indian incursions, the absence of
law and order, security and justice. Until the Articles of Confederation (which in
1777 set up a weak central government) had been approved by a majority of the
thirteen states, each state claimed sovereignty over those parts of the west granted to it
in its original charter. Virginia, indeed, had 'sea to sea' clauses by which its writ
extended to the 'Western ocean'. So columns of state militia were seeking territory in
the west in what was a no man's land; and Britain was, by way of Quebec, the Lakes,
the Ohio and its tributaries, seeking to hold the forts on the Mississippi that it had
acquired in 1763 on the defeat of the French. This war was a many-sided thing, and
the Indians, whose hunting routes did not coincide with the sketchy charts and claims
to possession of territory of the white men, were unpredictable, even treacherous,
whether as foe or friend.

British policy was clear, even if it was not always welcome. The Earl of Dartmouth
wrote from Whitehall to Colonel Guy Johnson on 24 July 1775:

It is therefore His Majesty's pleasure that you do lose no time in taking
such steps as may induce them to take up the hatchet against His
Majesty's rebellious subjects in America, and to engage them in His
Majesty's service upon such plan as shall be suggested to you by General
Gage to whom this letter is sent accompanied with a large assortment
of goods for presents to them upon this important occasion.

142

Germain also encouraged the use of Indian warriors, writing to John Stuart, the Indian agent, on 6 November 1776:

. . . I expect with some impatience to hear from you of the success of your negociation with the Creeks and the Choctaws and that you have prevailed with them to join the Cherokees who I find have already commenced hostilities against the Rebels in Carolina and Virginia. The Rebel government in the former province have, I also learn, not only offered considerable rewards for the scalps of those Indians but declared their children of a certain age which may be taken prisoners the slaves of the captors, a measure which I am sure must inflame the enmity of that nation to the highest pitch against them and excite the resentment of all the other Indians in so great a degree that I cannot doubt of your being able under such advantageous circumstances to engage them in a general confederacy against the Rebels in defence of those liberties of which they are so exceedingly jealous and in the full enjoyment of which they have always been protected by the King.

Chatham, before his collapse, gave a stirring speech in the Lords on 18 November 1777:

My lords, I am astonished to hear such principles confessed! I am shocked to hear them avowed in this house, or in this territory! Principles, equally unconstitutional, inhuman, and unchristian!

My lords, I did not intend to have encroached again on your attention; but I cannot repress my indignation. I feel myself impelled by every duty. My lords, we are called upon as members of this house, as men, as Christian men, to protest against such notions standing near the throne, polluting the ear of majesty. 'That God and nature put into our hands!' I know not what ideas that lord may entertain of God and nature; but I know that such abominable principles are equally abhorrent to religion and humanity.

What! to attribute the sacred sanction of God and nature to the massacres of the Indian scalping knife? to the cannibal savage, torturing, murdering, roasting and eating; literally, my lords, *eating* the mangled victims of his barbarous battles! Such horrible notions shock every precept of religion, divine or natural, and every generous feeling of humanity. And, my lords, they shock every sentiment of honor; they shock me as a lover of honorable war, and a detester of murderous barbarity.

143

Spain armed herself with blood-hounds to extirpate the wretched natives of America; and we improve on the human example even of Spanish cruelty. We turn loose these savage hell-hounds against our brethren and countrymen in America, of the same language, laws, liberty and religion, endeared to us by every tie that should sanctify humanity.

Washington, on the other hand, wrote to the Commissioners of Indian Affairs, from his headquarters at Valley Forge on 13 March 1778:

Gentlemen: You will perceive, by the inclosed Copy of a Resolve of Congress, that I am impowered to employ a body of four hundred Indians, if they can be procured upon proper terms. Divesting them of the Savage customs exercised in their Wars against each other, I think they may be made of excellent use, as scouts and light troops, mixed with our own Parties. I propose to raise about one half the number among the Southern and the remainder among the Northern Indians.

In May 1778, Butler's Tory Rangers and his Indian allies, 1200 strong, attacked a flourishing frontier settlement in the Wyoming valley on the banks of the Susquehanna, near present-day Wilkes-Barre, and, with most of its men fighting elsewhere, destroyed it savagely, as Hector St John de Crèvecoeur, a French-born American settler, recounted in his Letters:

The assailants formed a body of about eight hundred men who received their arms from Niagara; the whites under the conduct of Colonel Butler, the Indians under that of Brant. After a fatiguing march, they all met at some of the upper towns of the Susquehanna, and while they were refreshing themselves and providing canoes and every other necessary implement, parties were sent out in different parts of the country. Some penetrated to the west branch and did infinite mischief; it was easy to surprise defenceless, isolated families who fell an easy prey to their enemies. Others approached the New England settlements, where the ravages they committed were not less dreadful. Many families were locked up in their houses and consumed with all their furniture. Dreadful scenes were transacted which I know not how to retrace. The other party, who had taken their flight towards their forts, were all either taken or killed. It is said that those who were then made prisoners were tied to small trees and burnt the evening of the same day.

The body of the aged people, the women and children who were enclosed in the stockade, distinctly could hear and see this dreadful onset, the last scenes of which had been transacted close to the very

144

Lord Howe and Comte d'Estaing encounter off Rhode Island

The collapse of the Earl of Chatham in the House of Lords

John Paul Jones, whose raids on the English coast became legendary

Sir Henry Clinton succeeded Howe on 8 May 1778

The French attack on St Lucia

gates. What a situation these unfortunate people were in! Each wife, each father, each mother could easily distinguish each husband and son as they fell. But in so great, so universal a calamity, when each expected to meet the same fate, perhaps they did not feel so keenly for the deplorable end of their friends and relations. Of what powerful materials must the human heart be composed, which could hold together at so awful a crisis! This bloody scene was no sooner over than a new one arose of a very similar nature. They had scarcely finished scalping the numerous victims which lay on the ground when these fierce conquerors demanded the immediate entrance to the fort. It was submissively granted. Above a hundred of them, decorated with all the dreadful ornaments of plumes and colour of war, with fierce animated eyes, presented themselves and rushed with impetuosity into the middle of the area, armed with tomahawks made of brass with an edge of steel. Tears relieved some; involuntary cries disburdened the oppression of others, a general shriek among the women was immediately heard all around.

Thus perished in one fatal day most of the buildings, improvements, mills, bridges, etc., which had been erected there with so much cost and industry. Thus were dissolved the foundations of a settlement begun at such a distance from the metropolis, disputed by a potent province; the beginning of which had been stained with blood shed in their primitive altercations. Thus the ill-judged policy of these ignorant people and the general calamities of the times overtook them and extirpated them even out of that wilderness which they had come twelve years before to possess and embellish. Thus the grand contest entered into by these colonies with the mother-country has spread everywhere, even from the sea-shores to the last cottages of the frontiers.

Richard McGinnis, by trade a carpenter, was in the Tory ranks.

The loss on our side was one Indian killed and two white men wounded. One of the white men, Willson by name, died of his wound, it having mortefied. The other recovered.

With the defeat of the rebles followed a total confiscation of all their property, such as oxen, cows, horses, hogs, sheep and every other thing of that kind. Thus did Rebellion get a severe shock. The Rebles begged of us to restore them something back, but 'No,' we replyed. 'Remember how you served the peaceable subjects of his Majesty at Tankennick. Remember how you took their property and converted it to Reble porpesses, and their persons fell in your hands, you immediately sent them of[f] to prison clean into Connetticut and left their numerous familys in the utmost distress. And be contented, Rebles, that your lives are still spared and that you have not shared the same fate with your sedetious brethren.'

Joseph Brant who had taken his first scalp at thirteen, but who became a protégé of Sir William Johnson, learned Latin and Greek, translated the New Testament into his native language, and was presented at Court in London, appeared in different guise in the Mohawk Valley in September, where his Indians destroyed German Flats. In November, he led 500 Indians and 200 of Butler's Rangers in an attack on Cherry Valley, a village fifty miles west of Albany. A survivor told his tale to a Boston newspaper:

The enemy, 800 in number, consisting of some 500 Indians commanded by Brant, fifty regulars under Captain Colvill, and another captain with some of Johnson's Rangers, and about 200 Tories, the whole under Colonel Butler's command, immediately surrounded the fort, excluding several officers who were quartered out of the garrison and had gone to dinner. They commenced a very heavy fire on the fort, which held for three and a half hours, and was as briskly returned. They were so near as to call to the fort and bid the damn'd rebels surrender, which was answered with three cheers and a discharge of cannon and musketry. At four PM the enemy withdrew. Captain Ballard sallied out with a party which the enemy endeavored to cut off, but were prevented by a reinforcement. The next day they made it their whole business to collect horses, cattle and sheep, which they effected, and at sunset left the place.

On Friday morning the fort was reinforced by 800 militia. The enemy killed, scalp't, and most barbarously murdered thirty-two women and children . . . burnt twenty-four houses with all the grain, &c., took above sixty inhabitants prisoners, part of whom they released on going off. They committed the most inhuman barbarities on most of the dead: Robert Henderson's head was cut off, his skull bone cut out with his scalp – Mr Willis's sister was rip't up, a child of Mr Willis's, two months old, scalp't and arm cut off – the clergyman's wife's leg and arm cut off, and many others as cruelly treated. Many of the inhabitants and soldiers shut out from the fort, lay all night in the rain with children, which suffered very much. The cattle that were not easy to drive, they shot. We were informed by the prisoners they sent back, that the lieutenant colonel, all the officers and Continental soldiers were stript and drove naked before them.

The best-known operation in the west in 1778, however, was that led by the red-haired, blue-eyed Virginian George Rogers Clark. His ultimate target was Detroit, where the British Colonel Henry Hamilton, one of the four lieutenant-governors of Canada, was in charge of Indian operations. From his alleged readiness to pay for scalps, he had been given the name of the 'Hair Buyer'. Clark planned an expedition through the Illinois country, to capture the old French forts of Kaskaskia, Vincennes and Cahokia, to open up the Ohio (and the fur trade) to Americans – and to frighten the Indians. On 24 June 1778 his 175 men floated down the Ohio in flat-boats, disembarked ten miles below the mouth of the Tennessee River and marched 120 miles overland to take Kaskaskia.

I knew that my case was desperate, but the more I reflected on my weakness the more I was pleased with the enterprise. Joined by a few of the Kentuckians, under Col. Montgomery, to stop the desertion I knew would ensue on troops knowing their destination, I had encamped on a small island in the middle of the Falls, kept strict guard on the boats, but Lieutenant Hutchings of Dillards Company contrived to make his escape with his party after being refused leave to return. Luckily a few of his men was taken the next day by a party sent after them. On this island I first began to discipline my little army, knowing that to be the most essential point towards success. Most of them determined to follow me. The rest seeing no probability of making their escape, I soon got that subbordination as I could wish for. About twenty families that had followed me much against my inclination I found now to be of service to me in guarding a block house that I had erected on the island to secure my provisions.

I got every thing in readiness on the 26th of June, set off from the Falls, double manned our oars and proceeded day and night until we run into the mouth of the Tenesse River. The fourth day landed on an island to prepare ourselves for a march by land. A few hours after we took a boat of hunters but eight days from Kaskaskias; before I would suffer them to answer any person a question after their taking the oath of allegiance, I examined them particularly. They were Englishmen, and appeared to be in our interest; their intiligence was not favourable; they asked leave to go on the expedition. I granted it . . .

In the evening of the same day I run my boats into a small creek about one mile above the old Fort Missack, reposed ourselves for the night, and in the morning took a rout to the northwest and had a very fatigueing journey for about fifty miles, until we came into those level plains that is frequent throughout this extensive country. As I knew my success depended on secrecy, I was much afraid of being discovered in these meadows, as we might be seen in many places for several miles. Nothing extraordinary happened dureing our route excepting my guide loosing himself and not being able, as we judged by his confusion, of giving a just account of himself; it put the whole troops in the greatest confusion.

I never in my life felt such a flow of rage – to be wandering in a country where every nation of Indians could raise three or four times our number, and a certain loss of our enterprise by the enimie's getting timely notice. I could not bear the thoughts of returning; in short every

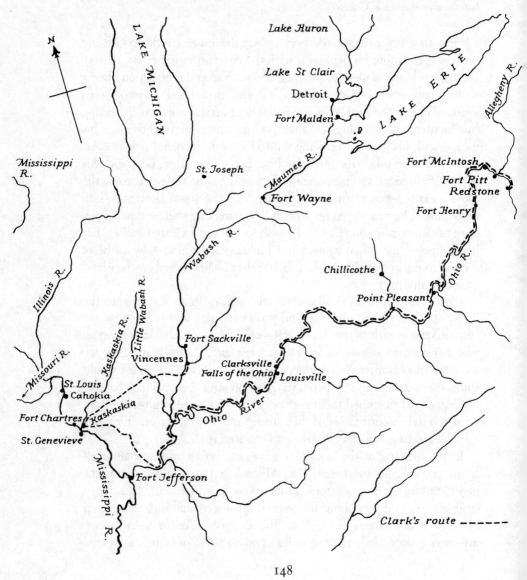

idea of the sort served to put me in that passion that I did not master for some time; but in a short time after our circumstance had a better appearance, for I was in a moment determined to put the guide to death if he did not find his way that evening. He begged that I would not be hard with him, that he could find the path that evening; he accordingly took his course and in two hours got within his knowledge.

His men had not eaten for two days when they emerged before the town, which surrendered in fifteen minutes. Like so much else in the War of Independence, its consequences were out of all proportion to the number of troops involved. 175 men won for Virginia — and thus in the end for the United States — a north-west empire larger than the present-day areas of France and West Germany. And Frederick the Great fought that same France in sixteen battles involving 500,000 men in the Seven Years' War — without one acre of German ground changing hands.

On hearing the news of their disasters, however, Hamilton matched Clark's courage with his own. He covered 600 miles in seventy-one days at the head of a motley group: thirty-four regulars of the 8th Regiment, 141 volunteers and 300 Indians. He reached Vincennes on 17 December, helped — or hindered — by snow and a freezing wind. The fort surrendered, and Clark narrowly escaped capture.

There was now, for Britain, a southern strategy based on the hoped — for Loyalist support. In November 1778, Clinton sent 3500 men under Lieutenant-Colonel Archibald Campbell to co-operate with a similar force from St Augustine under General Augustin Prévost. Two days before Christmas, Colonel Campbell's force landed near the mouth of the Savannah. The composition of the force was significant of British resources in 1778: two battalions of Highlanders, two Hessian battalions and four battalions of Loyalist troops. Defending Savannah was Major-General Robert Howe, commanding 700 Continentals and 150 militia — the only American army in the south. The British were led through the swamps by a Loyalist Negro, Quamino Dolly, in an epic journey, threading their way through creeks and swamps, living each day on a diet of oysters, and falling victim to a mosquito-ridden heat. This was country where it was the heat of the summer that brought pause to combat.

Despite the ordeal, Campbell's success was total, as his report indicates:

Having accidentally fallen in with a Negro [Quamino Dolly] who knew a private path through the wooded swamp upon the enemy's right, I ordered the first battalion of the Seventy-First to form on our right of the road and move to the rear of the light infantry, whilst I drew off that corps to the right as if I meant to extend my front in that quarter, where a happy fall of ground favored the concealment of this maneuver, and increased the jealousy of the enemy with regard to their left. Sir James

Baird had directions to convey the light infantry in this hollow ground, quite to the rear, and penetrate the wooded swamp upon our left, with a view to get . . . into the rear of the enemy's right flank . . .

Thirty-eight officers of different distinctions, and four hundred and fifteen non-commissioned officers and privates, one stand of colors, forty-eight pieces of cannon, twenty-three mortars, ninety-four barrels of powder, the fort, with all its stores . . . and in short, the capital of Georgia, the shipping in the harbor, with a large quantity of provisions, fell into our possession before it was dark, without any loss on our side than that of Captain Peter Campbell, a gallant officer of Skinner's light infantry, and two privates killed, one sergeant and nine privates wounded. Eighty-three of the enemy were found dead on the Common, and eleven wounded. By the accounts received from their prisoners, thirty lost their lives in the swamp, endeavoring to make their escape . . .

Many of the 400 prisoners were placed on board Commodore Hyde Parker's ships because of the lack of adequate quarters; in the hot and humid summer they died of disease and — as the patriots saw it — of Hyde Parker's neglect.

Georgia returned to British allegiance and stayed so until the end; and a royal governor, Sir James Wright, returned. The southern commanders blamed each other for the disaster.

Had General Howe retired from Savannah, and gone up the country, [declared Moultrie] we should soon have joined him, and made a body of 2,000 men; besides, such reinforcements were marching to us from Augusta, Ninety-Six and many other parts of Georgia and Carolina, that in a short time we should have had an army of 4 or 5,000 men; with them we could have marched down to Savannah, before the British had time to fortify . . .

Benjamin Franklin in Paris, always the optimist, saw disease as a valuable American ally, as he wrote to an English friend:

You have now got a little army into Georgia and are triumphing in that success . . . But if they stay through the summer in that climate there is a certain *General Fever* that I apprehend will give a good account of most of them.

As Captain Mackenzie bitterly noted:

So extraordinary an event as the present certainly never before occurred in the history of Britain! An army of 50,000 men, and a fleet of nearly 100 ships and armed vessels, are prevented from acting offensively by the appearance on the American coast of a French squadron of 12 sail of the line and 4 frigates, without troops. Some unpardonable faults have been committed somewhere and those whose duty it is to watch the motions of the enemy in every quarter should answer with their heads for risquing the fate of so large a portion of the national force by their supiness and total want of intelligence.

The entry of France had put a new factor into the Atlantic equation: a French fleet was in American waters. After the battle of Monmouth Courthouse, Clinton withdrew his force to Sandy Hook. The French Toulon fleets, under the Count d'Estaing, arrived before New York in July, just too late to prevent Admiral Lord Howe from ferrying the army across to the safety of Manhattan. A British fleet of thirteen ships under Howe's replacement, Admiral Byron — ominously nicknamed 'Foulweather Jack' — was chasing d'Estaing, from a home fleet that could ill spare them. The French planned to attack the British fleet off Manhattan but were worried about the shallow water across the harbour bar, and moved away.

Sullivan poured out his troubles to Washington in a letter on 13 August 1778:

I issued orders for the army to march the 11th at six in the morning, but fortune, still determined to sport longer with us, brought on a storm so violent that it, last night, blew down, tore & almost ruined all the tents I had. The arms were rendered useless, & almost the whole of the ammunition ruined. The much greater part of the army have no kind of covering, nor would tents, if they had them, prove a sufficient security against the severity of the storm. My men are lying under the fences, half covered with water, without ammunition, and with arms rendered useless. The communication between us and the main cut off by the violence of the wind, which will scarcely permit a whale boat to pass. Should the enemy come out to attack us, our dependence must be upon the superiority of our numbers and the point of the bayonet — how our militia may behave on such an occasion, I am unable to determine. To retreat is impossible; therefore we must conquer or perish . . .

To combat all these misfortunes, & to surmount all those difficulties requires a degree of temper and persevering fortitude which I could never boast of, & which few possess in so ample a manner . . .

And writing to Henry Laurens, the President of the Continental Congress, he made plain where he thought the responsibility lay:

I confess that I do most cordially resent the conduct of the Count, or rather the conduct of his officers who have, it seems, compelled him to go to Boston and leave us on an island without any certain means of retreat. And what surprises me exceedingly is that the Count could be persuaded that it was necessary for ten sail of the line to lay in the harbor to attend one which is refitting.

I begged the Count to remain only twenty-four hours, and I would agree to dismiss him, but in vain. He well knew that the original plan was for him to land his own troops with a large detachment of mine within their lines, under fire of some of his ships, while with the rest I made an attack in front. But his departure has reduced me to the necessity of attacking their works in front or doing nothing.

They have double lines across the island in two places, at near quarter of a mile distance. The outer line is covered in front by redoubts within musket shot of each other; the second in the same manner by redoubts thrown up between the lines. Besides this, there is an inaccessible pond which covers more than half the front line. A strong fortress on Tomminy Hill overlooks and commands the whole adjacent country.

The enemy have about six thousand men within these works. I have eight thousand, one hundred and seventy-four. With this force I am to carry their lines or retire with disgrace. Near seven thousand of my men are militia, unaccustomed to the noise of arms. Should I throw my men by stratagem within these lines, it must be my best troops. Should they be defeated, the want of ships will render their retreat impracticable, and most of the army must be sacrificed. You will, therefore, judge of my feelings, and of the situation which my inconstant ally and coadjutor has thrown me into. My feelings as a man press me to make the desperate attempt; my feelings as an officer cause me to hesitate.

Lord Howe rightly judged that d'Estaing would sail north to mount a joint American-French attack on General Pigot's force of 5000 men in Newport, Rhode Island. He sailed north in pursuit. D'Estaing landed 4000 men in Rhode Island, then re-embarked them over the vehement protests of General John Sullivan, the irascible New Hampshire Irishman, to whom Washington had given command. The French put to sea, but a gale on 11 August dispersed both fleets and dismasted the French flagship, the Languedoc, *before a battle could be fought. D'Estaing sailed away to refit in Boston; local militia drifted home to till their fields, Sullivan met an attack from Pigot but feared a major assault, and raised the blockade.*

Sullivan was not alone in his gloom. There was an anti-French riot in Boston, which shattered Lafayette's optimism.

I begin to see that, seduced by a false enthusiasm, I made a mistake to leave everything and run to America. But it would be a greater one to return. My cup is filled; I must drink it to the dregs, but the dregs can already be tasted.

As American forces withdrew, Clinton arrived too late to take part in the clash between Pigot's men and Nathanael Greene's rearguard. He attacked the privateering bases at Bedford and Martha's Vineyard as he returned to New York. The Americans blamed the French for the failure to take Newport, the French blamed the Americans. It was no good augury for the future. Washington began to play an additional role of arbitrator and soother of souls.

This was to be his major role over the next three years, with his men in position along the Hudson or at his headquarters in New Jersey. Britain had two islands: Manhattan Island and Rhode Island — or more accurately that tiny portion of it between Narragansett Bay and Serkonnett Passage. The Franco-American alliance was expected to bring total victory, but the French fleet, after their appearance off New York and Rhode Island, sailed away to the West Indies. In the northern theatre, the war was now confined to coastal raids and local skirmishes, and would stay so until the end.

Early in December, after months of comparative inactivity, Washington took his men into winter quarters, in a great forty-mile-wide semi-circle around his own headquarters at Middlebrook, New Jersey. Putnam's division was at West Point, De Kalb's at Patterson, New York, and Gates's at Danbury. In Connecticut, once the snows fell, movement of cannon, carts or even of men, was impossible. But a large shipment of clothes and shoes did get through from France, and — for the first time — the American Army had an almost uniform dress: Massachusetts, Delaware and Virginian units in blue, Pennsylvania's in brown with red facings. After the first snows, the winter was in fact much milder than at Valley Forge, but the shortages continued: of blankets and shoes, food and forage. A suit of clothes cost $1500, a handkerchief $100. Ironically, there was no shortage of money, for the Continental paper was losing value day by day, and no one would surrender good beef for worthless paper.

'A waggon load of money', said Washington, 'will scarcely purchase a waggon load of provisions.' His numbers dropped away, and discipline was still a problem.

John White, a merchant of Salem in Massachusetts, was equally gloomy.

We shall forever have reason (I fear) to lament our gloried Revolution, because I have only changed taskmasters, the later the worse, because they are poor creatures. Our country is too poor to be a separate nation. In 1775, April 19th was the first of our battling with the English troops sent here for to keep us in subjection to their unreasonable demands in taxation, etc. All or chiefly the men of knowledge made no resistance to government, and therefore men of little or no knowledge that took part in the opposition to Britain were preferred to places in our government. Thus come in men, poor, without moral virtue, blockheads, etc . . . The high sheriff of this country is a tanner; two magistrates, one a tanner, the other a joiner, neither of them could speak or read English . . . Why I describe our condition in the above manner is because it is impossible such men without education should be equal to the business. I bless God it is no worse with me, but I am too proud easily to submit to such things. I am now above sixty-six years old and am glad and rejoice my trial is almost over.

Strategically Middlebrook was an improvement on Valley Forge. It allowed movement north or south. To Clinton, however, the war would now be fought a long way away; his eyes were on the West Indies, on Georgia. An expedition under General Grant and Admiral Barrington, with veterans from Bunker Hill and Brandywine, seized and held the peninsula of La Vigie on St Lucia and held off a French attack: British killed, 13, and wounded, 150. The arrival of Admiral Byron's squadron on 28 December held St Lucia for Britain.

Raids and skirmishes may be less important than grand strategy, but for those involved they were just as important, for death when it comes is always personal. It was the Loyalists who suffered most by the strategic changes of 1778. They were said to be numerous, and in the end some forty Loyalist regiments of greater or lesser strength, and with exotic names (Butler's Rangers, the Royal Greens, the Roman Catholic Volunteers, Skinner's Greens, the Black Pioneers and the Ethiopian Regiment) fought for the king. Some Loyalist regiments became regular units of British infantry — the King's Royal Regiment (the 60th Foot), the Royal Highland Emigrants and the Volunteers of Ireland.

The Loyalists, however, were never coherently organised. The Board of Associated Loyalists was not set up until 1779, under the ineffective leadership of William Franklin, Benjamin's illegitimate son who had been, from 1762 until the outbreak of war, royal governor of the Jerseys. The Loyalists usually kept a low profile until the king's troops appeared, and then suffered acutely when they moved away. No doubt the majority of them were — like most people most of the time — willing to go with the tide, to be what John Adams called 'mongrels'.

But, Oh! God bless our honest King
The Lords and Commons, true.
And if, next, Congress be the thing,
Oh, bless that Congress, too!

*A Poor Man's Advice to his Poor Neighbors:
a ballad to the tune of Chevy Chase, New York 1774*

A number had gone into exile already – the Philipses from the Hudson Valley, some of the Fairfaxes, Washington's neighbour, and Sir John Randolph, father of Edmund Randolph, a future Governor of Virginia. Over 1000 sailed away from Boston with General Howe in 1776. They were the local British establishment but not exclusively so; there were Loyalist sentiments in all classes of society. When in June 1776 a number of people were arrested in New York, on suspicion of plotting to kill George Washington, they included the Mayor of New York and some officials, but also farmers, tavern-keepers, two tanners, two gunsmiths, two doctors, one saddler, one shoemaker, 'a pensioner with one arm', and an unfortunate, described only as 'a damned rascal'.

Governor Hutchinson, whose stubbornness in 1773 had caused so much trouble, had gone before them. Though he never liked London, its cold damp weather and his chilly reception, he was – with his daughter – to die there. Peggy was seventeen when she sailed away with her father. She wrote to her sister:

2 August 1774

MY DEAR POLLY,

. . . You wish for an account of what has passed since we saw each other; it seems a little age since the chariot drove from the door and conveyed me from so many dear friends, to suffer more than I should have thought possible for me to have borne. I had not left you many hours before I was the most miserable creature on earth: it is impossible for me to describe or give you any idea of what I endured the first fortnight; the second was bad enough, and I am not yet what I used to be. Your beloved [Elisha Hutchinson] has I suppose given you an account of our passage, though I recollect nothing material except the death of poor Mark, which happened when we were about half way over. London my dear is a world in itself: you ask me how I like it? very well for a little while: it will do to see once in ones life, and to talk of ever after; but I would not wish to fix my abode here. In the country methinks, had I my friends with me, I could not but be happy: for seventy miles round it is a perfect garden, and exceeds all that the most romantic fancy could paint. I cannot say much in favour of the climate; the weather has been as cold as our Novembers, and excessively damp, except two or three days, and I have not been free from a cold since I came.

Her father's diary is gloomy reading.

16 August 1777 Sensibly more feeble, and had a bad day. In this kind of life the days and nights pass incredibly swift, and I am six months older and nearer to my own death, than when my daughter's illness began; and it appears like the dream of a night.

19 March 1778 Called on Mr Ellis. Laments the universal despondency: should not wonder if this afternoon the Americans were acknowledged Independent – a term they always avoided as a Religious distinction, but will always boast of as a Civil character. After all, I shall never see that there were just grounds for this revolt. I see that the ways of Providence are mysterious, but I abhor the least thought that all is not perfectly right, and ordered by infinite rectitude and wisdom.

1 August 1778 The calm among all sorts of people is astonishing. It looks just the same as one might expect it would, if the English and French fleets were parading in the Channel upon friendly terms; and yet every minute some decisive stroke, some say, may be expected. The British forces in America are mouldering away – the Commissioners treated with neglect – and all considered as a matter of indifference. Why don't Government withdraw its forces, and leave the Americans to that Independence which the Ministry seem to expect they will attain to?

The Loyalists were weaker in numbers in Virginia. They were strongest in New York, and not only in New York City when the British occupied it. Westchester County, just north of the Harlem River, became the scene of a specially bitter civil war. James Delancey, a nephew of Oliver DeLancey and the former sheriff of Westchester County, fought for the British after Washington's withdrawal from New York in 1776, raised a troop of horse, the so-called 'Cowboys' or the 'Westchester Refugees', and annexed cattle. His guerilla operations took place in the 'Neutral Ground', that twenty-mile-wide area that became a no man's land between the two armies, extending from Kingsbridge and Morrisonia in the south to the mouth of the Croton River and across to the Sound. The rebel counterpart were the 'Skinners', so called because they often robbed and murdered their victims. Some of them were Patriots, some were banditti for whom patriotism was a cover-word for plunder.

Monmouth County, New Jersey, had its own local civil war. And in Virginia, where Loyalism was less obvious, Jefferson had a bill of attainder passed – the only bill of attainder passed by the Virginia legislature in this war – against a certain John Phillips, who led a group of banditti from the Dismal Swamp; he claimed to be an agent of Lord Dunmore, but to Jefferson he was 'a mere robber . . . availing himself of the troubles of the times'.

The line between Loyalists and Patriots was especially narrow in the Mohawk Valley where it was closer to a division between Mohawk Indians with their handsome leader Joseph Brant (and their British sponsors, the Johnson clan) and scattered white settlers. This was a war that did not begin in 1776 – or cease in 1783; it was a war marked by the use of tomahawk as well as rifle, fought usually in isolation from the other theatres of war, and unusually bloodthirsty.

1779

The dance of death

By 1779 the main theatre of war for Britain was the Atlantic – and the Channel. Both at the time, and since, Sandwich has been blamed for the Navy's failures, mainly because of his profligate private life. But he was by no means solely responsible: in one sense Lord North was responsible, because of his stringent economising. The decision not to commit the Navy to a tight blockade and to fight the war by costly and pointless forays into a wild hostile interior was a basic strategic error. For this, as North recognised, the Cabinet, not Sandwich, was responsible. When on 23 April 1779 the motion in the House of Lords to remove Sandwich from his post was defeated, Lord North made the position clear.

Every expedition, in regard to its destination, object, force and number of ships, is planned by the Cabinet, and is the result of the collective wisdom of all his Majesty's confidential ministers. The First Lord of the Admiralty is only the executive servant of these measures; and if he is not personally a Cabinet minister he is not responsible for the wisdom, the policy, and the propriety of any naval expedition. But if he is in the Cabinet, then he must share in common with the other ministers that proportional division of censure which is attached to him as an individual. In no situation is he more or less responsible to his country than his colleagues from any misconduct which flows from a Cabinet measure.

Early in the year, Franklin and Lafayette planned a full-scale invasion of Britain. It was made possible by the alliance of Spain with France, though Spain refused to ally, directly, with the republican United States. The French fleets in Brest put out for Corunna to rendezvous with the Spanish fleet. A joint force of sixty-six ships would control the Channel and allow a force of 31,000 men to cross from Le Havre and St Malo to the Portsmouth area. Sir Charles Hardy who was in command of the Channel fleet had not been to sea for twenty years . . .

Franklin gave Jones very clear orders for the invasion and was even clearer to Lafayette (at one point destined to lead the invasion) on 22 March:

It is certain that the Coasts of England and Scotland are extremely open and Defenceless; there are also many rich Towns near the Sea, which 4 or 5,000 Men, landing unexpectedly, might easily surprize and destroy, or extract from them a heavy Contribution, taking a part in ready Money and Hostages for the rest. I should suppose, for Example, that two Millions Sterling, or 48 Millions of Livres might be demanded of Bristol for the Town and Shipping; Twelve Millions of Livres from Bath; Forty-eight Millions from Liverpool, Six Millions from Lancaster and Twelve Millions from Whitehaven. On the East Side there are the Towns of New-Castle, Scarborough, Lyn and Yarmouth, from which very considerable sums might be exacted. And if among the Troops there were a few Horsemen to make sudden incursions at some little Distance from the Coast, it would spread Terror to much greater Distances, and the whole would occasion Movements and Marches of Troops that must put the Enemy to prodigious Expense and harass them exceedingly. Their Militia will probably soon be drawn from the different Counties to one or two Places of Encampment, so that little or no Opposition can be made to such a Force as this above mentioned in the Places where they may land. But the Practicability of such an Opposition and the Means of facilitating and executing it, military People can best judge of. I have not enough of Knowledge in such Matters to presume upon Advising it, and I am so troublesome to the Ministers on other Accounts, that I could hardly venture to solicit it if I were ever so confident of its Success. Much will depend on a prudent and brave Sea Commander, who knows the Coasts, and on a Leader of the Troops who has the affair at Heart, who is naturally active and quick in his Enterprises, of a Disposition proper to conciliate the Good-will and Affection of both the Corps, and by that Means to prevent or obviate such Misunderstandings as are apt to arise between them, and which are often pernicious to joint Expeditions.

On the whole it may be encouraging to reflect on the many Instances of History which prove that War, Attempts thought to be impossible, do often, for that very Reason become possible and practicable because nobody expects them and no Precautions are taken to guard against them. And those are the kind of Undertakings of which the Success affords the most glory to the Ministers who plan and to the Officers who execute them.

But the Spanish fleet was slow; the French were too long at sea, their crews sickly and ill-provisioned; and storms had arrived. By late August Hardy was back at Spithead and the French-American advantage had gone.

But John Paul Jones was not to be denied. A British officer in prison in Brest, got a letter out dated 15 June which was printed in the Gazetteer and New Daily Advertiser *on 7 July:*

Capt. Paul Jones, who some time since landed in Scotland and other places, has fitted out an Old East-Indiaman, to mount 50 guns, and has had her full manned except about 40. She is to carry 300; most of them are English prisoners, who are allowed to enter on board the American vessels. Numbers of them, I am sure, would never have gone on board, but for the bad treatment they experience in prison. The above ship is to sail in consort with an American frigate called the *Alliance*.

Jones put to sea in August with a tiny squadron, comprising the Pallas, *the* Vengeance, *the* Alliance *(commanded by the unstable and treacherous Pierre Landais) and the flagship, the* Bonhomme Richard.

The squadron passed round the north of Scotland and followed the east coast southward. A raid on Leith — to seize ships and demand a ransom — was, again, averted by a storm, and Jones made for the open North Sea. Here he found a merchant fleet of forty ships returning from the Baltic, escorted by the Serapis *of forty-four guns, and the* Countess of Scarborough, *of twenty-eight. The merchant fleet scurried to safety but Jones engaged the* Serapis, *outgunned forty-four to forty. It was a savage four-hour engagement.*

Lieutenant Richard Dale was commanding a battery of twelve-pounders on the Bonhomme Richard:

At about eight, being within hail, the *Serapis* demanded, 'What ship is that?'

He was answered, 'I can't hear what you say.'

Immediately after, the *Serapis* hailed again, 'What ship is that? Answer immediately, or I shall be under the necessity of firing into you.'

At this moment I received orders from Commodore Jones to commence the action with a broadside, which indeed appeared to be simultaneous on board both ships. Our position being to windward of the *Serapis* we passed ahead of her, and the *Serapis* coming up on our larboard quarter, the action commenced abreast of each other. The *Serapis* soon passed ahead of the *Bon Homme Richard*, and when he thought he had gained a distance sufficient to go down athwart the fore foot to rake us, found he had not enough distance, and that the *Bon Homme Richard* would be aboard him, put his helm a-lee, which brought the two ships on a line, and the *Bon Homme Richard*, having head way, ran her bows into the stern of the *Serapis*.

We had remained in this situation but a few minutes when we were again hailed by the *Serapis*, 'Has your ship struck?'

To which Captain Jones answered, 'I have not yet begun to fight!'

As we were unable to bring a single gun to bear upon the *Serapis* our top-sails were backed, while those of the *Serapis* being filled, the ships separated. The *Serapis* bore short round upon her heel, and her jibboom ran into the mizen rigging of the *Bon Homme Richard*. In this situation the ships were made fast together with a hawser, the bowsprit of the *Serapis* to the mizen-mast of the *Bon Homme Richard*, and the action recommenced from the starboard sides of the two ships. With a view of separating the ships, the *Serapis* let go her anchor, which manoeuver brought her head and the stern of the *Bon Homme Richard* to the wind, while the ships lay closely pressed against each other.

A novelty in naval combats was now presented to many witnesses, but to few admirers. The rammers were run into the respective ships to enable the men to load after the lower ports of the *Serapis* had been blown away, to make room for running out their guns, and in this situation the ships remained until between 10 and 11 o'clock PM, when the engagement terminated by the surrender of the *Serapis*.

From the commencement to the termination of the action there was not a man on board the *Bon Homme Richard* ignorant of the superiority of the *Serapis*, both in weight of metal and in the qualities of the crews. The crew of that ship was picked seamen, and the ship itself had been only a few months off the stocks, whereas the crew of the *Bon Homme Richard* consisted of part Americans, English and French, and a part of Maltese, Portuguese and Malays, these latter contributing by their want of naval skill and knowledge of the English language to depress rather than to elevate a just hope of success in a combat under such circumstances. Neither the consideration of the relative force of the ships, the fact of the blowing up of the gundeck above them by the bursting of two of the 18-pounders, nor the alarm that the ship was sinking, could depress the ardor or change the determination of the brave Captain Jones, his officers and men. Neither the repeated broadsides of the *Alliance*, given with the view of sinking or disabling the *Bon Homme Richard*, the frequent necessity of suspending the combat to extinguish the flames, which several times were within a few inches of the magazine, nor the liberation by the master-at-arms of nearly 500 prisoners, could change or weaken the purpose of the American commander. At the moment of the liberation of the prisoners, one of them, a commander of a 20-gun ship taken a few days before, passed through the ports on board the *Serapis* and informed Captain Pearson that if he would hold out only a little while longer, the ship alongside would either strike or sink, and that all the prisoners had been released to save their lives. The combat was accordingly continued with renewed ardor by the *Serapis*.

The fire from the tops of the *Bon Homme Richard* was conducted with so much skill and effect as to destroy ultimately every man who appeared upon the quarter deck of the *Serapis*, and induced her commander to order the survivors to go below. Not even under the shelter of the decks were they more secure. The powder-monkies of the *Serapis*, finding no officer to receive the 18-pound cartridges brought from the magazines, threw them on the main deck and went for more. These cartridges being scattered along the deck and numbers of them broken, it so happened that some of the hand-grenades thrown from the main-yard of the *Bon Homme Richard*, which was directly over the main-hatch of the *Serapis*, fell upon this powder and produced a most awful explosion. The effect was tremendous; more than twenty of the enemy were blown to pieces, and many stood with only the collars of their shirts upon their bodies. In less than an hour afterwards, the flag of England, which had been nailed to the mast of the *Serapis*, was struck by Captain Pearson's *own hand*, as none of his people would venture aloft on this duty; and this too when more than 1500 persons were witnessing the conflict, and the humiliating termination of it, from Scarborough and Flamborough Head.

Midshipman Nathaniel Fanning was perched in the maintop of the same ship and had a different view.

It was, however, some time before the enemy's colours were struck. The captain of the *Serapis* gave repeated orders for one of his crew to ascend the quarter-deck and haul down the English flag, but no one would stir to do it. They told the captain they were afraid of our riflemen, believing that all our men who were seen with muskets were of that description. The captain of the *Serapis* therefore ascended the quarter-deck and hauled down the very flag which he had nailed to the flag-staff a little before the commencement of the battle, and which flag he had at that time, in the presence of his principal officers, swore he never would strike to that infamous pirate J. P. Jones.

The enemy's flag being struck, Captain Jones ordered Richard Dale, his first lieutenant, to select out of our crew a number of men and take possession of the prize, which was immediately put into execution. Several of our men (I believe three) were killed by the English on board of the *Serapis* after she had struck her colours.

Thus ended this ever memorable battle, after a continuance of a few minutes.

A note of peace in that troubled year, however, came when Benjamin Franklin in Paris issued an advice to all armed ships engaged in the war between the United States of America and Britain to allow Captain Cook unharmed passage in his journey to 'unknown seas':

To all Captains and Commanders of armed Ships acting by Commission from the Congress of the United States of America, now in war with Great Britain

GENTLEMEN,

A Ship having been fitted out from England before the Commencement of this War, to make Discoveries of new Countries in Unknown Seas, under the Conduct of that most celebrated Navigator and Discoverer Captain Cook; an Undertaking truly laudable in itself, as the Increase of Geographical Knowledge facilitates the Communication between distant Nations, in the Exchange of useful Products and Manufactures, and the Extension of Arts, whereby the common Enjoyments of human Life are multiply'd and augmented, and Science of other kinds increased to the benefit of Mankind in general; this is, therefore, most earnestly to recommend to every one of you, that, in case the said Ship, which is now expected to be soon in the European Seas on her Return, should happen to fall into your Hands, you would not consider her as an Enemy, nor suffer any Plunder to be made of the Effects contain'd in her, nor obstruct her immediate Return to England, by detaining her or sending her into any other Part of Europe or to America, but that you would treat the said Captain Cook and his People with all Civility and Kindness, affording them, as common Friends to Mankind, all the Assistance in your Power, which they may happen to stand in need of. In so doing you will not only gratify the Generosity of your own Dispositions, but there is no doubt of your obtaining the Approbation of the Congress, and your other American Owners. I have the honour to be, Gentlemen, your most obedient humble Servant.

[Given] at Passy, near Paris, this 10th day of March, 1779.

B. FRANKLIN

Plenipotentiary from the Congress of the
United States to the Court of France.

Back on land, George Rogers Clark, having narrowly avoided capture by a scouting party of Indians in Kaskaskia, recruited a relief force of 170 men, half of whom were French volunteers. He set off in February 1779 across 240 miles of swamps, 'the drowned lands', swollen by winter rain. The two branches of the Little Wabash became a single broad river, five miles across in places. Writing to George Mason in November 1779 about the events of February, Clark described his watery march.

. . . We had now a rout before us of two hundred and forty miles in length, through, I suppose, one of the most beautiful country [sic] in the world; but at this time in many parts flowing with water and exceeding bad marching. My greatest care was to divert the men as much as possible in order to keep up their spirits.

The first obstruction of any consequence that I met with was on the 13th arriveing at the two Little Wabachces. Although three miles as-under they now make but one, the flowed water between them being at least three feet deep, and in many places four, being near five miles to the opposite hills. The shallowest place, except about one hundred yards, was three feet.

This would have been enough to have stopped any set of men that was not in the same temper that we was, but in three days we contrived to cross by building a large canoe, ferried across the two channels, the rest of the way we waded; building scaffolds at each to lodge our baggage on until the horses crossed to take them. It rained nearly a third of our march, but we never halted for it . . .

From the spot we now lay on was about ten miles to town, and every foot of the way put together that was not three feet and upwards under water would not have made the length of two miles and a half, and not a mouthful of provision. To have waited for our boat, if possible to avoid it, would have been impolitic . . .

I returned slowly to the troops, giving myself time to think. On our arrival all ran to hear what was the report. Every eye was fixed on me. I unfortunately spoke serious to one of the officers. The whole was alarmed without knowing what I said. They ran from one another, bewailing their situation. I viewed their confusion for about one min-ute, whispered to those near me to do as I did: immediately took some water in my hand, poured on powder, blacked my face, gave the war whoop and marched into the water without saying a word. The party gazed, and fell in one after another without saying a word, like a flock of sheep. I ordered those that was near me to begin a favorite song of theirs. It soon passed through the line, and the whole went on cheerfully.

I now intended to have them transported across the deepest part of the water, but when getting about waist deep, one of the men informed me that he felt a path (a path is very easily discovered under water by the feet). We examined and found it so, and concluded that it kept on the highest ground, which it did, and by pains to follow it, we got to the sugar camp without the least difficulty . . . where there was about half an acre of dry ground, at least, not under water where we took up our lodgings.

We moved on cheerfully, every moment expecting to see dry land, which was not discovered . . . By the evening we found ourselves encamped on a pretty height in high spirits, each laughing at the other in consequence of something that had happened in the course of this ferrying business, as they called it, and the whole at the great exploit as they thought they had accomplished; thus a little antic drummer afforded them great diversion by floating on his drum, &c. All this was greatly encouraged, and they really began to think themselves superior to other men, and that neither the rivers or seasons could stop their progress. Their whole conversation now was what they would do when they got about the enemy, and now began to view the main Wabash as a creek and made no doubt but that such men as they were could find a way across it. They wound themselves up to such a pitch, that they soon took Vincennes, divided the spoil, and before bed time was far advanced on their route to Detroit . . .

But to our inexpressible joy in the evening of the 23rd we got safe on terra firma within half a league of the fort, covered by a small grove of trees, had a full view of the wished for spot (I should have crossed at a greater distance from the town but the White River comeing in jest below us we were afraid of getting too near it). We had already taken some prisoners that was coming from the town. Laying in this grove some time to dry our clothes by the sun, we took another prisoner known to be a friend, by which we got all the intiligence we wished for, but would not suffer him to see our troops except a few.

A thousand ideas flashed in my head at this moment. I found that Governor Hamilton was able to defend himself for a considerable time, but knew that he was not able to turn out of the fort; that if the siege continued long a superior number might come against us, as I knew there was a party of English not far above the river, that, if they found out our numbers, might raise the disaffected savages and harass us. I resolved to appear as darring as possible, that the enemy might conceive by our behaviour that we were very numerous and probably discourage them.

Henry Hamilton detailed his own downfall:

About five minutes after candles were lighted, we were alarmed by hearing a musket discharged; presently after, some more. I concluded that some party of Indians was returned or there was some riotous frolic in the village. Going upon the parade to enquire, I heard the balls whistle, ordered the men to the blockhouses, forbidding them to fire till they perceived the shot to be directed against the fort. We were shortly out of suspense, one of the sergeants receiving a shot in the breast. The fire was now returned, but the enemy had a great deal of advantage from their rifles, and the cover of the church, houses, barns, &c. . . .

The firing was but slack after sunrise, and about eight o'clock a flag of truce from the rebels appeared, carried by Nicholas Cardinal, a captain of the militia of St Vincennes, who delivered me a letter from Colonel Clark, requiring me to surrender with discretion, adding with an oath that if I destroyed any stores or papers I should be treated as a murderer. Having assembled the officers and read this letter, I told them my intention was to undergo any extremity rather than trust to the discretion of such sort of people as we had to deal with. They all approved of this resolution, on which I assembled the men and informed them of our determination. The English assured me that they would defend the King's colors to the last, adding a homely, but hearty, phrase, that they would stick to me as the shirt to my back. They then gave three cheers. The French, on the contrary, hung their heads. I returned for answer to Colonel Clark's note, that threats would not prevent us from doing our duty as British subjects, and the flag having returned, the firing recommenced.

La Mothe's volunteers now began to murmur, saying it was very hard to be obliged to fight against their countrymen and relations, who, they now perceived had joined the Americans. As they made half our number, and after such a declaration were not to be trusted, the Englishmen wounded, six in number, were a sixth of those we could depend on, and duty would fall every hour on the remaining few. Considering we were at a distance of six hundred miles from succor, that if we did not burn the village we left the enemy most advantageous cover against us, and that if we did, we had nothing to expect after rejecting the first terms, but the extremity of revenge, I took up the determination of accepting honorable terms if they were to be procured, else to abide the worst . . .

About two o'clock a party of Indians with some whites returned from a scout with two Canadians whom they had taken prisoner near the falls of Ohio, probably with information for the rebels at the fort. Colonel Clark sent off a detachment of seventy men against them. The Indian party of fifteen or sixteen men, who seeing the British flag flying at the fort, discharged their pieces (an usual compliment with these people). They were immediately fired upon by the rebels and Canadians, two killed on the spot, one shot in the belly who, however, escaped. The rest were surrounded and taken bound to the village, where being set in the street opposite the fort they were put to death, notwithstanding a truce at the moment existed . . .

One of them was tomahawk'd immediately. The rest, sitting on the ground in a ring, bound, seeing by the fate of their comrade what they had to expect, the next on his left sung his death song and was in turn tomahawk'd; the rest underwent the same fate, one only was saved at the intercession of a rebel officer who pleaded for him, telling Colonel Clark that the savage's father had formerly spared his life.

The chief of this party, after having had the hatchet stuck in his head, took it out himself and deliver'd it to the inhuman monster who struck him first, who repeated his stroke a second and a third time, after which the miserable spectacle was dragged by the rope about his neck to the river, thrown in, and suffer'd to spend still a few moments of life in fruitless strugglings. Two sergeants who had been volunteers with the Indians escaped death by the intercession of a father and a sister who were on the spot . . .

Colonel Clark, yet reeking with the blood of these unhappy victims, came to the esplanade before the fort, where I had agreed to meet him and treat of the surrender of the garrison. He spoke with rapture of his late achievement, while he wash'd off the blood from his hand, stained in this inhuman sacrifice . . .

Clark justified the slaughter by the reasoning:

I now had a fair opportunity of making an impression on the Indians that I could have wished for; that of convincing them that Governor Hamilton could not give them that protection that he had made them to believe he could, in some measure to incense the Indians against him for not exerting himself to save his friends.

Hamilton surrendered on 25 February. He and his officers were marched off to Virginia, where the 'Hair Buyer' was confined. Thomas Jefferson, then Governor of Virginia, refused to exchange him or to release him on parole for fear of his influence on the frontier.★ *Clark, whose expedition was one of the most heroic episodes of the war, claimed all the surrounding countryside in Virginia's name, and became conqueror of a territory more than half the size of all the thirteen colonies. He bound the Indians of the Ohio and Mississippi Valleys to the American cause but — largely for lack of Virginian support, when it was itself invaded — never realised his dream of an assault on Detroit.*

An end to the war seemed no nearer and Washington was melancholy.

I never was, much less reason have I now, to be afraid of the enemy's *arms*' [he wrote to General John Armstrong on May 18th] but I have no scruple in declaring to *you*, that I have never yet seen the time in which our affairs (in my opinion) were at so low an ebb as they are at present; and without a speedy and capital change, we shall not be able to call out the strength and resources of the country.

He had also — without success — urged on Congress the need to reward officers with half-pay pensions for life after the war. In May 1778, Congress compromised by agreeing to half-pay for seven years for those officers in the service throughout the war. In 1779 Washington was still asking for half-pay for life.
　It had become an even uglier war, too, as William Gipson of South Carolina recalled some fifty years later when he claimed his war pension.

. . . sometime in the summer of 1779, at one Wm. Brazleton's in Guilford county, he and his party were in the house, when suddenly two armed men stood at the door. They, seeing the party within, immediately wheeled, and Colonel Moore knocked down one of the men, who proved to be the notorious Hugh McPherson, a Tory. His party soon took the other one, who proved to be one Campbell and brother to the Campbell taken prisoner and made his escape during the first campaign. His party took both these Tories to Guilford Court-house, about fifteen miles from the place of capturing them. There, a court-martial was held, composed of the officers of his party, and McPherson was condemned and shot in the presence of this applicant. And Campbell was condemned *to be spicketed*, that is, he was placed with one foot upon a sharp pin drove in a block, and was turned round by

★But eventually he *was* paroled and sent to New York. In due course his fortunes changed for the better: he became Lieutenant-Governor of Quebec in 1784 (for one year), and was Governor of Bermuda from 1790 to 1794 and of Dominica, 1794–5. He died in 1796.

one Thomas Archer, to the best of his recollection, until the pin run through his foot. Then he was turned loose. The applicant cannot forbear to relate that as cruel as this punishment might seem to be to those who never witnessed the unrelenting cruelties of the Tories of that day, yet he viewed the punishment of those two men with no little satisfaction, as they were then supposed to belong to the identical band who inhumanly inflicted corporal punishment upon his helpless parent, who had committed no other offense than that of earnestly exhorting her sons to be true to the cause of American liberty. So notorious was the conduct of this applicant and his party towards the Tories of that neighborhood, that they were compelled to range the country, not daring to return home to stay anytime or separate until about Christmas 1779, when he separated from his party, where he stayed for the most part of his time until about October or November 1780.

As in all wars, the press found its own special human interest stories, diverse as they may be.

Last week died, at Hammersmith, in England, Mrs Ross, celebrated for her beauty and constancy. Having met with opposition in her engagement with Captain Charles Ross, she followed him, in men's clothes, to America, where, after such a research and fatigue as scarce any of her sex could have undergone, she found him in the woods lying for dead, after a skirmish with the Indians, and with a poisoned wound. Having previously studied surgery in England, she, with an ardor and vigilance which only such a passion could inspire, saved his life by sucking his wound, the only expedient that could have effected it at the crisis he was in, and nursing him with scarce a covering from the sky for the space of six weeks. During this time she remained unsuspected by him, having dyed her skin with lime and bark; and keeping to a man's habit, still supported by the transport of hearing his unceasing aspirations of love and regret for that dear though (he then thought) distant object of his soul, being charged by him with transmitting to her (had the captain died) his remains, and dying asseverations of constancy and gratitude for the unparalleled care and tenderness of his nurse, the bearer of them; but, recovering, they removed into Philadelphia, where, as soon as she had found a clergyman to join her to him forever, she appeared as herself, the priest accompanying her. They lived for the space of four years in a fondness almost ideal to the present age of corruption, and that could only be interrupted by her declining health, the fatigue she had undergone, and the poison not properly expelled which she had imbibed from his wound, undermining her constitution. The knowledge he had of it, and piercing regret of having been the occasion, affecting him still more sensibly, he died with a broken heart last spring at John's Town, in New York. She lived to return and implore forgiveness of her family, whom she had distressed so long by their ignorance of her destiny. She died, in consequence of her grief and affection, at the age of twenty-six.

New York Gazette and Weekly Mercury, 4 OCTOBER

That wretched tool of a brutish tyrant, Sir Harry Clinton, in a proclamation, dated this day, has declared, 'That all Negroes taken in arms, or upon any military duty, shall be purchased, and the money paid to the captors.' He likewise invites all Negroes to desert the States, and 'take refuge with his army', meaning, no doubt, (like the noted Negro thief, *Lord Dunmore*,) to put such refugees in his pocket. However, I am not much concerned, nor is the cause of freedom much interested, how Sir Henry and his *black* and *white* refugees, settle their accounts; as they are all villains, it matters little which may prove in the end the *greatest*. But justice, honor, and freedom, are concerned for all men, of whatever nation or kindred, who are in the service of the United States, and fight under the banners of freedom; therefore I have long expected some notice from authority, would have been taken of that insulting and villanous proclamation. Justice demands retaliation for every man in the service of these States who may be injured by the ruffian tyrant or any of his slaves; and his slave Sir Harry ought to be told what retaliation he is to expect from the insulted majesty of our nation in this instance.

'American Soldier', *New York Packet*, 18 NOVEMBER

In May 1779 Clinton sent a naval force under Admiral Collier, with support from General Matthews and 2500 troops, to devastate Virginia, whose salted beef fed the Continental Line, and whose tobacco financed any credit Congress might obtain abroad. It was now war against non-combatants, with wharfs, warehouses and women attacked. Of the £2 million worth of damage done in the destruction of Portsmouth, most of it went into soldiers' — and officers' — kitbags. Similar depredation marked the raids in July on New Haven, Fairfield and Norfolk, the last two of which were gutted. According to the New York Journal, *the redcoats*

plundered the houses of everything they could carry away or convert to their own use, and broke or destroyed every whole article of household goods and furniture, together with the window glass and sashes.

At Fairfield, according to the New London Gazette:

They entered the houses, attacked the persons of Whig and Tory indiscriminately, breaking open desks, trunks, chests, closets, and taking away everything of value; they robbed women of buckles, rings, bonnets, aprons, and handkerchiefs . . .

Congress had already protested against the mounting evidence of violence and rape, and the increasing attacks on civilians.

We, therefore, the Congress of the United States of America, do solemnly declare and proclaim, that if our enemies presume to execute their threats, or persist in their present career of barbarity, we will take such exemplary vengeance, as shall deter others from a like conduct.

In London, as reports percolated back, the Opposition voiced its indignation. General Conway in the House of Commons was eloquent.

The robe and the mitre animating us in concert to massacre, we plunged ourselves into rivers of blood, spreading terror, devastation and death over the whole continent of America, exhausting ourselves at home both of men and money, dishonouring forever our church, we become the objects of horror in the eyes of indignant Europe! It was our reverend prelates who led on this dance, which may justly be styled the dance of death . . . Such is the horrid war which we have maintained for five years.

Washington, at his headquarters at Middlebrook in New Jersey, was seething. He had chosen this location lest Clinton move south against Philadelphia but, with only 12,000 men at his headquarters in New York, Clinton launched a raid on Penobscot and personally attacked posts in the Hudson Valley, seizing Verplanck's Point and Stony Point in June in order to control King's Ferry on the Hudson — posts so important that Washington Irving likened them to the Pillars of Hercules.
Washington feared an attack on West Point and put his army south of it to block Clinton's path. In July, the Americans, led by Anthony Wayne, who had the disaster at Paoli to avenge, struck back at Stony Point. He took it at bayonet point, killing sixty-three British and capturing 545. Nathanael Greene wrote to Colonel Cox from Stony Point on 17 July:

I wrote you a hasty account yesterday morning of a surprize Gen. Wayne had effected upon the garrison at this place. He marched about two o'clock in the afternoon from Fort Montgomery with part of the light infantry of the army, amounting to about 1,400 men. The garrison consisted of between 5 and 600 men, including officers. The attack was made about midnight and conducted with great spirit and enterprise, the troops marching up in the face of an exceeding heavy fire with cannon and musketry, without discharging a gun. This is thought to be the perfection of discipline and will for ever immortalize Gen. Wayne, as it would do honor to the first general in Europe. The place is as difficult of access as any you ever saw, strongly fortified with lines and secured with a double row of abatis. The post actually looks more formidable on the ground than it can be made by description, and, contrary to almost all other events of this nature, increases our surprize by viewing the place and the circumstances.

The darkness of the night favoured the attack and made our loss much less than might have been expected. The whole business was done with fixed bayonets. Our loss in killed and wounded amounted to 90 men, including officers – eight only of which were killed. Gen. Wayne got a slight wound (upon the side of the head) and three or four other officers – among the number is Lieut. Col. Hay, of Pennsylvania – but they are all in a fair way of recovery.

Colonel Christian Febiger wrote to his American bride the next day.

MY DEAR GIRL:
I have just borrowed pen, ink and paper to inform you that yesterday we march'd from Fort Montgomery, and at 12 o'clock last night we stormed this confounded place . . . I can give you no particulars as yet. A musquet ball scraped my nose. No other damage to 'Old Denmark.' God bless you.

Farewell—

FEBIGER.

On 19 August American forces led by Major Henry Lee ('Light Horse Harry'), the father of Robert E. Lee, carried out a raid that was a duplicate of Stony Point. Four hundred picked men crossed the Hackenseck River in New Jersey after dark, and stormed the British fort at Paulus Hook (now Jersey City) at bayonet point, at two in the morning. Not a shot was fired and fifty British were killed or wounded, and 158 taken prisoner. It was a brilliant thirty-mile march in the dark, on difficult terrain.

Washington planned a three-part strategy for the war in the west, with Gates in command of a force of 4000 men. This was the largest ever force in the Western

Campaign, but Gates refused the command, which passed to Sullivan. Sullivan himself was to move up the Susquehanna to the New York border; General James Clinton was to strike at Indian camps in the Mohawk country and then move down Lake Oswego to join Sullivan; and Colonel Daniel Brodhead was to move from Pittsburgh up the Allegheny into the Indian country. The orders: that the country was not to be 'merely overrun but destroyed'. This was an area stretching from Lake Ontario to the Susquehanna, and from the Catskills on the east to Lake Erie on the west. It was not a country of wigwams but of settled villages with log and stone cabins and well-cultivated orchards.

Nathan Davis wrote an account of the battle of New Town on 29 August 1779 when Sullivan's column out of Wyoming and Clinton's force met their first Indian resistance, from Brant's Mohawks.

When our front had advanced within a short distance of them, they commenced a fire from behind every tree, and at the same time gave a war whoop. Not all the infernals of the Prince of Darkness, could they have been let loose from the bottomless pit, would have borne any comparison to these demons of the forest.

We were expressly ordered not to fire, until we had obtained permission from our officers, but to form a line of battle as soon as possible and march forward. This we did in good order, and at the same time the Indians kept up an incessant fire upon us from behind trees; firing and retreating back to another tree, loading and firing again, still keeping up the war whoop. They continued this mode of warfare till we had driven them halfway up the hill, when we were ordered to charge bayonets and rush on. No sooner said than done. We then, in our turn, gave our war whoop, in the American style, which completely silenced the unearthly voice of their stentorian throats. We drove them, at once, to the opposite side of the hill, when we were ordered to halt, as the Indians were out of sight and hearing.

How many we killed I never could exactly ascertain, but some were killed, and one scalped to my knowledge, and much blood was seen on their track. We also took two prisoners, one Negro and one white man, said to be a Tory. The white man was found painted black, lying on his face, and pretending to be dead. As no blood was seen near him, after a proper discipline he was soon brought to his feelings. He was then stripped and washed, and found to be white. A rope was then tied round his neck, and he was led in front of the troops, whilst every one gave him his sentence, 'You shall be hung tomorrow.' This, however, was not put into execution.

Lieutenant William Barton was among those who were dispatched along the trail to count dead Indians.

Towards noon they found them and skinned two of them from their hips down for boot legs; one pair for the Major and the other for myself.

It was a war of easy plunder as Major Jeremiah Fogg reported at Seneca Town.

But oh! sad mishap! When our commander advanced to complete his part, to his great mortification, he found the detachments either misled by their guards, or else had mistaken a field of pumpkins for the town. But whatever might have been the cause, the whole party from the monkey to the rat, had armed themselves with almost every species of the vegetable creation, each man with three pumpkins on his bayonet and staggering under the weight of a bosom filled with corn and beans, when he broke out, 'You damned unmilitary set of rascals! What, are you going to storm the town with pumpkins! Turn aside, open to the right and left, that men unaccustomed to plundering, and such scandalous conduct, may execute the design! Ye officers, never more show your heads with military characters.' In an instant the whole band was disrobed of their vegetable accoutrements and armor, and pumpkins, squashes, melons and mandrakes rolled down the hill like hail stones in a tempest.

Twenty-year-old Lieutenant (later Major) Erkuries Beatty recorded in September the fate that overtook Lieutenant Boyd's scouting party that probed ahead of Sullivan's column.

The whole army was under arms this morning an hour before day and remained so till sunrise: about 7 oclock fatigue parties was sent out to destroy corn, which was there in great abundance, and beans. About 12 o'clock we marched, crossed over the branch of the Jinasee River and came upon a very beautiful flat of great extent growing up with wild grass higher in some places than our heads. We marched on this flat 2 mile and crossed the Jinasee River, which is about as big as the Tyoga but very crooked. Left the flats and marched thro the woods 3 mile and arrived at Chenesee Town, which is the largest we have yet seen; it lies in a crook of the river on extraordinary good land, about 70 houses, very compact and very well built, and about the same number of out houses in cornfields, etc. On entering the town we found the body of Lt Boyd and another rifle man in a most terrible mangled condition. They was both stripped naked and the flesh of Lt Boyds head was intirely taken of[f] and his eyes punched out. The other mans hed was not there. They was stabed, I supose, in 40 diferent places in the body with a spear and great gashes cut in their flesh with knifes, and Lt Boyds privates was nearly cut of[f] and hanging down, his finger and toe nails was bruised of[f], and the dogs had eat part of their shoulders away; likewise a knife was sticking in Lt Boyds body. They was immediately buried with the honour of war.

In Seneca Town Lieutenant Beatty reported finding white captives.

On the first entrance of our brigade, a young child, I believe about three years old, found running about the houses which one of our officers picked up and found it to be a white child, but it was so much tanned and smoked that we could hardly distinguish it from an Indian child and was exceeding poor, scarcely able to walk. It could talk no English, nothing but Indian, and I believe, but little of that. The officer took great care of it and clothed it, as it was naked when he found it, and could give no account of itself; only said 'His Mammy was gone.' The men got very little plunder, or anything in the town as the Indians had taken everything with them.

By 15 September the campaign was drawing to a close. It was soon after the burial of Lieutenant Boyd that Major Fogg heard the welcome command:

This day was spent in destroying corn which had become so ripe that we were obliged to burn it in kilns. Some corn stalks were seventeen feet long. The whole army was employed, but at three o'clock we *faced to the right about*. A most joyful day! Marched back to the east end of the great flat and encamped.

Sullivan's expedition must be counted a military success: forty-one Indian towns (their so called 'castles') destroyed, along with 1500 fruit trees and over 200 acres of corn — for a loss of only forty-one men, not all of whom had died in combat. Was it effective? Major Fogg, with General Sullivan, expressed his doubts.

The question will naturally arise, what have you to show for your exploits? Where are your prisoners? To which I reply that the rags and emaciated bodies of our soldiers must speak for our fatigue, and when the querist will point out a mode to tame a partridge or the expediency of hunting wild turkeys with light horse, I will show them our prisoners.

The nests are destroyed but the birds are still on the wing.

The Indians fell back to Niagara, to be supplied by Britain from Canada. Daniel Brodhead's column moved through the Allegheny country on a similar mission of 'discover and destroy'. He covered 400 miles without losing a man, a record in the Revolution.

In the south, 1779 brought no success to the American cause. Britain, having regained Savannah, had sent royal governor Sir James Wright back to Georgia to restore royal government. He would be there for almost three years. Major-General Benjamin Lincoln was the American commanding general in the Southern Department — middle-aged, stout and going bald. He sent a column, mainly militia, led by John Ashe, into British-held Georgia, but they broke and ran when attacked by a column led by Colonel Mark Prevost. Thus encouraged, Prevost moved north towards Charleston, which Governor John Rutledge offered to surrender if its harbour, and the state as a whole, would be considered neutral for the rest of the war. Prevost insisted on unconditional surrender, and withdrew towards Savannah.

The initiative now swung to the Americans. With the support of d'Estaing's fleet, fresh from the capture of St Vincent and Grenada in the West Indies, Lincoln marched on Savannah with 2000 men in September. The royalist Chief Justice of Georgia, Anthony Stokes, described the terrors of bombardment.

I had some distance to go before I got out of the line of fire, and did not know the way under Savannah bluff, where I should have been safe from cannon balls, and therefore, whenever I came to an opening of a street, I watched the flashes of the mortars and the guns, and pushed on until I came under cover of a house, and when I got to the Common and heard the whistlings of a shot or shell, I fell on my face . . .

The appearance of the town afforded a melancholy prospect, for there was hardly a house which had not been shot through, and some of them were almost destroyed . . . In the streets and on the Common there was a number of large holes made in the ground by the shells . . . The troops in the lines were much safer from the bombardment than the people in town . . . In short, the situation of Savannah was at one time deplorable. A small garrison in an extensive country was surrounded on the land by a powerful enemy, and its seacoast blocked up by one of the strongest fleets that ever visited America. There was not a single spot where the women and children could be put in safety, and the numerous desertions daily weakened that force which was at first inadequate to man such extensive lines, but the situation of the ground would not permit the able engineer to narrow them. However, with the assistance of God, British valor surmounted every difficulty.

Comte d'Estaing insisted upon an all-out assault, despite the objections of Lincoln. Major Thomas Pinckney of the South Carolina militia blamed d'Estaing for the fiasco that followed:

By the time the French column had arrived at the open space, day had fairly broke, when Count d'Estaing, without waiting until the other columns had arrived at their positions, placed himself at the head of his first column and rushed forward to the attack. But this body was so severely galled by the grape shot from the batteries as they advanced, and by both grape shot and musketry when they reached the abatis that, in spite of the efforts of the officers, the column got into confusion and broke away to their left toward the wood in that direction. The second and third French column shared successively the same fate, having the additional discouragement of seeing, as they marched to the attack, the repulse and loss of their comrades who had preceded them.

Count Pulaski who, with the cavalry, preceded the right column of the Americans, proceeded gallantly until stopped by the abatis, and before he could force through it, received his mortal wound. In the meantime, Colonel Laurens at the head of the light infantry, followed by the 2nd South Carolina Regiment and 1st Battalion Charlestown militia, attacked the Spring Hill redoubt, got into the ditch and planted the colors of the 2nd Regiment on the berm, but the parapet was too steep for them to scale it under so heavy a fire, and after much slaughter they were driven out of the ditch.

By this time the 2nd American column, headed by General McIntosh, to which I was attached, arrived at the foot of the Spring Hill redoubt, and such a scene of confusion as there appeared is not often equalled . . . Count d'Estaing was wounded in the arm, and endeavoring to rally his men, a few of whom with a drummer he had collected. General McIntosh did not speak French, but desired me to inform the Commander-in-Chief that his column was fresh, and that he wished his directions, where, under the present circumstances, he should make the attack. The Count ordered that we should move more to the left, and by no means to interfere with the troops he was endeavoring to rally. In pursuing this direction we were thrown too much to the left, and before we could reach Spring Hill redoubt, we had to pass through Yamacraw Swamp, then wet and boggy, with the galley at the mouth annoying our left flank with grape shot.

'Six Pence a day' — life for the British soldier could be very hard

The Bonhomme Richard *engaging* H.M.S. Serapis

Henry Lee, 'Light Horse Harry'

Count Casimir Pulaski

Nathanael Greene, a kind and able Quaker

While struggling through this morass, the firing slacked, and it was reported that the whole army had retired. I was sent by General McIntosh to look out from the Spring Hill, where I found not an assailant standing. On reporting this to the General, he ordered a retreat, which was effected without too much loss, notwithstanding the heavy fire of grape shot with which we were followed.

The loss of both armies in killed and wounded amounted to 637 French and 457 Americans . . . The loss of the British amounted only to fifty-five.

Twice Franco-American co-operation had failed. As the Loyalist officer, John Harris Cruger, put it:

They came in so full of confidence of succeeding, that they were at some loss where to lay the blame, each abusing the other for deceiving them . . . We are all hands sufferers by this unfortunate invasion. The difference is we have acquired glory and our Enemies, Disgrace.

1780

Washington is certainly to be bought – honours will do it

The year began in piercing cold. It would end in high treason. It was to be the grimmest year in Washington's experience.

When it was clear that Clinton was to winter in New York, Washington chose Morristown as his site for winter quarters. The weather turned so cold that the Hudson was frozen solid from New York to Paulus Hook, New Jersey. Staten Island could be supplied by sleigh, and a cavalry troop rode from there to the Battery. 'It has been amazing cold to such a Degree that I who never yet flinched to old Boreas', wrote Simeon De Witt, 'had t'other day one of my Ears froze as hard as a Pine gnut.' It brought only one relief: the snow was so thick – in drifts twelve feet high – that it ended Steuben's continual drilling, and paperwork lessened because ink froze.

It was not just a question of climate. By April, Washington's command amounted to no more than 10,400 rank and file, on paper, of whom 2800 were due to complete their term of service in May. He had written on 18 December 1779 to the governors of several neighbouring states.

The situation of the army in respect to supplies is beyond description alarming. It has been five or six weeks past on half allowance and we have not more than three days bread at a Third allowance on hand, nor any where within reach . . . Our magazines are absolutely empty everywhere and our commissaries entirely destitute of money or credit to replenish them. We have never experienced a like extremity at any period of the war . . . Unless some extraordinary and immediate exertions are made by the States from which we draw our supplies, there is every appearance that the army will infallibly disband in a fortnight.

They have borne their distress . . . with as much fortitude as human nature is capable of; but they have been at last brought to such dreadful extremity that no authority or influence of the officers could any longer restrain them from obeying the dictates of their own sufferings. The

Soldiery have in several instances plundered the neighbouring Inhabitants even of their necessary subsistence.

Surgeon Thacher's memories of that winter were grim.

On the 3rd instant, we experienced one of the most tremendous snow storms ever remembered; no man could endure its violence many minutes without danger of his life. Several marquees were torn asunder and blown down over the officers' heads during the night, and some of the soldiers were actually covered while in their tents, and buried like sheep under the snow. My comrades and I were roused from sleep by the calls of some officers for assistance; their marquee had blown down, and they were almost smothered in the storm before they could reach our marquee, only a few yards, and their blankets and baggage were nearly buried in the snow. We were greatly favored in having a supply of straw for bedding; over this we spread our blankets, and with our clothes and large fires at our feet, while four or five are crowded together, preserve ourselves from freezing. But the sufferings of the poor soldiers can scarcely be described, while on duty they are unavoidably exposed to all the inclemency of storms and severe cold. At night they now have a bed of straw upon the ground, and a single blanket to each man. They are badly clad, and some are destitute of shoes. We have contrived a kind of stone chimney outside, and an opening at one end of our tents gives us the benefit of the fire within.

The snow is now from four to six feet deep, which so obstructs the roads as to prevent our receiving a supply of provisions. For the last ten days we have received but two pounds of meat per man, and we are frequently for six or eight days entirely destitute of meat, and then as long without bread . . .

As if to make up the full measure of grief and embarrassment to the Commander-in-Chief, repeated complaints have been made to him that some of the soldiers are in the practice of pilfering and plundering the inhabitants of their poultry, sheep, pigs, and even their cattle, from their farms. This marauding practice has often been prohibited in general orders, under the severest penalties, and some exemplary punishments have been inflicted.

Death has been inflicted in a few instances of an atrocious nature, but, in general, the punishment consists in a public whipping, and the number of stripes is proportioned to the degree of offence. The Law of Moses prescribes forty stripes save one, but this number has often been exceeded in our camp. In aggravated cases, and with old offenders, the culprit is sentenced to receive one hundred lashes or more. It is always the duty of the drummers and fifers to inflict the chastisement, and the drum-majors must attend and see that the duty is faithfully performed. The culprit being securely tied to a tree, or post, receives on his naked back the number of lashes assigned him, by a whip formed of several small knotted cords, which sometimes cut through the skin at every stroke. However strange it may appear, a soldier will often receive the severest stripes without uttering a groan, or once shrinking from the lash, even while the blood flows freely from his lacerated wounds. This must be ascribed to a stubbornness or pride. They have, however, adopted a method . . . which, they say, mitigates the anguish in some measure; it is by putting between the teeth a leaden bullet, on which they chew while under the lash, till it is made quite flat and jagged . . .

Another mode of punishment is that of running the *gauntlet*. This is done by a company of soldiers standing in two lines, each one furnished with a switch, and the criminal is made to run between them and receive the scourge from their hands on his naked back. But the delinquent runs so rapidly, and the soldiers are so apt to favor a comrade, that it often happens in this way that the punishment is very trivial, but on some occasions a soldier is ordered to hold a bayonet at his breast to impede his steps.

By April Washington had only 4000 men fit for duty. In May, although officers put themselves on bread and water to save what meat there was for the men, there came open mutiny among the Connecticut Line, as the long-suffering Joseph Martin reported.

. . . At evening roll call they began to show their dissatisfaction by snapping at the officers and acting contrary to their orders. After their dismissal from the parade, the officers went as usual to their quarters, except the Adjutant who happened to remain, giving details for next day's duty to the orderly sergeants, or some other business, when the men (none of whom had left the parade) began to make him sensible that they had something in train. He said something that did not altogether accord with the soldiers' ideas of propriety. One of the men retorted. The Adjutant called him a mutinous rascal or some such epithet and then left the parade.

This man, then stamping the butt of his musket upon the ground . . . in a passion, called out, 'Who will parade with me?'

The whole regiment immediately fell in and formed. We had made no plans for our future operations, but while we were consulting how to proceed, the Fourth Regiment, which lay on our left, formed and came and paraded with us. We now concluded to go in a body to the other two regiments that belonged to our brigade and induce them to join with us . . .

After our officers had left us to our own option, we dispersed to our huts and laid by our arms of our own accord, but the worm of hunger knawing so keen kept us from being entirely quiet. We, therefore, still kept upon the parade in groups, venting our spleen at our country and government, then at our officers, and then at ourselves for our imbecility in staying there and starving . . . for an ungrateful people who did not care what became of us . . .

While we were thus venting our gall against we knew not who, Colonel [Walter] Stewart of the Pennsylvania Line, with two or three other officers of that Line, came to us and questioned us respecting our unsoldierlike conduct, (as he termed it).

'Your officers', he said, 'are gentlemen. They *will* attend to you. I know them. They cannot refuse to hear you. But . . . your officers suffer as much as you do. We all suffer. The officers have no money to purchase supplies with, any more than the private men have, and if there is nothing in the public store, we must fare as hard as you . . .

'Besides,' said he, 'you know not how much you injure your own characters by such conduct. You Connecticut troops have won immortal honor to yourselves the winter past by your performance, patience, and bravery, and now you are shaking it off at your heels. But I will go and see your officers and talk with them myself.'

He went, but what the result was, I never knew. This Colonel Stewart was an excellent officer, much loved and respected by the troops of the Line he belonged to. He possessed great personal beauty. The Philadelphia ladies styled him the *Irish Beauty*.

Our stir did us some good in the end, for we had provisions directly after . . .

In the end Washington granted pardons to all, except those who had actually shouldered their packs with a view to desertion.

By contrast, Clinton had at his disposal by now a force of some 28,500 men, since he had withdrawn his garrison from Newport, and Cornwallis had arrived with reinforcements from England. Of these, 13,848 were British regulars, 10,836 were Hessians, and 4072 were Loyalist 'Provincials'. British raids were carried out against turbulent Westchester County and towns in Connecticut were sacked, at the indiscriminate expense of homes, wharfs and warehouses. But his personal attention was elsewhere: Britain at last had a southern strategy.

VIRGINIA

Boyd's Ferry

Roanoke R.

Dan R.

NORTH

Guilford ×
Courthouse

Hillsborough

CAROLINA

Salisbury

Northeast Cape Fear

King's Mountain

Charlotte

Cross Creek

Cowpens ×

Waxhaws

Cape Fear R.

Fishing Creek

Cheraw

Blackstocks

Catawba

Rocky Mount

× Hanging Rock
× Rugeley's Mills
× Hobkirk's Hill

Wilmington

Winnsborough

Camden

Wateree

SOUTH

Great Peedee R.

Ninety six

Saluda R.

Congaree R.

Cape Fear

Fort Granby

North Fork

Fort Motte

CAROLINA

South Fork

Orangeburg

Fort
Watson

Santee R.

Georgetown

Eutaw Springs ×

Edisto R.

GEORGIA

Savannah R.

Monck's Corner

Charleston

Fort Moultrie
Sullivan's I.
James I.
John's I.

Long I.

Black Swamp

Ebenezer

Edisto I.

Purysburg

Port Royal I.

Savannah
Tybee I.

Port Royal Sd.

→←× Gates' route 1780
—— Cornwallis' route 1780
–←– Cornwallis' pursuit of Greene
and subsequent retreat to
Wilmington 1781
·←··· Cornwallis' route to Virginia,
1781
←······ Retreat of Greene (including
Morgan and Huger) and the
subsequent pursuit of
Cornwallis 1781
←←← Tarleton's route to and from
Cowpens 1781
o·←o·o Rawdon's relief of Ninety-six
1781

182

Clinton took command of it in person. He recalled the Rhode Island garrison of 3000 men so he would then have 5000 troops to spare, and crews of 5000 in a fleet of ninety transports. D'Estaing's departure left the sea lanes open to him. He sailed on 26 December 1779. The voyage was stormy: horses perished, stores were damaged, part of the fleet was dispersed. One dismasted transport drifted for eleven weeks before reaching St Ives in Cornwall. He even lost most of his guns. Clinton did not land on John's Island, thirty miles south of Charleston, until 11 February where inexplicably he waited for eight weeks.

General Lincoln had less than 4000 men, half of them militia. Aided by 600 slaves who built redoubts across Charleston Neck, from the Ashley to the Cooper, he prepared for a siege. He was strengthened by 1500 Virginian and North Carolina militia; Clinton called on 1500 more men from Savannah and another 2500 from New York.

Recalling the failure in 1776 of the attack from the sea past Sullivan's Island, Clinton planned to strangle the city's lifeline by a siege operation across Charleston Neck between the Ashley and the Cooper Rivers. Admiral Arbuthnot's fleet blockaded the harbour and on 8 April, without serious opposition, sailed past Fort Moultrie on Sullivan's Island. The garrison refused to surrender and a siege began. Lincoln relied on an escape route, protected by General Isaac Huger and 500 mounted men stationed at Monck's Corner, thirty miles to the north. This was attacked on 13 April by a British force of 500 dragoons led by Colonel Banastre Tarleton, the short, muscular and tireless cavalry leader who fought a ruthless war, and whose name soon became a synonym for terror in the south. In his own — sometimes vainglorious — narrative of the campaign he recalled:

At three o'clock in the morning, the advanced guard of dragoons and mounted infantry, supported by the remainder of the Legion and [Major Patrick] Ferguson's corps [of American Loyalists] approached the American post. A watch word was immediately communicated to the officers and soldiers which was closely followed by an order to charge the enemy's grand guard on the main road, there being no other avenue open, owing to the swamps upon the flanks, and to pursue them into their camp.

The order was executed with the greatest . . . success. The Americans were completely surprised. Major [Paul] Vernier of Pulaski's Legion and some other officers and men who attempted to defend themselves were killed or wounded. General Huger, Colonels Washington and [John] Jameson with many officers and men fled on foot to the swamps close to their encampment, where being concealed by the darkness, they effected their escape. Four hundred horses belonging to officers and dragoons with their arms and appointments (a valuable acquisition for the British cavalry in their present state) fell into the hands of the victors. About one hundred officers, dragoons, and hussars, together with fifty wagons loaded with arms, clothing, and ammunition shared the same fate. Without loss of time, Major [Charles] Cochrane was ordered to force the bridge and the meetinghouse with the infantry of the British legion. He charged the militia with fixed bayonets, got possession of the pass, and dispersed everything that opposed him . . .

The British had one officer and two men wounded . . .

The American line of retreat was severed. By 19 April, Clinton's lines were within 250 yards of Lincoln's. The result could not be in doubt, and Benjamin Smith warned his wife:

This will give a rude shock to the Independence of America, and a Lincolnade will become as common a term as a Burgoynade . . . Nothing prevents Lincoln's surrender but a point of honor of holding out to the last extremity. This is nearly at hand, as our provisions will soon fail, and my plan is to WALK off as soon as I can obtain permission . . . A mortifying scene must first be encountered. The thirteen stripes will be leveled in the dust and I owe my life to the clemency of a conqueror.

General Moultrie recorded the death throes.

Tuesday, [April] 25th. Between twelve and one this morning, a heavy fire of cannon and musketry commenced from our advanced redoubt and the right of the lines, occasioned, as it was said, by the enemy's advancing in column. It is certain they gave several huzzas, but whether they were out of their trenches is not clear. They kept up a very heavy and incessant fire with musketry for thirty minutes. The enemy threw several light balls into the town . . .

Wednesday, 26th. The *Lord George Germain* and a sloop joined the enemy's fleet. The enemy were very quiet all day and last night. We suppose they are bringing cannon into their third parallel. They are strengthening their approaches. Lord Cornwallis took possession of Mount Pleasant yesterday. Brigadier General du Portail arrived from Philadelphia. The garrison ordered to be served with the usual quantity of provisions, a plentiful supply having been received . . .

On General du Portail declaring that the works were not tenable, a council was again called upon for an evacuation, and to withdraw privately with the Continental troops. When the citizens were informed upon what the council were deliberating, some of them came into

184

council and expressed themselves very warmly, and declared to General Lincoln that if he attempted to withdraw the troops and leave the citizens, they would cut up his boats and open the gates to the enemy. This put a stop to all thoughts of an evacuation of the troops, and nothing was left for us but to make the best terms we could.

After Clinton rejected Lincoln's surrender terms, Moultrie on 7 May recounted the last hurrah of Lincoln's guns:

At length, we fired the first gun and immediately followed a tremendous cannonade, and the mortars from both sides threw out an immense number of shells. It was a glorious sight to see them like meteors crossing each other and bursting in the air. It appeared as if the stars were tumbling down. The fire was incessant almost the whole night, cannon balls whizzing and shells hissing continually amongst us, ammunition chests and temporary magazines blowing up, great guns bursting, and wounded men groaning along the lines. It was a dreadful night! It was our last great effort, but it availed us nothing. After this, our military ardor was much abated. We began to cool . . . and, on the eleventh of May, we capitulated.

The British showed soldierly restraint in their triumph.

The LINCOLNADE was acted . . . General [Alexander] Leslie with the Royal English Fusiliers and Hessian Grenadiers and some Artillery took possession of the town and planted the British colors by the gate, on the ramparts, and Lincoln limped out at the head of the most ragged rabble I ever beheld. It however, pleased me much better than the Meschianza.

They were indulged with beating a drum and to bring out their colors eased. They laid down their arms between their abatis and surrendered prisoners of war . . . The militia, poor creatures, could not be prevailed upon to come out. They began to creep out of their holes the next day . . .

By the capitulation they are allowed to go home and plow the ground. There only they can be useful.

Five thousand men surrendered at Charleston, with their stores. American casualties were eighty-nine killed and 138 wounded against Clinton's seventy-six killed and 189 wounded. It was the greatest American surrender of the war — and indeed the greatest in American history until Bataan.

Yet in the larger sense it was a pointless victory, for there was danger in a war fought in two widely separated theatres, cut off by a sea link now imperilled by the French. New York and Charleston alike survived as British bases by permission of Neptune. Who commanded the Atlantic commanded the future. Dispersion of forces meant ultimate defeat.

Clinton moved to occupy South Carolina: one column moved to Fort Ninety-Six on the western frontier, another to Augusta, and the main force under Lord Cornwallis, Clinton's second-in-command, 'Old Corncob' to his men, moved towards Camden, where an American force was believed to be gathering. Part of this supply force of 350 Virginia troops under Colonel Abraham Buford, having heard of the fall of Charleston, was now retreating northwards. Tarleton was ordered after them, his green-uniformed cavalry covering over a hundred miles in fifty-four hours. He overtook them on the lush green valleys near the North Carolina line known as the 'Waxhaws'. The first Buford knew of his approach was the cry of a British bugle as his rearguard under Lieutenant Pearson was attacked. As Dr Robert Brownfield, a surgeon with Buford, later recorded:

Not a man escaped. Poor Pearson was inhumanely mangled on the face, as he lay on his back. His nose and lip were bisected . . . several of his teeth were broken out in the upper jaw and the under, completely divided on each side. These wounds were inflicted after he had fallen, with several others on his head, shoulders and arms . . .

This attack gave Buford the first confirmation of Tarleton's declaration by his flag. Unfortunately, he was then compelled to prepare for action on ground which presented no impediment to the full action of cavalry. Tarleton having arranged his infantry in the center and his cavalry on the wings, advanced to the charge with the horrid yells of infuriated demons. They were received with firmness and completely checked until the cavalry were gaining the rear. Buford, now perceiving that further resistance was hopeless, ordered a flag to be hoisted and the arms to be grounded, expecting the usual treatment by civilized warfare.

This, however, made no part of Tarleton's creed. His ostensible pretext for the relentless barbarity that ensued was that his horse was killed under him, just as the flag was raised. He affected to believe that this was done afterwards and imputed it to treachery on the part of Buford . . .

Ensign Cruit, who advanced with the flag, was instantly cut down. Viewing this as an earnest of what they were to expect, a resumption of their arms was attempted, to sell their lives as dearly as possible. But before this was fully affected, Tarleton . . . was in the midst of them . . .

The demand for quarter, seldom refused to a vanquished foe, was at once found to be in vain. Not a man was spared, and it was the concurrent testimony of all the survivors that for fifteen minutes after every man was prostrate, they went over the ground, plunging their bayonets into everyone that exhibited any signs of life, and in some instances, where several had fallen one over the other, these monsters were seen to throw off on the point of the bayonet the uppermost, to come to those beneath.

Only fifty-three Virginians survived; Tarleton's losses were five killed, fourteen wounded. Clinton issued proclamations offering pardons and the promise of eventual self-government, with exemption from taxation except by their own assemblies. A chain of British posts, as far west as Ninety-Six, were the strong points. 'We may', he thought, 'have conquered the two Carolinas in Charleston . . . a few works which, if properly reinforced, will give us all between this and Hudson's River . . .' He sailed north, leaving Cornwallis as military administrator in South Carolina, where all was – he thought – 'tranquility, submission' – and he was charged to do the same in North Carolina and Virginia.

On 31 May Cornwallis entered Camden. Clinton left behind not only Tarleton's soldiery but a proclamation of 3 June restoring citizenship but requiring an oath of allegiance to Britain; without this, there would be no protection of property or job; those who did not help the king's cause would be treated as 'rebels'; all men must choose. It caused acute anguish and rebels with no scruples could, of course, take the oath and secure the benefits of being faithful Loyalists. The contemporary historian Charles Stedman recorded:

Even the most violent revolutionist, unless he chose to leave the country, was obliged to assume the appearance of loyalty . . . The loyalists murmured because notorious rebels, by taking the oath of allegiance, and putting on a shew of attachment, became entitled to the same privileges as themselves.

There was booty too. Two thousand Negroes were sent to the West Indies for sale; farms and plantations were confiscated. A greedy general might collect as much as £4000 by seizing stores or tobacco.

Eliza Wilkinson, whose plantation was some thirty miles from Charleston, described the horrors of this partisan war, now disturbingly becoming a civil war:

Well, now comes the day of terror – the 3d of June [1780]. (I shall never love the anniversary of that day.) In the morning, fifteen or sixteen horsemen rode up to the house. We were greatly terrified, thinking them the enemy, but from their behavior were agreeably deceived and found them friends. They sat a while on their horses, talking to us; and then rode off, except two, who tarried a minute or two longer and then followed the rest, who had nearly reached the gate. One of them said two must needs jump a ditch — to show his activity I suppose; for he might as well, and better, have gone in the road. However, he got a sad fall; we saw him, and sent a boy to tell him, if he was hurt, to come up to the house, and we would endeavor to do something for him. He and his companion accordingly came up; he looked very pale and bled much; his gun somehow in the fall had given him a bad wound behind the ear, from whence the blood flowed down his neck and bosom plentifully. We were greatly alarmed on seeing him in this situation, and had gathered around him, some with one thing, some with another, in order to give him assistance.

We were very busy examining the wound when a Negro girl ran in, exclaiming, 'O! the King's people are coming! It must be them, for they are all in red!' Upon this cry, the two men that were with us snatched up their guns, mounted their horses and made off, but had not got many yards from the house before the enemy discharged a pistol at them. Terrified almost to death as I was, I was still anxious for my friends' safety. I tremblingly flew to the window, to see if the shot had proved fatal, when, seeing them both safe, 'Thank heaven,' said I, 'they've got off without hurt!'

I'd hardly uttered this when I heard the horses of the inhuman Britons coming in such a furious manner that they seemed to tear up the earth, and the riders at the same time bellowing out the most horrid curses imaginable, oaths and imprecations, which chilled my whole frame. Surely, thought I, such horrid language denotes nothing less than death; but I'd no time for thought. They were up to the house — entered with drawn swords and pistols in their hands. Indeed, they rushed in, in the most furious manner, crying out, 'Where're these women rebels?' (pretty language to ladies from the *once famed Britons!*). That was the first salutation!

The moment they espied us, off went our caps (I always heard say none but women pulled caps!). And for what, think you? Why, only to get a paltry stone and wax pin, which kept them on our heads; at the same time uttering the most abusive language imaginable, and making as if they'd hew us to pieces with their swords. But it's not in my power to describe the scene. It was terrible to the last degree; and, what augmented it, they had several armed Negroes with them, who threatened and abused us greatly. They then began to plunder the house of every thing they thought valuable or worth taking; our trunks were split to pieces, and each man, pitiful wretch, crammed his bosom with the contents, which were our apparel, etc., etc., etc.

I ventured to speak to the inhuman monster who had my clothes. I represented to him the times were such we could not replace what they'd taken from us, and begged him to spare me only a suit or two; but I got nothing but a hearty curse for my pains; nay, so far was his callous heart from relenting that, casting his eyes towards my shoes, 'I want them buckles,' said he, and immediately knelt at my feet to take them out, which, while he was busy about, a brother villain, whose enormous mouth extended from ear to ear, bawled out, 'Shares there! I say, shares!' So they divided my buckles between them.

The other wretches were employed in the same manner; they took my sister's ear-rings from her ears; hers, and Miss Samuells's buckles. They demanded her ring from her finger. She pleaded for it, told them it was her wedding ring, and begged they'd let her keep it. But they still demanded it, and, presenting a pistol at her, swore if she did not deliver it immediately, they'd fire. She gave it to them, and, after bundling up all their booty, they mounted their horses. But such despicable figures! Each wretch's bosom stuffed so full they appeared to be all afflicted with some dropsical disorder. Had a party of rebels (as they called us) appeared, we should soon have seen their circumference lessen . . .

These recurring features, of Loyalty oaths, British ruthlessness and guerilla war, indicate that the character of the war was changing. Four years had passed; there were new men and new tactics; civilians were no longer seen to be immune; and the locale in itself dictated a change of plan. This vast plantation world covered some 15,000 square miles, stretching from the rich and easy tidal rivers of Virginia to the dark jungles of Florida; it was intersected by creeks and swamps; and its sandy roads allowed the use of cavalry for almost the first time. Moreover, it was thinly peopled; there were many slaves; and though many planters might still be loosely loyal to a distant king they lived remote lives, in isolated pockets. Here Loyalist support was essential, but erratic, and unpredictable. Tarleton found Mecklenburg and Rowan Counties in North Carolina 'more hostile to England than any in America'.

The vehemence of Tarleton's campaigning as well as the topography helps to explain the appearance of American guerilla forces. They were fighting less for Congress than in self-defence against a brutal and licentious British and Loyalist soldiery. They had able leaders in Thomas Sumter, the 'Carolina gamecock' whose plantation near Eutaw Springs was burned and who fought his own war in the War; in Francis Marion, the 'swamp fox' who, though the grandson of Huguenot immigrants and by nature gentle, brave and humane, learned to outdo Tarleton in ruthlessness. A moody, introverted man, he became, nevertheless, in legend, largely through Parson Weems' telling, an American Bayard; as William Cullen Bryant's poem The Song of Marion's Men *testifies:*

> Our band is few, but true and tried
> Our leader frank and bold;
> The British soldier trembles
> When Marion's name is told.

Captain Tarleton Brown of South Carolina remembered Marion too:

For prudence sake, Marion never encamped over two nights in one place, unless at a safe distance from the enemy. He generally commenced the line of march about sun-set, continuing through the greater part of the night. By this policy he was enabled effectually to defeat the plans of the British and to strengthen his languishing cause. For while the one army was encamping and resting in calm and listless security, not dreaming of danger, the other, taking advantage of opportunity and advancing through the sable curtains of the night unobserved, often effectually vanquished and routed their foes. It was from the craftiness and ingenuity of Marion, the celerity with which he moved from post to post, that his enemies gave to him the significant appellation of the 'Swamp Fox'. Upon him depended almost solely the success of the provincial army of South Carolina, and the sequel has proven how well he performed the trust reposed in him. His genuine love of country and liberty, and his unwearied vigilance and invincible fortitude, coupled with the eminent success which attended him through his brilliant career, has endeared him to the hearts of his countrymen, and the memory of his deeds of valor shall never slumber so long as there is a Carolinian to speak his panegyric.

Nor should one omit Andrew Pockets, the taciturn Presbyterian elder from Ninety-Six who had taken a loyalty oath but who turned to guerilla war when his home was burnt, William Davie and his 'Bloody Corps', or William Lee Davidson from the Catawba bottom lands.

Davie failed to dislodge a British post at Rocky Mounts in July, but when successful (with Thomas Sumter) on another post twelve miles away at Hanging Rock, the Patriots plundered the stores and got drunk. Here the battle was especially bitter, and was between Patriots and Tories – not a single British soldier took part. In August, Tarleton struck back at Fishing Creek, finding Sumter's force bathing, killing 150 and capturing 300. 'The whole country between the Peedee and the Santee', Cornwallis admitted, 'was in an absolute state of rebellion.'

In the post of Commander in the South, Congress insisted — against Washington's preference for Nathanael Greene — on Horatio Gates, the British-born hero of Saratoga. He planned to strike at Camden. He moved towards it slowly, through wilderness and swamps, thin in provisions (and especially short of the army staple — rum) and thick with Loyalists. He issued a Burgoyne-style proclamation, declaring that

... exertions of the virtuous citizens of America in the State, and by the approach of a numerous, well appointed and formidable army, [he intended] to compel our late triumphant and insulting foes to retreat from their most advantageous posts with precipitation and dismay.

Colonel Otho Williams, deputy adjutant general, noted the results.

The distresses of the soldiery daily increased; they were told that the banks of the Pee Dee River were extremely fertile, and so indeed they were. But the preceding crop of corn (the principal article of commerce) was exhausted, and the new grain, although luxuriant and fine, was unfit for use. Many of the soldiery, urged by necessity, plucked the green ears and boiled them with the lean beef which was collected in the woods, made for themselves a repast, not unpalatable to be sure, but which was attended with painful effects. Green peaches were also substituted for bread, and had similar consequences. Some officers, aware of the risk of eating such vegetables, and in such a state, with poor fresh beef, and without salt, restrained themselves from taking anything but the beef itself, boiled or roasted. It occurred to some that the hair powder which remained in their bags, would thicken soup, and it was actually applied ...

As there were no spirits yet arrived in camp, and as . . . it was unusual for troops to make a forced march, or prepare to meet an enemy without some extraordinary allowance, it was unluckily conceived that molasses would, for once, be an acceptable substitute. Accordingly the hospital stores were broached, and one gill of molasses per man, and a full ration of corn meal and meat were issued to the army previous to their march, which commenced, according to orders at about ten o'clock at night of the 15th . . . The troops of General Gates's army had frequently felt the bad provision; but at this time, a hasty meal of quick-baked bread and fresh beef, with a dessert of molasses, mixed with mush, or dumplings, operated so cathartically, as to disorder very many of the men, who were breaking ranks all night, and were certainly much debilitated before the action commenced in the morning.

191

*Gates assumed that the town was his to take, and marched on the night of 15
August, by way of Gum Swamp. Cornwallis had arrived to take command from
Rawdon and was determined to attack Gates. He marched also by way of Gum
Swamp. At two in the morning, to each party's surprise, the armies did not so much
meet as collide. Otho Williams was deeply involved in subsequent events.*

The General's astonishment could not be concealed. He ordered the
deputy adjutant general to call another council of war. All the general
officers immediately assembled in the rear of the line; the unwelcome
news was communicated to them. General Gates said, 'Gentlemen,
what is best to be done?' All were mute for a few moments, when the
gallant Stevens exclaimed, 'Gentlemen, is it not too late *now* to do
anything but fight?' No other advice was offered, and the General
desired the gentlemen would repair to their respective commands . . .

Frequent skirmishes happened during the night between the two
advanced parties, which served to discover the relative situation of the
two armies, and as a prelude to what was to take place in the morning.
General Stevens, observing the enemy to rush on, put his men in mind
of their bayonets; but, the impetuosity with which they advanced,
firing and huzzaing, threw the whole body of the militia into such a
panic, that they generally threw down their *loaded* arms and fled in the
utmost consternation. The unworthy example of the Virginians was
almost instantly followed by the North Carolinians; only a small part of
the brigade, commanded by Brigadier General Gregory, made a short
pause. A part of Dixon's regiment, of that brigade, next in line to the
second Maryland brigade, fired two or three rounds of cartridge. But a
great majority of the militia (at least two-thirds of the army) fled
without firing a shot . . .

The second Maryland brigade, including the battalion of Delawares,
on the right, were engaged with the enemy's left, which they opposed
with a very great firmness. They even advanced upon them and had
taken a number of prisoners, when their companions of the first brigade
(which formed the second line) being greatly outflanked, and charged
by superior numbers, were obliged to give ground . . .

The enemy, having collected their corps, and directing their whole
force against these two devoted brigades, a tremendous fire of musketry
was, for some time, kept up on both sides with equal perseverance and
obstinacy, until Lord Cornwallis, perceiving there was no cavalry opposed to him, pushed forward his dragoons and his infantry charging at
the same moment with fixed bayonets, put an end to the contest.

His victory was complete. All the artillery and a great number of

Banastre Tarleton. His name became a synonym for terror in the South

General Horatio Gates, hero of Saratoga, defeated at Camden

prisoners fell into his hands. Many fine fellows lay on the field, and the rout of the remainder was entire (not even a company retired in any order), every one escaped as he could. If, in this affair, the militia fled too soon, the regulars may be thought almost blamable for remaining too long on the field, especially after all hope of victory must have been despaired of . . .

The torrent of unarmed militia bore away with it Generals Gates, Caswell, and a number of the others, who *soon* saw that all was lost. General Gates, at first, conceived a hope that he might rally at Clermont a sufficient number to cover the retreat of the regulars, but the farther they fled the more they were dispersed, and the generals soon found themselves abandoned by all but their aides . . .

They left hundreds of dead and wounded behind. Among the dying was the Frenchman de Kalb — sent originally by the French to see if a French professional commander was not required to lead the American cause — with eleven wounds in him, and plundered as he lay of his gold-braided uniform coat and of his shirt — a fate Williams noted, avoided by other generals only by an opportune retreat. In three days on a charger sired by a racehorse named Fearnought, Gates covered the 180 miles between Camden and Hillsboro. As he passed through the Moravian settlement at Salem it was noted that 'General Gates and several officers breakfasted with us this morning, but seemed in haste'. Cornwallis drove Gates to flight — and disgrace — from Camden, and Alexander Hamilton★ was shocked by his behaviour. In a personal letter he wrote:

What think you of the conduct of this great man? I am his enemy personally, for unjust and unprovoked attacks upon my character, therefore what I say of him ought to be received as from an enemy, and have no more weight than is consistent with fact and common sense. But did ever anyone hear of such a disposition or such a flight?

★Alexander Hamilton, Washington's penman until 1781 when they quarrelled over Hamilton's anxiety to take a more active part in the war (Hamilton won — and fought at Yorktown), was born in the West Indies, the illegitimate son of a wandering Scots merchant who deserted his family when Alexander was a boy. The young Hamilton took over the running of his father's store but his fortunes changed when, on submitting to the local minister an essay he wrote on surviving a hurricane, he was sent to New York to be educated at what is now Columbia University. He joined the students' radical movement and his talent was remarked by Washington whose staff he joined as speech writer and scribe. He was appointed secretary to the Treasury when Washington became President and it was believed that, were it not for the circumstances of his birth, he might have become President himself. He was certainly the brains of Washington's administration and a financial expert.

But was there ever an instance of a general running away, as Gates had done, from his whole army? And was there ever so precipitate a flight? One hundred and eighty miles in three days and a half! It does admirable credit to the activity of a man at his time of life, but it disgraces the general and the soldier. I always believed him to be very far short of a Hector or a Ulysses. All the world, I think, will begin to agree with me.

Rivington's Loyalist New York Royal Gazette *reported:*

MILLIONS! MILLIONS! MILLIONS!

REWARD

Strayed, deserted or stolen, from the subscriber on the 16th August last, near Camden, in the State of South Carolina, a whole army, consisting of Horse, Foot and Dragoons, to the amount of near ten thousand (as has been said) with all their baggage, artillery, wagons, and camp equipage. The subscriber has very strong suspicions from information received from his Aid de Camp, that a certain Charles, Earl Cornwallis, was principally concerned in carrying off the said army with their baggage.

As Cornwallis moved steadily north, his left flank column was composed of Loyalists led by Major Patrick Ferguson, already distinguished by his rifle company's role at Brandywine, where he had been badly wounded. His right arm was useless and he was learning to use his left, but with difficulty. He communicated with his troops by blowing a whistle. He was highly esteemed for his professional marksmanship and for the qualities that won him the nickname 'Bulldog', but he was in fact gentle and affable by nature. He had been angered by the behaviour of Tarleton's men at the Waxhaws, and he had himself raised some seven battalions of Loyalist militia. The rebels he saw as 'backwater plunderers'.

Hearing that a force of 'Over the Mountain Men' led by Colonels John Sevier, William Campbell and Isaac Shelby, and outnumbering his 1000 men by three to one, was moving against him, he fell back towards Charlotte, and stationed himself on King's Mountain, a wooded and rocky outlying spur of the Blue Ridge near the border of North Carolina and South Carolina, sixty feet above the farmland. He said he was on King's Mountain and was king of the mountain, and 'God Almighty could not drive him from it'.

David Vance, a young Patriot volunteer, tells of the hunt for Ferguson:

The day and night were occasionally showery. We marched on, cross-

194

ing Ferguson's trail in the track, and proceeded on to the Cowpens and came to a Tory's house, pulled him out of bed, treated him roughly, and asked him at what time Ferguson had passed that place. He said he had not passed at all; that he had torch pine, that we might light it and search, and if we could find any trace of any army, we might hang him or do what we pleased with him, and if no sign of an army could be found, he would expect more mild treatment. Search was made and no sign of an army found.

We then camped, and began to send persons to find Ferguson's track. Chronicle proposed to send Enoch Gilmer as one; it was objected to because he was not acquainted with the country. Chronicle said that he could find out anything better than those acquainted, for he could act any character he pleased; that he could cry and laugh in the same breath, and those best acquainted would believe that he was in earnest in both; that he could act the fool so that those best acquainted with him would believe him to be deranged; that he was a shrewd, cunning fellow, and a stranger to fear. Hence he was sent, among others.

He went to a Tory's house on Ferguson's trail, and stated to him that he had been waiting on Ferguson's way from Twitty's Ford to Ninety-Six, but missed finding him; that he wished to join the army. The Tory replied that after Ferguson had crossed the river at Twitty's Ford, he had received an express from Lord Cornwallis for him to join the main army at Charlotte, that he had called in Tarleton, and would call in his outposts, and give Gates another defeat, and reduce North Carolina to British rule as he had South Carolina and Georgia, and would enter Virginia with a larger army than ever had been seen in America. Gilmer gave this account to the officers . . .

They then commenced marching to the Cherokee Ford on Broad River. Night came on, and our pilots missed their way, the night being dark, and occasionally raining, so that when we came to the river it was near daylight. It was agreed that we would send Enoch Gilmer to see whether Ferguson had not been apprised of us and would attack us in the river. Orders were given to keep our guns dry, for it was raining. Gilmer was gone for some time, when his voice was heard in the hollow singing 'Barney Linn', a favorite black-guard song. This was notice that all was right . . . After passing the river it was agreed that Enoch Gilmer should go ahead and make all the discoveries about Ferguson that he could. He went off in a gallop . . .

After travelling some miles, the officers saw Gilmer's horse at a gate three-quarters of a mile ahead. They gave whip to their horses, and went full speed to the gate – alighted, and went into the house. Gilmer was sitting at a table eating. Campbell exclaimed, 'We have got you, you damned rascal.'

Gilmer replied, 'A true King's man, by God.'

Campbell, in order to try Gilmer's metamorphosis, had provided himself with a rope with a running noose in it, threw it over Gilmer's neck. Gilmer commenced crying and begging. Campbell swore they would hang him on the bow of the gate – when Chronicle stated that it would be wrong to hang him there, for his ghost would haunt the women, who were now in tears. Campbell observed that was right, that we will hang him on the first stooping limb of a tree that they should pass on the road. Then sending Gilmer along one or two hundred yards, Gilmer crying and begging for his life, the rope was taken from his neck, and he mounted his horse, and was asked what news he had obtained.

He stated as follows. That when he came to the Tory's house, he professed to be a true King's man; that he was wishing to join Colonel Ferguson, and desired to know where he was; and that he had kissed the two Tory women; that the youngest of the two informed him that she had been in Ferguson's camp that morning; that the camp was about three miles distant from that place; that she had carried him some chickens; that he was camped on a ridge between two branches where some deer hunters had a camp the last fall. Major Chronicle and Captain Mattocks stated that the camp referred to was their camp, and that they well knew the ground Ferguson was on . . .

They immediately began to arrange their men, without stopping, and assigning to each officer the part he was to take in surrounding the hill. By the time this was done, we were close to our enemy. The last whose duty was to be prescribed was Colonel William Graham with his men, who desired a leave of absence, alleging that he had received certain intelligence that his wife was dying with the colic about sixteen miles off, near Armstrong's Ford on the South Fork. Campbell stated to him that should be the greatest inducement for him to stay, that he could carry the news, and if we were successful, it would be to her as good as a dose of medicine.

Graham exclaimed, 'Oh my dear wife! Must I never see her again?'

Campbell in an angry tone of voice turned to Major Chronicle and said, 'Shall Colonel Graham have leave of absence?'

To which Chronicle replied, 'It is woman's business, let him go.'

Graham said he must have an escort. Chronicle told him he might have one; Graham chose David Dickey. Dickey said he would rather be shot than go. Chronicle said, 'Dave, you must go.' Dickey said he would rather be shot on the spot, 'But if I must go, I must go, I must.'

Then Colonel Graham and Dickey immediately took to the woods and disappeared.

The American force was a motley company, with no clear commander: on 25 September, Colonel Isaac Shelby arrived with 250 men from Sullivan County, North Carolina; Colonel Charles McDowell with 160 men from Burke and Rutherford Counties, North Carolina; Colonel William Campbell with 400 from Washington County, Virginia; Colonel John Sevier with 240 from Washington County, North Carolina; and Colonel Benjamin Cleveland with 350 men from Wilkes and Surrey Counties. The colonels, awaiting a field commander, did not sit idle. According to Shelby:

On the morning after the appointment of Colonel Campbell, we proceeded towards Gilbert Town, but found that Ferguson, apprised of our approach, had left . . . a few days before. On the next night it was determined . . . to pursue him unremittingly with as many of our troops as could be well armed and well mounted, leaving the weak horses and footmen to follow on as fast as they could.

James Collins, a sixteen-year-old lad who had marched to war with his father, adjusted himself like an old campaigner:

Everyone ate what he could get, and slept in his own blanket, sometimes eating raw turnips and often resorting to a little parched corn, which, by the by, I have often thought, if a man would eat a mess of parched corn and swallow two or three spoonfuls of honey, then take a good draught of cold water, he could pass longer without suffering than with any other diet he could use.

Collins was with Major William Chronicle's regiment, which got into position on the north-east, the broad end of the mountain, where the ascent was extremely steep.

Each leader made a short speech in his own way to his men, desiring every coward to be off immediately. Here I confess I would willingly have been excused, for my feelings were not the most pleasant. They may be attributed to my youth, not being quite seventeen . . . but I could not well swallow the appellation of coward . . .

We were soon in motion, every man throwing four or five balls in his mouth to prevent thirst, also to be in readiness to reload quick. The shot of the enemy soon began to pass over us like hail. The first shock was quickly over, and for my own part, I was soon in a profuse sweat.

My lot happened to be in the center where the severest part of the battle was fought. We soon attempted to climb the hill, but were fiercely charged upon and forced to fall back to our first position. We tried a second time, but met the same fate. The fight then seemed to become more furious.

The American advance to King's Mountain, through the dripping woods, had caught Ferguson completely unprepared. Captain Alexander Chesney, a South Carolina Loyalist officer, had been on reconnaissance:

So rapid was their attack that I was in the act of dismounting to report that all was quiet and the pickets on the alert when we heard their firing [on the pickets] about half a mile off. I immediately paraded the men and posted the officers . . .

King's Mountain, from its height, would have enabled us to oppose a superior force with advantage, had it not been covered with wood, which sheltered the Americans and enabled them to fight in the favorite manner. In fact, after driving in our pickets, they were able to advance . . . to the crest . . . in perfect safety, until they took post and opened an irregular but destructive fire from behind trees and other cover.

Thomas Young, another sixteen-year-old private, had lost his shoes but fought his way up the north slope.

The orders were at the firing of the first gun, for every man to raise a whoop, rush forward, and fight his way as best he could. When our division came up to the northern base of the mountain, Colonel Roebuck drew us a little to the left and commenced the attack. I well remember how I behaved. Ben Hollingworth and myself took right up the side of the mountain, and fought from tree to tree, our way to the summit. I recollect I stood behind one tree and fired until the bark was nearly all knocked off, and my eyes pretty well filled with it. One fellow shaved me pretty close, for his bullet took a piece out of my gun stock. Before I was aware of it, I found myself apparently between my own regiment and the enemy, as I judged, from seeing the paper the Whigs wore in their hats, and the pine knots the Tories wore in theirs, these being the badges of distinction.

On top of the mountain, in the thickest of the fight, I saw Colonel Williams fall, and a braver or better man never died upon the field of battle. I had seen him fall but once before that day; it was in the beginning of the action, as he charged by me at full speed around the mountain. Towards the summit a ball struck his horse just under the jaw, when he commenced stamping as if he were in a nest of yellow jackets. Colonel Williams threw his reins over the animal's neck, sprang to the ground, and dashed onward.

The moment I heard the cry that Colonel Williams was shot, I ran to his assistance, for I loved him as a father; he had been ever so kind to me and almost always carried a cake in his pocket for me and his little son, Joseph. They carried him into a tent, and sprinkled some water in his face. He revived, and his first words were, 'For God's sake, boys, don't give up the hill!' . . . I left him in the arms of his son, Daniel, and returned to the field to revenge his fate.

Robert Henry was in Graham's regiment when the command was given to Chronicle:

We then advanced up the hill close to the Tory lines. There was a log across a hollow that I took my stand by, and stepping one step back, I was safe from British fire. I there maintained firing until the British charged bayonets . . . The Fork boys fired and did considerable execution. I was preparing to fire when one of the British advancing, I stepped [back] and was in the act of cocking my gun when his bayonet was running along the barrel of my gun, and gave me a thrust through my hand and into my thigh. My antagonist and I both fell. The Fork boys retreated and loaded their guns. I was then lying under the smoke and it appeared that some of them were not more than a gun's length in front of the bayonets, and the farthest could not have been more than twenty feet in front when they discharged their rifles. It was said that every one dropped his man. The British then retreated in great haste, and were pursued by the Fork boys.

William Caldwell saw my condition, and pulled the bayonet out of my thigh, but it hung to my hand; he gave my hand a kick and it went out. The thrust gave me much pain, but the pulling of it was much more severe. With my well hand I picked up my gun and found her discharged. I suppose that when the soldier made the thrust, I gripped the trigger and discharged her; the load must have passed through his bladder and cut a main artery of his back, as he bled profusely . . .

In Colonel Shelby's column was the boy James Collins:

Their leader, Ferguson, came in full view, within a rifle shot as if to encourage his men, who by this time were falling very fast; he soon disappeared. We took to the hill a third time; the enemy gave way. When he had gotten near the top, some of our leaders roared out: 'Hurrah, my brave fellows! Advance! They are crying for quarter!'

And Shelby's own account describes Ferguson's death:

Still Ferguson's proud heart could not think of surrender. He swore 'he never would yield to such a d———d banditti,' and rushed from his men, sword in hand, and cut away until his sword was broken and he was shot down. His men, seeing their leader fall, immediately surrendered. The British loss, in killed and prisoners, was eleven hundred and five.

Collins continued:

By this time the right and left had gained the top of the cliff; the enemy was completely hemmed in on all sides, and no chance of escaping. Besides, their leader had fallen. They soon threw down their arms and surrendered. After the fight was over, the situation of the poor Tories appeared to be really pitiable; the dead lay in heaps on all sides, while the groans of the wounded were heard in every direction. I could not help turning away from the scene before me, with horror, and though exulting in victory, could not refrain from shedding tears . . .

On examining the body of their great chief, it appeared that almost fifty rifles must have been leveled at him at the same time. Seven rifle balls had passed through his body, both his arms were broken, and his hat and clothing were literally shot to pieces. Their great elevation above us had proved their ruin; they overshot us altogether, scarce touching a man except those on horseback, while every rifle from below seemed to have the desired effect. In this conflict I had fired my rifle six times, while others perhaps fired nine or ten.

He confirmed the scale of the casualties:

The wives and children of the poor Tories came in, in great numbers. Their husbands, fathers, and brothers lay dead in heaps, while others lay wounded or dying . . . We proceeded to bury the dead, but it was badly done. They were thrown into convenient piles and covered with old logs, the bark of old trees and rocks, yet not so as to secure them from becoming a prey to the beasts of the forest, or the vultures of the air; and the wolves [later] became so plenty, that it was dangerous for anyone to be out at night for several miles around. Also the hogs in the neighborhood gathered into the place to devour the flesh of men, in-as-much as numbers chose to live on little meat rather than eat their hogs, though they were fat. Half of the dogs in the country were said to be mad and were put to death. I saw myself in passing the place, a few weeks after, all parts of the human frame . . . scattered in every direction . . .

In the evening, there was a distribution . . . of the plunder, and we were dismissed. My father and myself drew two fine horses, two guns, and some articles of clothing with a share of powder and lead. Every man repaired to his tent or home. It seemed like a calm after a heavy storm . . . and for a short time, every man could visit his home, or his neighbor without being afraid . . .

Ferguson, wrapped in a green ox hide, was buried beneath a pile of rocks. Of his men, 157 were dead, 163 wounded and 698 prisoners; hardly one of his force managed to escape. Ferguson was in fact the only man at King's Mountain who was not an American. Hatreds were local and savage. Campbell had to issue an order: 'I must request the officers of all ranks in the army to endeavor to restrain the disorderly manner of slaughtering and disturbing the prisoners.'

Tarleton, who was on his way to help Ferguson, was hastily recalled. Cornwallis feared that the Patriot forces — whose numbers he exaggerated — would move on Camden. On 14 October, a week after King's Mountain, he began a hurried withdrawal southward. The rainy season had begun and the roads were deep in mud. Wagons and food were lost, and sickness spread among the men. He encamped at Winnsboro, with his plans for a winter campaign now in disarray.

On 14 October, the same day as the battle of King's Mountain, Nathanael Greene was ordered south to replace Gates. He wrote to his wife expressing his feelings about the order:

MY DEAR ANGEL

What I have been dreading has come to pass. His Excellency General Washington by an order of Congress has appointed me to the command of the Southern Army, Gen. Gates being recalled to undergo an examination into his conduct. This is so foreign from my wishes that I am distressed exceedingly: especially as I have just received your letter of the 2d of this month where you describe your distress and sufferings in such a feeling manner as melts my soul into the deepest distress.

I have been pleasing my self with the agreeable prospect of spending the winter here with you; and the moment I was appointed to the command I sent off Mr Hubbard to bring you to camp. But alas, before we can have the happiness of meeting, I am ordered to another quarter. How unfriendly is war to domestic happiness! . . .

Earlier in the year — on 10 July — a French fleet had disembarked 6000 troops under the Comte de Rochambeau and made Newport their headquarters. (It had been evacuated by Clinton since he needed all the men he could find for the south.) In answer to an address of welcome by the Rhode Island Assembly, the French general proved himself a diplomat.

The King, my master, hath sent me to the assistance of his good and faithful allies, the United States of America. At present, I only bring over the vanguard of a much greater force destined for their aid; and the King has ordered me to assure them, that his whole power shall be exerted for their support.

The French troops are under the strictest discipline, and acting under the orders of General Washington, will live with the Americans as their brethren, and nothing will afford me greater pleasure than contributing to their success.

Louis XVI's instructions to Rochambeau were clear:

In sending this corps which His Majesty has furnished with its proper complement of artillery for sieges and service in the field, in sending such considerable succours to co-operate with General Washington, commander in chief of the troops of the Congress of the United States of North America, in the military operations which he may determine upon the intentions of His Majesty are:

1 That the General to whom His Majesty entrusts the command of his troops should always and in all cases be under the command of General Washington.

2 That the projects and plans for the campaign, or for private expeditions, should be decided upon by the American General, keeping in view the harmony which His Majesty hopes to see maintained between the two commanders in chief as well as the generals and the soldiers of the two nations.

3 The French troops, being only auxiliaries, should, on this account, as was done in Germany in the campaign of 1757, yield precedence and the right to the American troops; and this decision is to hold good in all general or particular cases which may occur.

4 In consequence of the above article the American officers with equal rank and the same date of commission shall have the command, and in all cases the American troops shall take the right. In all military proceedings and capitulations the American General and Troops shall

be named first and will sign first, as has always been the custom, and in accordance with the principles above laid down in regard to auxiliary troops.

5 It is His Majesty's expectation and very positive order to Count de Rochambeau that he will see to the exact and literal execution of the above four Articles.

Abbé Claude Robin, who marched with Soissonais regiment only when he could not ride, explained more clearly perhaps than the other diarists why the French contingent under Rochambeau was received in some quarters so coldly:

Before the war the Americans regarded the French as enslaved to despotism, a prey to all manner of superstitions and prejudices; as people quite incapable of solid and consistent effort, only occupied in such matters as curling their hair and painting their faces, and far from being respectors of the most sacred duties. These prejudices had been spread and emphasized by the English; then, at the beginning of the war, not a few things happened to confirm these unfavourable opinions. The great majority of the French who came to America when the rumour of revolution reached them were men who had lost their reputations and were wholly in debt and who generally presented themselves under false names and titles of nobility to which they had no manner of right. Under these false pretences some of them obtained high rank in the American Army, also considerable advances in money, and then disappeared. The simplicity of the Americans and their lack of world experience made tricks of this nature very easy.

These prejudices were in full control when Rochambeau arrived and we all saw the extreme importance of dissipating them. High officers established the most strict discipline and the others were careful to exhibit that politeness and amenity which has always characterized the French nobility. Even our common soldiers became mild, careful, and moderate, and in the course of our long sojourn not a single complaint was brought against them. Our young nobles who, because of their birth and fortune and their residence at court, should have been most attached to dissipation, to luxury, and all the *appareils de la grandeur*, were the very first to give an example of complete simplicity and to accept the requirements of the frugal life. They always showed themselves most affable to their new neighbours, quite as though they had never come in contact with any other kind of men; and when this line of conduct had been maintained for a few weeks a complete revolution in

203

the spirit of the people was noticed. Even the Tories and Royalists could not help loving the French.

Washington did not meet Rochambeau until September, by which time not only was Newport firmly blockaded by the British fleet (three days in fact after Rochambeau's arrival) but the promised reinforcements were similarly bottled up in Brest by the British Channel fleet. Britain still ruled the waves — though only just.

Both in Paris and in North America the secret service played a key role, facilitated by Loyalist sentiment. Invisible ink and notes left in trees in the Tuileries Gardens, hollow bullets and templates to fit over coded letters were some of the devices. All the commanders relied on spies and intelligence just before battle for the latest reports on enemy locations. In both armies the Adjutant General was in charge of this intelligence.

John André had come to Clinton's notice as staff officer in the occupation of Philadelphia and became his Adjutant General. His papers show that he had a list of the American generals he thought corruptible — it did not include Arnold, whose courage and reputation suggested he was beyond such reproach. Colonel Zedwitz of the 1st New York Continental Line was caught offering information in 1776. William Demont, adjutant of the 5th Penn Regiment gave plans to Britain of Fort Washington. Major Daniel Hammill served both sides, as, in his own eccentric way, did Charles Lee. Putnam, Schuyler, Morgan, Samuel Parsons of Connecticut were all approached by Britain and all said firmly no. Arnold's was not the only, but it was the most conspicuous, act of treason in the war, and probably the most dramatic in American history.

For years Arnold had been living beyond his means, with a splendid wife, a splendid home and splendid food and drink. In January 1780 he had been reprimanded after a court-martial for improper conduct, and Washington moved him to the strategic post of West Point to remove him from the probing eyes of Congressmen. He was one of the most courageous and dashing of field officers. Benjamin Rush was many years later to describe him:

His person was low but well made, and his face handsome. His conversation was uninteresting and sometimes indelicate. His language was ungrammatical and his pronunciation vulgar. I once heard him say 'his courage was acquired, and that he was a coward till he was 15 years of age.' His character in his native state, Connecticut, was never respectable, and hence its vote was withheld from him when he was created a general by the Congress of the United States.

His wife, as a wealthy eighteen-year-old socialite, had been friendly with British officers, notably André, during the British occupation of Philadelphia, and Arnold had himself been in correspondence with André for at least eighteen months. Now commanding at West Point, Arnold became especially valuable: he was willing to surrender the post for £20,000 and a British major-generalcy.

André came up the Hudson on HMS Vulture *in September to lay the groundwork for the treason. After his meeting with Arnold at William Smith's house at King's Ferry, André returned. The* Vulture, *however, had been fired on by a Patriot battery, and had dropped downstream. He would now have to make his way back overland, in civilian clothing, and through difficult country, where allegiances were sharply divided and banditry frequent. He called himself John Anderson.*

He was caught by three militiamen near Tarrytown on his return, and had on his person a military inventory of West Point and a pass signed by Benedict Arnold. Lieutenant Joshua King, who first had André under his care, remembered:

He said he came up the North River in the *Vulture* sloop-of-war, for the purpose of seeing a person by flag.

Nothing occurred to disturb him in his route until he arrived at the last place, excepting at Crampound. He told me his hair stood erect, and his heart was in his mouth, on meeting Colonel Samuel B. Webb, of our army, plump in the face; an acquaintance of his. He said the Colonel stared at him, and he thought he was gone, but they kept moving and soon passed each other.

He then thought himself past all danger. Whilst ruminating on his good luck, and his hair-breadth escape, he was assailed [on September 23] by three bushmen near Tarrytown, who ordered him to stand. He says to them, 'I hope, gentlemen, you belong to the Lower [Tory] Party.'

'We do,' says one.

'So do I,' says he, 'and by the token of this ring and key you will let me pass. I am a British officer on business of importance, and must not be detained.'

One of them took his watch from him and ordered him to dismount. The moment this was done, he said he found he was mistaken and he must shift his tone. He says, 'I am happy, gentlemen, to find that I am mistaken. You belong to the Upper Party, and so do I. A man must make use of any shift to get along, and to convince you of it, here is General Arnold's pass,' handing it to them, 'and I am at your service.'

'Damn Arnold's pass,' says they, 'You said you was a British officer; where is your money?'

'Gentlemen, I have none about me,' he replied.

'You a British officer and no money,' says they, 'Let's search him.' They did so, but found none. Says one, 'He has got his money in his

205

boots,' and there they found his papers, but no money. Then they examined his saddle, but found none.

He said he saw they had such a thirst for money, he could put them in a way to get it, if they would be but directed by him. He asked them to name their sum for to deliver him to King's Bridge.

They answered him in this way, 'If we deliver you at King's Bridge, we shall be sent to the Sugar House [a local prison] and you will save your money.'

He says to them, 'If you will not trust my honor, two of you may stay with me, and one shall go with a letter I shall write. Name your sum.'

The sum was agreed upon, but I cannot recollect whether it was five hundred or a thousand guineas, the latter, I think, was the sum. They held a consultation a considerable time, and finally they told him, if he wrote, a party would be sent out to take them, and then they would all be prisoners. They said they had concluded to take him to the commanding officer on the lines. They did so, and retained the watch, until General Washington sent for them to Tappan, where the watch was restored to Major Andre. Thus you see, had money been at the command after the imprudent confession of Major Andre, or any security given that the patriots could put confidence in, he might have passed on to Sir Henry Clinton's headquarters, with all papers, and Arnold's papers in the bargain.

On hearing of André's arrest, Arnold deserted to the HMS Vulture.

A moment before his [Arnold] setting out, he went into Mrs Arnold's apartment, and informed her that certain transactions had just come to light, which must forever banish him from his country. She fell into a swoon at this declaration, and he left her in it, to consult his own safety, till the servants, alarmed by her cries, came to her relief.

She remained frantic all day, accusing everyone who approached her with an intention of murdering her child (an infant in her arms) and exhibiting every mark of the most agonizing affliction. Exhausted by the fatigue and tumult of her spirits, her frenzy sudsided towards evening, and she sank into all the sadness of distress. It was impossible not to have been touched with her situation, everything affecting in female fears, or in the misfortunes of beauty, everything pathetic in the wounded tendencies of a wife or in the apprehensive fondness of a mother, and every appearance of suffering innocence, conspired to make her an object of pity to all who were present. She experienced the most delicate attentions and every friendly office, till her departure for Philadelphia.

Lieutenant-Colonel Benjamin Tallmadge, head of Washington's intelligence, felt strongly about Arnold's conduct.

Treason! treason! treason! black as Hell! That a man so high on the lists of fame should be guilty as Arnold, must be attributed not only to original sin, but actual transgressions. Heaven and earth! we are all astonishment – each peeping at his next neighbor to see if any treason was hanging about him; nay, we even descended to a critical examination of ourselves.

There was no doubt of André's guilt, and for it sentence was pronounced by a board that included six major-generals, presided over by Major-General Nathanael Greene. The sentence for spying was hanging.
André wrote to Washington:

SIR:
Buoyed above the terror of death by the consciousness of a life devoted to honorable pursuits, and stained with no action that can give remorse, I trust that the request I make to your Excellency at this serious period, and which is to soften my last moments, will not be rejected.

Sympathy towards a soldier will surely induce your Excellency and a military tribunal to adapt the mode of my death to the feelings of a man of honor.

Let me hope, sir, that if aught in my character impresses you with esteem towards me, if aught in my misfortune marks me as the victim of policy and not of resentment, I shall experience the operations of those feelings in your breast by being informed that I am not to die on the gibbet.

I have the honor to be your Excellency's most obedient and most humble servant.

The request was refused.
Surgeon Thacher, keen recorder of events, wrote of events of the final day on 2 October:

I was so near during the solemn march to the fatal spot, as to observe every movement, and participate in every emotion which the melancholy scene was calculated to produce. Major André walked from the stone house in which he had been confined between two of our subaltern officers, arm in arm. The eyes of the immense multitude were fixed upon him, who, rising superior to the fears of death, appeared as if conscious of the dignified deportment which he displayed. He betrayed no want of fortitude, but retained a complacent smile on his countenance, and politely bowed to several gentlemen whom he knew, which was respectfully returned. It was his earnest desire to be shot, as the mode of death most comfortable to the feelings of a military man, and he had indulged the hope that his request would be granted. At the moment, therefore, when suddenly he came in view of the gallows, he involuntarily started backward, and made a pause.

'Why this emotion, Sir?' said an officer by his side.

Instantly recovering his composure, he said, 'I am reconciled to my death, but I detest the mode.'

The rope being appended to the gallows, he slipped the noose over his head and adjusted it to his neck, without the assistance of the awkward executioner. Colonel Scammel now informed him that he had an opportunity to speak, if he desired it. He raised the handkerchief from his eyes and said, 'I pray you to bear me witness, that I meet my fate like a brave man.' The wagon being now removed from him, he was suspended and instantly expired; it proved indeed 'but a momentary pang'. He was dressed in his royal regimentals and boots, and interred at the foot of the gallows, and the spot was consecrated by the tears of thousands.

Arnold was a traitor, André a spy. Yet chance was the central fact in the story. It was pure chance that led three 'bushmen' in Patriot militia dress, if Patriots in intent they really were, to stop and search the passing traveller in New York's uneasy Neutral Ground. They were like other 'skinners', not out for glory or for cause, but for booty. A New York Act permitted such raiders to claim as prize any property they might find on a captured enemy. To them, all who passed by were for plundering.

Washington wrote several days later:

In no instance since the commencement of the war has the interposition of Providence appeared more remarkably conspicuous than in the rescue of the post and garrison at West Point. How far Arnold meant to involve me in the catastrophe of this place, does not appear by any indubitable evidence, and I am rather inclined to think he did not wish to hazard the more important object, by attempting to combine two events, the lesser of which might have marred the greater. A combina-

The execution of John André

The Comte de Rochambeau

General Daniel Morgan, whose sharpshooters defeated Tarleton at Cowpens

tion of extraordinary circumstances, and unaccountable deprivation of presence of mind in a man of the first abilities, and the virtue of three militiamen, threw the adjutant-general of the British forces, with full proof of Arnold's intention, into our hands, and but for the egregious folly or the bewildered conception of Lieutenant-Colonel Jamison, who seemed lost in astonishment, and not to have known what he was doing, I should undoubtedly have gotten Arnold. Andre has met his fate, and with that fortitude which was to be expected from an accomplished man and a gallant officer; but I mistake if Arnold is suffering at this time the torments of a mental hell. He wants feeling. From some traits of his character which have lately come to my knowledge, he seems to have been so hacknied in crime, so lost to all sense of honor and shame, that while his faculties still enable him to continue his sordid pursuits, there will be no time for remorse.

Meanwhile, back at sea Sir George Rodney wrote privately to Lord George Germain in December:

Believe me, my dear Lord, you must not expect an end of the American war till you can find a general of active spirit, and who hates the Americans from principle. Such a man with the sword of war and justice on his side will do wonders, for in this war I am convinced the sword should cut deep. Nothing but making the Americans feel every calamity their perfidy deserves can bring them to their senses . . .

Believe me, my Lord, this man Arnold, with whom I had many conferences, will do more towards suppressing the rebellion than all our generals put together. He perfectly knows every inch of the country, is greatly beloved by the American troops, and if entrusted with a body of what is called Royalists will induce great part of [the] rebels to desert. I am perfectly of his opinion that upon a certainty of their being paid their arrears and a portion of land given after the war, Washington would soon have no army. Jealousy, my Lord, unless commands from home signifies his Majesty's pleasure, will prevent Arnold being employed to advantage. He certainly may be trusted, as the Americans never forgive, and the Congress to a man are his personal enemies. Give him but a command and thousands will join him who are sick of the war and have a great opinion of his generalship . . .

Thus, my Lord, have I endeavoured to make you truly acquainted with affairs at present in America, but believe me the acting in North Carolina will only prolong the war. The Northern Colonies should feel the fatal results of their treason. There and there only the war must be finished. I cannot conclude without being of opinion that a new Commission with the same powers of Lord Carlisle's, taking care the majority of Commissioners are not *military men*, may have such effect as to bring about a peace. Washington is certainly to be bought – honours will do it.

1781

Your Lion shall growl –
but never bite more

Washington established winter quarters at New Windsor on the Hudson, with the Pennsylvania Line at Morristown, the New Jersey Line at Pompton, and the New England troops stationed at West Point and other posts along the Hudson. Army grumbling became something more serious than the customary grousing. Six regiments of the Pennsylvania Line, unpaid, ill-clothed and ill-fed, broke the bonds of discipline on New Year's Day 1781 when they learned that money was being distributed as a bounty for new recruits. Dr James Thacher witnessed the scene:

General Howe ordered that three of the ring-leaders should be selected as victims for condign punishment. These unfortunate culprits were tried on the spot, Colonel Sprout being president of the court-martial, standing on the snow, and they were sentenced to be immediately shot. Twelve of the most guilty mutineers were next selected to be their executioners . . . the first that suffered was a sergeant and an old offender . . . The second criminal was, by the first fire, sent into eternity in an instant.

To this, add inflation, as Washington indicated:

The history of this war is a history of false hopes and temporary devices, instead of system and of economy. We have no magazines nor money to form them, and in a little time we shall have no men if we had money to pay them. We have lived upon expedients till we can live no longer.

Indeed, he wrote to Morris, the Superintendent of Finance, exposing his predicament:

I must entreat you, if possible, to procure one month's pay in specie for the detachment under my command. Part of the troops have not been paid anything for a long time past and have upon several occasions

211

shown marks of great discontent. The service they are going upon is disagreeable to the Northern regiments; but I make no doubt that a *douceur* of a little hard money would put them in proper temper. If the whole sum cannot be obtained, a part of it will be better than none, as it may be distributed in proportion to the respective wants and claims of the men.

Lieutenant Enos Reeves welcomed the New Year:

We had a elegant regimental dinner and entertainment . . . We spent the day very pleasantly and the evening till about ten o'clock as cheerfully as we could wish, when we were disturbed by the huzzas of the soldiers upon the Right Division, answered by those on the left.

I went on parade and found numbers in small groups whispering and busily running up and down the line. In a short time a gun was fired upon the right and answered by one on the right of the Second Brigade, and a skyrocket thrown from the center of the first, which was accompanied by a general huzza throughout the line, and the soldiers running out with their guns, accoutrements and knapsacks.

I immediately found it was a mutiny, and that the guns and skyrocket were the signals. The officers in general exerted themselves to keep the men quiet, and keep them from turning out. We each applied himself to his own company, endeavored to keep them in their huts and lay by their arms, which they would do while we were present, but the moment we left one hut to go to another, they would be out again. Their excuse was they thought it was an alarm and the enemy coming on.

A revolt in the Jersey Line followed. The leaders were executed. Concessions were granted by Congress, but many left the service, and one soldier summed up his feelings in a lament.

My time it has expired all on the tenth of June,
Where the pretty birds were singing, and flowers in their bloom,
Where the pretty birds were singing, so sweet from every tree,
Farewell unto the army where they beat the revillee.

And to you my lovely officers, a word I have to say,
Before you go to battle, consider well I pray,
See how you kept our wages back, and rob'd us of our clothes,
That we so dearly paid for in hard fatiguing blows.

And to you my lovely officers, those lines were written for,
I'd have you to pray for a short and moderate war,
Pray for the strength of Sampson and great King David slight,
For there's scarcely one to twenty of you that's courage enough to
    fight.

Hear a word unto our counsel, that rules through every state,
I pray be honest hearted, for knavery I hate,
Try for once to do justice, be liberal and free,
Deal fairly with a soldier, and he'll deal fair with thee.

What think you of a soldier that fights for liberty,
Do you think he fights for money, or to set his country free?
I'd have you consider, and bear it on your mind,
Lest you should want their help again, it might be hard to find.

Our officers on the right of us, our country on the left,
Our enemy in front of us firing at our breasts,
The devil he comes up behind, and brings up the rear,
And a soldier that escapes them all has never need to fear.

My time it has expired, my song is at an end.
Here's a health to General Washington and every soldier's friend,
And he that cheats a soldier out of his little pay,
May the devil take him on his back, to hell with him straightway.

*On 16 December 1780, Greene, now commander in the south, ordered Morgan —
who for fifteen months had retired from the service because of lack of recognition, and
complaining of arthritis — to the west side of the Catawba, in western South
Carolina, where with 1000 men and any volunteers he could raise he was 'to give
protection to that part of the country and spirit up the people, to annoy the enemy in
that quarter, collect the provisions and forage out of the way of the enemy'. One of his
columns, under William Washington — a relative of the commander-in-chief —
attacked 250 Loyalists at Hammond's Store, near Ninety-Six, and killed or wounded
150 of them, without a single loss.*

    *Cornwallis, based at Winnsboro, sent Tarleton with 1200 men in pursuit of
Morgan. But Daniel Morgan, at Cowpens — once a pasture for backwoods cattle —
took a stand. He stayed up all night before the battle, moving among his men and
rallying the militia in particular: two shots each were all that was required of them;
and they must aim at the officers. He put his raw troops in the front and centre, and
the picked troops in the rear 'to shoot down the first man that runs'. On 16 January,
Tarleton's men drove with the bayonet in a straight attack that should have had the
new militia running as they had always before. They did not, as James Collins recounted:*

About sunrise on the 17th of January, 1781, the enemy came in full view. The sight, to me at least, seemed somewhat imposing. They halted for a short time, and then advanced rapidly as if certain of victory. The militia under Pickins and Moffitt was posted on the right of the regulars some distance in advance, while Washington's cavalry was stationed in the rear. We gave the enemy one fire; when they charged us with their bayonets, we gave way and retreated for our horses. Tarleton's cavalry pursued us. 'Now,' thought I, 'my hide is in the loft.'

Just as we got to our horses, they overtook us and began to make a few hacks at some, however without doing much injury. They, in their haste, had pretty much scattered, perhaps thinking they would have another Fishing Creek frolic, but in a few moments Col Washington's cavalry was among them like a whirlwind, and the poor fellows began to keel from their horses without being able to remount. The shock was so sudden and violent they could not stand it and immediately betook

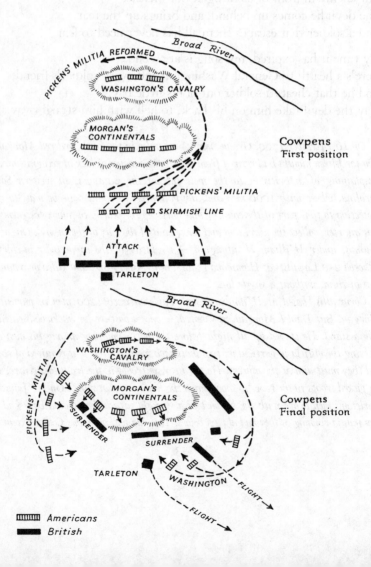

Cowpens
First position

Cowpens
Final position

▦▦▦ Americans
■■ British

themselves to fight. There was no time to rally, and they appeared to be as hard to stop as a drove of wild Choctaw steers going to a Pennsylvania market. In a few moments the clashing of swords was out of hearing and quickly out of sight.

By this time both lines of the infantry were warmly engaged and we, being relieved from the pursuit of the enemy, began to rally and prepare to redeem our credit, when Morgan rode up in front and, waving his sword, cried out, 'Form, form, my brave fellows! Give them more fire and the day is ours. Old Morgan was never beaten.'

We then advanced briskly and gained the right flank of the enemy, and they, being hard pressed in front by Howard and falling very fast, could not stand it long. They began to throw down their arms and surrender themselves prisoners of war. The whole army, except Tarleton and his horsemen, fell into the hands of Morgan, together with all the baggage . . .

General Daniel Morgan wrote to Nathanael Greene from Cain Creek:

The troops I have the honour to command have been so fortunate as to obtain a complete victory over a detachment from the British army, commanded by Lieut. Col. Tarleton. The action happened on the 17th inst., about sunrise, at the Cowpens. It, perhaps, would be well to remark, for the honour of the American arms, that although the progress of this corps was marked with burning and devastation, and although they waged the most cruel warfare, not a man was killed, wounded or even insulted after he surrendered. Had not Britons during this contest received so many lessons of humanity, I should flatter myself that this might teach them a little. But I fear they are incorrigible.

Lieutenant Mackenzie of the 71st Regiment of Highlanders, wounded in the battle, savaged Tarleton in the Morning Chronicle *in August of the following year, and Tarleton's reputation never recovered.*

You got yourself and the party completely ambuscaded, completely surrounded, upon all sides, by Mr Morgan's rifle men. What was the consequence? The two detachments of British were made prisoners after a great slaughter was made among them, your legion dragoons were so broke by galling fire of rifle shot that your charging was in vain, till prudence, on your side, with about twenty more who were well mounted, made your retreat good, by leaving the remains of the poor blended legion in the hands of Mr Morgan, who I must say, though an enemy, showed great masterly abilities in this manoever.

Thus fell, at one blow, all the Provincial Legion, with about three hundred veterans.

The British lost in one hour 1000 men (killed, wounded or captured), two three-pounders, 800 muskets, thirty-five wagons of stores, 100 horses and sixty slaves. The Americans lost only twelve lives. And in London Horace Walpole reflected:

America is once more not quite ready to be conquered, although every now and then we fancy it is. Tarleton is defeated, Lord Cornwallis is checked, and Arnold not sure of having betrayed his friends to much purpose.

The Reverend John Miller of Rutherford County in North Carolina offered up a fulsome prayer of thanks from his Presbyterian flock on hearing the news of Morgan's victory over Tarleton at Cowpens. It was in fact more fulsome than accurate.

Good Lord, our God who art in Heaven, we have great reason to thank thee for the many favours we have received at thine hands, the many battles we have won. There is the great and glorious battle of King's Mountain, where we Kilt the great General Ferguson, and took his whole army . . . and ever-memorable and glorious Battle of the Coopens where we made the proud Gineral Tarleton run down the road helter-skelter, and good Lord, if ye had na suffered the Cruel Tories to burn Belly hell's [Billy Hill's] Iron Works we would na' have asked any mair favours at thy hands. Amen.

Morgan moved to rejoin Greene, across swollen streams and on muddy, icy roads. The rendezvous was Guilford Courthouse. Despite his 'cectick' — the weather had brought on his sciatica again — he covered 100 miles in five days, and left behind him fords made impassable by felled trees. Cornwallis with 2500 men gave chase, having told his men to burn all unnecessary stores, including rum, and transforming them into a light corps. It was the beginning of his country dance, the steps of which were recorded:

> Cornwallis led a country dance,
> the like was never seen, Sir,
> much retrograde and much advance,
> and all with General Greene, Sir.

On 15 February, the last of Greene's men crossed the Dan into Virginia, after a four-day march, practically without sleep. In Virginia, they believed, there were reinforcements and supplies, and safety. But the speed of the movement prevented the embodiment of the militia, and there were few of them around. As Lewis Morris Jr, aide to Greene, wrote:

The militia . . . gave us no assistance. They were more intent upon saving their property by flight than by embodying to protect it.

Greene's army was ragged and hungry, and losing numbers. It appeared as if the south from Virginia to the Floridas, was now the king's country again. But Cornwallis was now 250 miles from base, and active king's men were very few in number. He was in fact dangerously isolated.

My force being ill-suited to enter . . . so powerful a province as Virginia, and North Carolina being in the utmost confusion, after giving the troops a halt of one day I proceeded by easy marches to Hillsboro, where I erected the King's Standard and invited by proclamation all loyal subjects to repair to it and to . . . take an active part in assisting me to restore order and constitutional government.

As Patriot guerilla forces assembled to move against him, his commissary, Charles Stedman, reported:

There being few cattle to be had in its neighborhood and those principally draught oxen, Lord Cornwallis had promised that they should not be slaughtered but in case of absolute necessity; but that necessity did exist and compelled the author to direct that several of the draught oxen should be killed. This measure . . . caused murmuring amongst the loyalists, whose property these cattle were. Most of the cattle in the neighborhood of Hillsboro had been consumed by the Americans who held a post for a very considerable time in that town . . .

Lord Cornwallis could not have remained as long as he did at Hillsboro had it not been for a quantity of salt beef, pork, and some hogs found in the town. Such was the situation of the British army that the author, with a file of men, was obliged to go from house to house . . . to take provisions from the inhabitants, many of whom were greatly distressed by this measure, which could be justified only by extreme necessity.

As the winter rains ceased and the dogwood blossomed, the two armies manoeuvred along the Dan River for advantage. The spring brought Greene reinforcements, and a mood of optimism, caught by the young Virginian, St George Tucker, who had risen from private to major of militia, in a letter to his wife:

The lark is up, the morning gray, and I am seated by a smoky fire to let my dearest Fanny know that her soldier is as blithe as the mockingbird which is at this moment tuning his pipe within a dozen yards of me. If the fatigues of the remainder of the campaign sit as well upon my limbs as those which I have hitherto experienced, you may be assured that I shall return to Cumberland the most portly, genteel fellow that the country will be able to boast of.

The battle of Guilford Courthouse in March was a repeat of Cowpens, although Cornwallis claimed the victory since he kept the field. Greene reported:

The battle was fought at or near Guilford Court-House, the very place from whence we began our retreat after the Light Infantry joined the army from the Pedee. The battle was long, obstinate and bloody. We were obliged to give up the ground and lost our artillery, but the enemy have been so soundly beaten that they dare not move towards us since the action, notwithstanding we lay within ten miles of him for two days. Except the ground and the artillery, they have gained no advantage. On the contrary, they are little short of being ruined. The enemy's loss in killed and wounded cannot be less than between six and seven hundred, perhaps more.

Victory was long doubtful, and had the North Carolina militia done their duty, it was certain. They had the most advantageous position I ever saw, and left it without making scarcely the shadow of opposition. Their general and field officers exerted themselves, but the men would not stand. Many threw away their arms and fled with the utmost precipitation, even before a gun was fired at them. The Virginia militia behaved nobly and annoyed the enemy greatly. The horse, at different times in the course of the day, performed wonders. Indeed, the horse is our great safeguard, and without them the militia could not keep the field in this country . . . Never did an army labour under so many disadvantages as this; but the fortitude and patience of the officers and soldiery rise superior to all difficulties. We have little to eat, less to drink, and lodge in the woods in the midst of smoke. Indeed, our fatigue is excessive. I was so much overcome night before last that I fainted.

Our army is in good spirits, but the militia are leaving us in great numbers to return home to kiss their wives and sweethearts.

I have never felt an easy moment since the enemy crossed the

Catawba until since the defeat of the 15th, but now I am perfectly easy, being persuaded it is out of the enemy's power to do us any great injury. Indeed, I think they will retire as soon as they can get off their wounded. My love to your family and all friends . . .

In all, Cornwallis had at his disposal about 2200 men and was heavily out-numbered. In Webster's Brigade was Sergeant Roger Lamb, who had escaped from Burgoyne's Convention troops back to the British army, and had been sent south. After the brigade was formed, he wrote:

Colonel [Webster] rode on to the front and gave the word, 'Charge!' Instantly, the movement was made in excellent order, in a smart run, with arms charged. When arrived within forty yards of the enemy's lines, it was perceived that their whole force had their arms presented and resting on a rail fence . . . They were taking aim with the nicest precision . . .

At this awful period, a general pause took place. Both parties surveyed each other for the moment with the most anxious suspense. Nothing speaks the general more than seizing on decisive moments: Colonel Webster rode forward in the front of the Twenty-third Regiment and said . . . 'Come on, my brave fusiliers' . . . They rushed forward amidst the enemy's fire. Dreadful was the havoc on both sides . . . At last the Americans gave way and the brigade advanced to the attack of their second line.

The second line, 300 yards behind the first, gave way, but the Continentals behind it remained firm. They even counter-attacked, but Greene dared not follow up the counter-attack — to lose would be to lose an army. With one horse already shot under him, and now mounted on a second, Cornwallis was in the middle of the action. Finally he ordered his artillery to fire grapeshot at the Continental Line, halting them and driving them back. His artillery was indiscriminate and killed many men — on both sides. At the end, however, Cornwallis held the field.

Henry Lee ('Light Horse Harry') for the Americans left a vivid account:

The night . . . was rainy, dark, and cold. The dead unburied, the wounded unsheltered, the groans of the dying and the shrieks of the living, cast a deeper shade over the gloom of nature. The victorious troops, without tents and without food, participated in sufferings which they could not relieve. The ensuing morning was spent in performing the last offices to the dead and in providing comfort for the wounded . . . The British general regarded with equal attention friends and foes. As soon as this service was over, he put his army in motion for New Garden, where his rear guard with his baggage met him. All his wounded, incapable of moving (about seventy . . .) he left to the humanity of General Greene.

Cornwallis lost a quarter of his army (killed, wounded or missing) at Guilford, including some of his best officers. He had been led 250 miles from his base, the ocean; he had been harried all the way; and he had in the end paid a heavy price for a Pyrrhic victory. As Charles James Fox put it, echoing Clinton's comment after Bunker Hill, 'Another such victory would destroy the British army'. Cornwallis, feeling isolated in a hostile countryside, withdrew to the coast at Wilmington, and Greene moved south to reconquer South Carolina and Georgia.

Frederick Mackenzie, observing the campaign from New York, wrote:

Greene is however entitled to great praise for his wonderful exertions; the more he is beaten, the further he advances in the end. He has been indefatigable in collecting troops and leading them to be defeated . . . Greene is this, to be the Fabius of the age, and the people of this country almost adore him.

Or as Greene put it himself: 'We fight, get beat, rise and fight again.'

Greene wrote to George Washington in March from his headquarters at Colonel Ramsay's on Deep River:

In this critical and distressing situation, I am determined to carry the war immediately into South Carolina. The enemy will be obliged to follow us or give up their posts in that State. If the former takes place it will draw the war out of this State and give it an opportunity to raise its proportion of men. If they leave their posts to fall, they must lose more than they can gain here. If we continue in this State, the enemy will hold their possessions in both. All things considered, I think the movement is warranted by the soundest reasons, both political and military. The manoeuvre will be critical and dangerous, and the troops exposed to every hardship. But as I share it with them, I hope they will bear up under it with that magnanimity which has already supported them, and for which they deserve everything of their country.

That a British victory still left the British chained to their posts was the effective comment on the war in the south. They had a number of posts at Camden, Augusta and Ninety-Six, Orangeburg and Fort La Motte (which fell to Marion's attack by flaming arrows) and some 8000 troops scattered across what was now plainly hostile country. Clinton recognised that by moving to the coast 'Old Corncob' had

exposed the two valuable Colonies behind him to be overrun and conquered by that very army which he boasts to have completely routed
only a week or two before.

William Dickson, meanwhile, wrote to his cousin in Ireland:

The whole country was struck with terror; almost every man quit his
habitation and fled, leaving his family and property to the mercy of
merciless enemies. Horses, cattle, and sheep, and every kind of stock
were driven off from every plantation, corn and forage taken for the
supply of the army and no compensation given, houses plundered and
robbed, chests, trunks, etc; broke; women and children's clothes, etc.,
as well as men's wearing apparel and every kind of household furniture
taken away. The outrages were committed mostly by a train of loyal
refugees, as they termed themselves, whose business it was to follow
the camps and under the protection of the army enrich themselves on
the plunder they took from the distressed inhabitants who were not
able to defend it.

We were also distressed by another swarm of beings (not better than
harpies). These were women who followed the army in the character of
officers' and soldiers' wives. They were generally considered by the
inhabitants to be more insolent than the soldiers. They were generally
mounted on the best horses and side saddles, dressed in the finest and
best clothes that could be taken from the inhabitants as the army
marched through the country.

*Andrew Jackson was only fourteen when he witnessed the battles of Hanging
Rock and Hobkirk's Hill, but he remembered enough to pass on his recollections to
Francis Blair.*

I witnessed two battles, Hanging Rock and Hobkirk's Hill, but did not
participate in either. I was in one skirmish – that of Sands House – and
there they caught me, along with my brother Robert and my cousin,
Tom Crawford. A lieutenant of Tarleton's Light Dragoons tried to
make me clean his boots and cut my arm with his sabre when I refused.
After that they kept me in jail at Camden about two months, starved
me nearly to death and gave me the small-pox. Finally my mother
succeeded in persuading them to release Robert and me on account of
our extreme youth and illness. Then Robert died of small-pox and I

barely escaped death. When it left me I was a skeleton – not quite six feet long and a little over six inches thick! It took me all the rest of that year [1781] to recover my strength and get flesh enough to hide my bones. By that time Cornwallis had surrendered and the war was practically over in our part of the country.

I was never regularly enlisted, being only fourteen when the war practically ended. Whenever I took the field it was with Colonel Davie, who never put me in the ranks, but used me as a mounted orderly or messenger, for which I was well fitted, being a good rider and knowing all the roads in that region. The only weapons I had were a pistol that Colonel Davie gave me and a small fowling-piece that my Uncle Crawford lent to me. This was a light gun and would kick like sixty when loaded with a three-quarter-ounce ball or with nine buckshot. But it was a smart little gun and would carry the ball almost as true as a rifle fifteen or twenty rods, and threw the buckshot spitefully at close quarters – which was the way I used it in the defence of Captain Sands's house, where I was captured.

I was sorry about losing the gun there as about the loss of my own liberty, because Uncle Crawford set great store by the gun, which he had brought with him from the old country; and, besides, it was the finest in that whole region. Not long afterwards – while I was still in the Camden jail or stockade – some of Colonel Davie's men under Lieutenant Curriton captured a squad of Tories, one of whom had that gun in his possession, together with my pistol that Colonel Davie had given to me. This Tory's name was Mulford. The gun and pistol cost him his life. Davie's men regarded his possession of them as prima facie evidence that he had been a member of the party that captured Captain Sands's house, sacked and burned it and insulted the womenfolks of his family. He pleaded that he was not there; that he had bought the gun and pistol from another Tory. Davie's men told him it would do him no good to add lying to his other crimes, hanged him forthwith and afterward restored the gun and pistol to their proper owners.

Conditions were grim for Lord Cornwallis as he wrote to Sir Henry Clinton from his camp near Wilmington in April.

With a third of my army sick and wounded, which I was obliged to carry in waggons or on horseback, the remainder without shoes and worn down with fatigue, I thought it was time to look for some place of rest and refitment. I, therefore, by easy marches, taking care to pass through all the settlements that had been described to me as most friendly, proceeded to Cross-Creek. On my arrival there, I found to my great mortification and contrary to all former accounts, that it was impossible to procure any considerable quantity of provisions, and that there was not four days forage within twenty miles. The navigation of Cape Fear River, with the hopes of which I had been flattered, was totally impracticable, the distance from Wilmington by water being 150 miles, the breadth of the river seldom exceeding one hundred yards, the banks generally high, and the inhabitants on each side almost universally hostile. Under these circumstances I determined to move immediately to Wilmington. By this measure the Highlanders have not had so much time as the people of the upper country to prove the sincerity of their former professions of friendship. But, tho' appearances are rather more favourable amoung them, I confess they are not equal to my expectations . . .

He also wrote to his old gunner William Phillips:

Now, my dear friend, what is our plan? Without one, we cannot succeed, and I assure you that I am quite tired of marching about the country in quest of adventure. If we mean an offensive war in America, we must abandon New York and bring our whole force into Virginia; we then have a stake to fight for and a successful battle may give us America. If our plan is defensive, mixed with desultory expeditions, let us quit the Carolinas (which cannot be held defensively while Virginia can be so easily armed against us) and stick to our salt pork at New York, sending now and then a detachment to steal tobacco, etc.

Gates, writing to Governor Jefferson in Virginia, predicted a blow at Virginia.

If Lord Cornwallis conquers the southern and eastern parts of North Carolina, and extends his posts of communication to Portsmouth, you must expect the weight of the war will penetrate into your bowels and cause such an inflammation there as may (if timely remedies are not applied) consume the life blood of the state. Have you cried aloud to Congress and to the Commander-in-Chief of the Army for succour? Have they listened to your cry? If they have not, are you doing the best thing for yourselves? Military wisdom has ever heretofore been imputed to Virginia. Is there a rottenness in the State of Denmark? Find it out and cut it off. This is a letter of one chess player to another, not a letter of General Gates to Governor Jefferson. I am now at my unhappy house; you are acting in the busy scene of public life, and in a most exalted station, in which I sincerely wish you all the honor and success; happiness, I know, you cannot have.

Major-General Phillips was already in Virginia, along with the traitor Benedict Arnold, now a British brigadier-general, leading an expedition sent in January by Clinton to cut off Virginian supplies to the south and perhaps to carry operations into Pennsylvania. All plans were dashed by Cornwallis' decision to set off along the coast and to join up with the British in the Chesapeake. Bitter words followed between Clinton and Cornwallis.

I am very anxious to receive your Excellency's commands, being as yet totally in the dark as to the intended operations of the summer. I cannot help expressing my wishes that the Chesapeak may become the seat of war, even (if necessary) at the expense of abandoning New York. Until Virginia is in a manner subdued, our hold of the Carolinas must be difficult, if not precarious. The rivers in Virginia are advantageous to an invading army; but North Carolina is of all the provinces in America the most difficult to attack (unless material assistance could be got from the inhabitants, the contrary of which I have sufficiently experienced), on account of its great extent, of the numberless rivers and creeks, and the total want of interior navigation.

And to Germain Clinton wrote:

I hope Lord Cornwallis may have gone back to Carolina . . . If he joins Phillips I shall tremble for every post except Charleston, and even for Georgia.

What Clinton feared was a Franco-American attack, which might be against New York, or in Virginia. He wanted to establish an anchorage in Chesapeake Bay for ships of the line, and it was because of this instruction that Cornwallis chose to fortify Yorktown. It held a commanding position seaward, but was vulnerable to land attack. Clinton had always differed from Cornwallis on the role of Virginia: to Cornwallis it was always the place where the war could be won. But then to him it had never been a war of posts.

On 9 June Phillips died of fever, and Cornwallis took over command; and yet another revised strategy was improvised: the attempt at the conquest of Washington's own side of Virginia, where active Loyalist support was at a minimum.

Clinton, still anticipating a Franco-American assault on New York, and uneasy at the incapacity of the Royal Navy to dominate local waters, could but acquiesce. His orders were 'to take up a defensive station in any healthy position he preferred'.

Cornwallis wrote to Clinton from Byrd's Plantation, north of the James:

. . . I shall now proceed to dislodge La Fayette from Richmond, and with my light troops to destroy any magazines or stores in the neighbourhood which may have been collected either for his use or for General Greene's army. From thence I purpose to move to the Neck at Williamsburgh, which is represented as healthy and where some subsistence may be procured, and keep myself unengaged from operations which might interfere with your plans for the campaign, untill I have the satisfaction of hearing from you. I hope I shall then have an opportunity to receive better information than has hitherto been in my power to procure, relative to a proper harbour and place of arms.

Richard Henry Lee wrote to Arthur Lee from Epping Forest on 4 June 1781:

The enemy affect to leave harmless the poor and they take everything from those they call the rich. Tis said that 2 or 3000 Negroes march in their train, that every kind of stock which they cannot remove they destroy — eating up the green wheat and by destroying of the fences expose to destruction the other growing grains. They have burnt a great number of warehouses full of tobacco and they are now pressing on to the large ones on Rappahanock and Potomac rivers and the valuable iron works in our northern parts.

The fine horses on James River have furnished them with a numerous and powerful cavalry — 'tis said to consist of 800. I hope that these afflictions are intended to do away some of our overcharge of wickedness, and that we shall be relieved in due season.

Cornwallis is the scourge — and a severe one he is. The doings of more than a year in the South are undoing very fast, whilst they rush to throw ruin into other parts.

I have got your keys from Richmond. Half of our militia is this day to be drafted for the Marquis, but how to get at him I know not, as the enemy are between us and him.

Tarleton, who had a grandiloquent taste for the third person, later wrote a History of Campaigns in Southern Provinces, *in which he gave his version of events that summer:*

To frustrate these intentions, and to distress the Americans by breaking up the assembly at Charlotteville and by taking or destroying the arms and other stores at Point of Fork, his Lordship employed

225

Lieutenant-Colonel Tarleton on the former expedition, as most distant and on that account more within the reach of cavalry, whilst he committed the latter enterprize to the execution of Lieutenant-Colonel Simcoe, with the yagers, the infantry and the hussars of the rangers.

Tarleton imagined that a march of seventy miles in twenty-four hours, with the caution he had used, might perhaps, give him the advantage of a surprise, and concluded that an additional celerity to the object of his destination would undoubtedly prevent a formidable resistance. He therefore approached the Rivanna, which runs at the foot of the hill on which the town is situated, with all possible expedition. The advanced dragoons reported that the ford was guarded. An attack was nevertheless ordered. The cavalry charged through the water with very little loss and routed the detachment posted at that place.

As soon as one hundred cavalry had passed the water, Lieutenant-Colonel Tarleton directed them to charge into the town, to continue the confusion of the Americans and to apprehend, if possible, the governor and assembly. Seven members of assembly were secured; a Brigadier-General Scott and several officers and men were killed, wounded or taken. The attempt to secure Mr Jefferson was ineffectual; he discovered the British dragoons from his house, which stands on the point of a mountain, before they could approach him, and he provided for his personal liberty by a precipitate retreat.

Jefferson's prestige never fully recovered from his sudden flight, and Tarleton's raid effectively ended his period as Governor. It might, in extenuation, be added that at least he did not join the legislature in their flight over the Blue Ridge to Staunton, and that the American troops were as panic-stricken as he was.

Colonel Otho Williams, a Marylander serving as Greene's adjutant, left a vivid description of the civil war savagery at Eutaw Springs in September, the last major battle in the lower south that year. Greene was destroying British outposts at the time.

The field of battle was, at this instant, rich in the dreadful scenery which disfigures such a picture. On the left, Washington's cavalry routed and flying, horses plunging as they died or coursing the field without their riders, while the enemy with poised bayonet issued from the thicket upon the wounded or unhorsed rider. In the fore-ground, Hampton covering and collecting the scattered cavalry while Kirkwood, with his bayonets, rushed furiously to revenge their fall, and a road strewed with the bodies of men and horses, and the fragments of dismounted artillery. Beyond these, a scene of indescribable confusion, viewed over the whole American line advancing rapidly and in order. And, on the right, Henderson borne off in the arms of his soldiers, and Campbell sustained in his saddle by a brave son, who had sought glory at his father's side.

Eutaw Springs was, again, modelled on Cowpens: a first line of militia, a second line of regulars, with Washington's cavalry and Kirkwood's light infantry in reserve. The militia on this occasion fired seventeen rounds before showing any sign of weakening. The second line then drove the British back. As Washington and Kirkwood then drove the British into full retreat, the discipline of the Virginian and Maryland Continentals could not resist the liquor they found in the British camp and they drank themselves silly. The British cavalry drove the 'victors' into the woods in disorder. It was a confused, bloody and three-hour battle fought in murderous heat.

John Chaney, a twenty-four-year-old volunteer in the South Carolina infantry, had his own clear memory of Eutaw Springs. One of Colonel William Washington's dragoons, Billy Lunsford, asked a special favour:

One of his dragoons, Billy Lunsford, requested of his captain leave to steal upon and shoot a British sentinel. The captain told him it could not do the cause any good, and, as the sentinel was doing his duty, it was a pity to shoot him. Billy swore his time was out, and, as he was going home to Virginia, he would have it to tell that he had killed 'one damned British son of a bitch.' Accordingly, Billy commenced passing backwards and forwards with a pistol, creeping on his all fours and grunting like a hog. The sentinel was heard to slap his cartouche box and fired, and Billy changed his grunting to groaning, being shot through the body, entering his right and coming out his left side. It was as pretty a shot as could have been made in daylight. The British sentinel, being reinforced, carried Billy a prisoner into their camp, where, by the kind attention of a British surgeon who nursed him and had him nursed all night to prevent his bleeding inwardly and to make him bleed outwardly, he recovered.

Philip Freneau commemorated 'the brave Americans' who fell in action at the battle:

> At Eutaw Springs the valiant died;
>   Their limbs with dust are covered o'er –
> Weep on, ye springs, your tearful tide;
>   How many heroes are no more!

If in this wreck of ruin, they
    Can yet be thought to claim a tear,
O smite your gentle breast and say
    The friends of freedom slumber here!

Thou, who shalt trace this bloody plain,
    If goodness rules thy generous breast,
Sigh for the wasted rural reign;
    Sigh for the shepherds, sunk to rest!

Stranger, their humble graves adorn;
    You too may fall and ask a tear;
Tis not the beauty of the morn
    That proves the evening shall be clear.

They saw their injured country's woe:
    The flaming town, the wasted field;
Then rushed to meet the insulting foe;
    They took the spear — but left the shield.

Led by thy conquering genius, Greene,
    The Britons they compelled to fly;
None distant viewed the fatal plain,
    None grieved, in such a cause to die —

But, like the Parthian, famed of old,
    Who, flying, still their arrows threw,
These routed Britons, full as bold,
    Retreated, and retreating slew.

Now rest in peace, our patriot band;
    Though far from nature's limits thrown,
We trust they find a happier land,
    A brighter sunshine of their own.

Eutaw Springs was again a British victory but, again, at the cost of one quarter (some 600 men) of the troops engaged. The British remnants fell back towards Charleston. Greene now controlled all the lower south except for their umbilical cords to the Atlantic — Wilmington, Charleston and Savannah. The only effective British force was now confined to the lower reaches of the James River in Virginia.

On 1 August, Cornwallis occupied Yorktown and began to fortify it. The showdown at Yorktown was the result of British contradictions, coincidence and not least military co-ordination, and courage. De Grasse, then in the Caribbean, agreed to sail for the Chesapeake on 3 August and to stay for two months — he could not stay

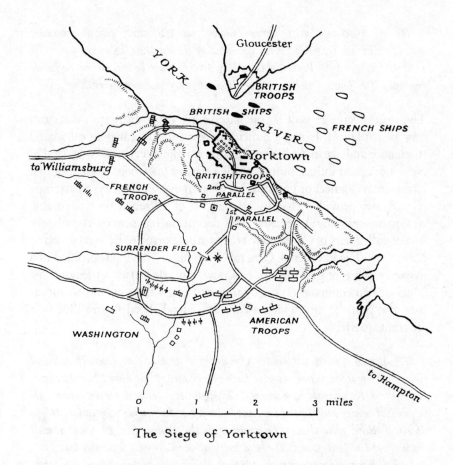

The Siege of Yorktown

longer because he had joint plans with the Spanish fleet planned for mid-October and by that time the hurricane season was in prospect. With de Grasse's support promised, Washington dropped his original plan for a diversion against New York to relieve the pressures on Greene, and he took a risk.

Matters having now come to a crisis and a decisive plan to be determined on, I was obliged from the shortness of Count de Grasses promised stay on this Coast, the apparent disinclination in their Naval Officers to force the harbour of New York and the feeble compliance of the States to my requisition for Men, hitherto, and little prospect of greater exertion in the future, to give up all idea of attacking New York; and instead thereof to remove the French Troops and a detachment from the American Army to the Head of Elk to be transported to Virginia for the purpose of co-operating with the force from the West Indies against the Troops in that State.

229

He left 2500 men on the lower Hudson and, with 2000 picked Americans and 5000 French troops under the command of Rochambeau, he moved south. By 1 September he was in Philadelphia and by 26 September he was on the Yorktown peninsula. Dr James Thacher describes Washington's 'masterly generalship'.

The great secret respecting our late preparation and movements can now be explained. It was a judiciously concerted strategem calculated to menace and alarm Sir Henry Clinton for the safety of the garrison of New York, and induce him to recall a part of his troops from Virginia, for his own defence; or perhaps, keeping an eye on the city, to attempt its capture, provided that by the arrival of a French fleet, favorable circumstances should present. The deception has proved completely successfull; a part of Cornwallis' troops are reported to have returned to New York. His Excellency General Washington, having succeeded in a masterly piece of generalship, has now the satisfaction of leaving his adversary to ruminate on his own mortifying situation, and to anticipate the perilous fate which awaits his friend, Lord Cornwallis, in a different quarter.

The French fleet set sail for the Chesapeake with siege equipment. If Admiral Graves, who was conducting the hunt for a French fleet off fog-bound New England, had realised this, he could have occupied Chesapeake Bay before de Grasse arrived. De Grasse had twenty-nine ships of line, and he landed 4000 men on 2 September. When Admiral Hood reached the Chesapeake with the British fleet he found himself outnumbered and outgunned. The hard battle off the Cape on 5 September lasted two and a half hours and was indecisive; the ships lay refitting within sight of each other. When the French fleet, under the Comte de Barras, arrived from Rhode Island, Graves withdrew to New York on 14 September, leaving the French with a tactical advantage at the key moment.

Colonel St George Tucker, still serving with the Virginia militia, wrote to his wife from Williamsburg on 5 September.

. . . Hear then, my Fanny, from me what perhaps you have not heard yet from good authority. About the middle of last week twenty-nine ships of the line and four frigates arrived in our bay, with four thousand land forces sent to our assistance by Louis the Great. Besides these there are three thousand marines to be landed in case of an emergency. Of the fleet there are ten sixty-fours; eighteen seventy-fours, and one ship of an hundred and ten guns! A fleet of twelve sail of the line has arrived in the West Indies to keep the enemy still employed in that quarter. Of the troops, three thousand five hundred landed at James Town three days ago and are now on their march to this city. Five hundred are left on board to land at York River. The fleet lies from Lynnhaven bay to the mouth of York River, and some, we are informed, have proceeded within two or three miles of the town. The British fleet still lies at York, and their land forces are now in the town.

Nor is this all, for, to my great suprise and pleasure, I was this morning informed from undoubted authority that General Washington is at the Head of Elk with five thousand troops, which are to be embarked from thence in transports sent there for that purpose, of which the Marquis last night received official accounts from General Washington in a letter dated at Chatham.

Colonel Jonathan Trumbull, former Governor of Connecticut, now secretary to George Washington, wrote in his journal on 28 September:

The General and family sleep in the field without any other covering than the canopy of the heavens and the small spreading branches of a tree, which will probably be rendered venerable from this circumstance for a length of time to come. Previous to this movement the enemies post at Glocester on the opposite side of York River had been invested by a body of militia under the command of Gen. Wedon, the French Legion of the Duke de Lauzun, and a body of French troops from the fleet all under the command of Brig. Gen. De Choisey.

The French and American troops had an immense advantage — 15,000 troops against 7000, naval superiority, siege artillery. The siege began on 28 September and on the next day Cornwallis withdrew to his outer defences. On 9 October, his earthworks were bombarded, ceremonially started by French guns, and with Washington touching off the first American blast.

'We cannot hope to make a very long resistance,' wrote Cornwallis. On 16 October, he attempted to evacuate across the York River to Gloucester, but was prevented by stormy weather.

Inside Yorktown was Captain Samuel Graham of the 76th Regiment of Foot, who had come to Virginia with his Highland regiment early in the spring. So far he had enjoyed thoroughly the Virginia campaign; now that he faced besiegement, his ardour only increased, as did that of his comrades:

On the twenty-eighth September, information was given by a picket . . . that the enemy were advancing in force by the Williamsburg road. The army immediately took post in the outward position. The French and Americans came on in the most cautious and regular order. Some shots were fired from our fieldpieces. The French also felt the redoubt on our right flank, defended by the Twenty-third and a party of marines, but did not persist. The two armies remained some time in this position observing each other. In ours there was but one wish, that they would advance. While standing with a brother captain . . . we overheard a soliloquy of an old Highland gentleman, a lieutenant, who drawing his sword, said to himself, 'Come on Maister Washington, I'm unco' glad to see you. I've been offered money for my commission, but I could na think of gangin' hame without a sight of you! Come on!'

Captain James Duncan's diary reported:

A militia man this day, possessed of more bravery than prudence, stood constantly on the parapet and d——d his soul if he would dodge for the buggers. He had escaped longer than could have been expected, and growing foolhardy, brandished his spade at every ball that was fired till, unfortunately, a ball came and put an end to his capers.

The next day two deserters fled from Yorktown into the allied lines. They told that Cornwallis' army was

very sickly to the amount of two thousand in the hospital and that the troops had scarce ground to live upon their shipping in a very naked state, and their cavalry very scarce of forage.

This was no revelation to Washington and his officers; they had been able to determine almost as much solely by observation.

Dr James Thacher recounted in his journal:

From the 10th to the 15th [of October], a tremendous and incessant firing from the American and French batteries is kept up, and the enemy return the fire, but with little effect. A red-hot shell from the French battery set fire to the *Charon*, a British 44-gun ship, and two or three smaller vessels at anchor in the river, which were consumed in the night. From the bank of the river I had a fine view of this splendid conflagration.

During the assault, the British kept up an incessant firing of cannon and musketry from their whole line. His Excellency General Washington, Generals Lincoln and Knox, with their aids having dismounted, were standing in an exposed situation waiting the result.

Colonel Cobb, one of General Washington's aids, solicitous for his

232

safety, said to His Excellency, 'Sir, you are too much exposed here. Had you not better step a little back?'

'Colonel Cobb,' replied his Excellency, 'if you are afraid, you have liberty to step back.'

Colonel Philip van Cortlandt, of the 2nd New York Regiment, later reminisced:

. . . the first gun which was fired I could distinctly hear pass through the town . . . I could hear the ball strike from house to house, and I was afterwards informed that it went through the one where many of the officers were at dinner, and over the tables, discomposing the dishes, and either killed or wounded the one at the head of the table. And I also heard that the gun was fired by the Commander-in-Chief, who was designedly present in the battery for the express purpose of putting the first match.

That night, Lieutenant Ebenezer Denny thought:

The scene viewed from the camp now was grand . . . A number of shells from the works of both parties passing high in the air and descending in a curve, each with a long train of fire, exhibited a brilliant spectacle.

Meanwhile, Stephen Popp in the British lines, remembered:

We could find no refuge in or out of the town. The people fled to the waterside and hid in hastily contrived shelters on the banks, but many of them were killed by bursting bombs. More than eighty were thus lost, besides many wounded, and their houses utterly destroyed. Our ships suffered, too, under the heavy fire, for the enemy fired in one day thirty-six hundred shot from their heavy guns and batteries. Soldiers and sailors deserted in great numbers. The Hessian Regiment von Bose lost heavily, although it was in our rear in the second line, but in full range of the enemy's fire. Our two regiments lost very heavily too. The Light Infantry posted at an angle had the worst position and the heaviest loss. Sailors and marines all served in defending our lines on shore.

The climax came with the storming at bayonet point of two redoubts, Number Nine, taken by the French, and Number Ten, taken by Alexander Hamilton. Hamilton's 'forlorn hope', led by a detachment of sappers and miners, under New York Captain, James Gilliland, included Sergeant Martin:

We arrived at the trenches a little before sunset. I saw several officers fixing bayonets on long staves. I then concluded we were about to make a general assault upon the enemy's works, but before dark I was informed of the whole plan . . .

The sappers and miners were furnished with axes and were to proceed in front and cut a passage for the troops through the abatis . . . At dark the detachment . . . advanced beyond the trenches and lay down on the ground to await the signal for . . . the attack, which was to be three shells from a certain battery . . . All the batteries in our line were silent, and we lay anxiously waiting for the signal . . . Our watchword was, 'Rochambeau' . . . Being pronounced, 'Ro-sham-bow,' it sounded when pronounced quick like, 'Rush on boys.'

We had not lain here long before the . . . signal was given for us and the French . . . the three shells with their fiery trains mounting the air in quick succession. The word, 'up up' was then reiterated through the detachment. We . . . moved toward the redoubt we were to attack with unloaded muskets.

Cornwallis wrote in October to Clinton that

My situation now becomes very critical. We dare not show a gun to their old batteries, and I expect that their new ones will open tomorrow morning. Experience has shown that our fresh earthen works do not resist their powerful artillery, so that we shall soon be exposed to an assault in ruined works, in a bad position, and with weakened numbers. The safety of the place is, therefore, so precarious that I cannot recommend that the fleet and army should run great risk in endeavoring to save us.

Ebenezer Denny wrote on 17 October:

Before relief came [I] had the pleasure of seeing a drummer mount the enemy's parapet and beat a parley, and immediately an officer, holding up a white handkerchief, made his appearance outside their works. The drummer accompanied him, beating. Our batteries ceased. An officer from our lines ran and met the other and tied the handkerchief over his eyes. The drummer [was] sent back, and the British officer conducted to a house in rear of our lines. Firing ceased totally.

Correspondence was exchanged between Cornwallis and Washington on 17 October:

SIR,

I propose a cessation of hostilities for twenty-four hours, and that two officers may be appointed by each side, to meet at Mr Moore's house, to settle terms for the surrender of the posts of York and Gloucester.

I have the honor to be, &c.

CORNWALLIS

MY LORD,

I have had the honor of receiving your Lordship's letter of this date. An ardent desire to spare the further effusion of blood will readily incline me to listen to such terms for the surrender of your posts of York and Gloucester, as are admissible.

I wish, previously to the meeting of commissioners, that your Lordship's proposals in writing may be sent to the American lines, for which purpose a suspension of hostilities, during two hours from the delivery of this letter, will be granted.

I have the honor to be, &c.

GEORGE WASHINGTON

St George Tucker recorded the memorable day:

At dawn of day [the eighteenth] the British gave us a serenade with the bagpipes, I believe, and were answered by the French with the band of the Regiment of Deux-Ponts. As soon as the sun rose, one of the most striking pictures of war was displayed . . . . From the point of Rock battery on one side our lines completely manned and our works crowded with soldiers were exhibited to view. Opposite these at the distance of two hundred yards, you were presented with a sight of the British works, their parapets crowded with officers looking at those who were assembled at the top of our works. The Secretary's [Thomas Nelson's] house with one of the corners broke off and many large holes through the roof and walls, part of which seemed tottering . . . afforded a striking instance of the destruction occasioned by war. Many other houses in the vicinity contributed to accomplish the scene.

On 19 October 1781 the surrender took place – on the same day as Clinton was finally setting sail with a rescue fleet. He reached the Chesapeake five days too late. At their head rode a splendid-looking, ruddy Irishman, Brigadier Charles O'Hara of the Guards, come to act for Lord Cornwallis – too indisposed to appear. Count Matthieu Dumas was deputised to ride forward to meet the garrison troops and direct them.

235

I placed myself at General O'Hara's left hand . . . He asked me where General Rochambeau was. 'On our left,' I said, 'at the head of the French line.' The English general urged his horse forward to present his sword to the French general. Guessing his intention, I galloped on to place myself between him and M. de Rochambeau, who at that moment made me a sign, pointing to General Washington who was opposite to him . . .

'You are mistaken,' said I to General O'Hara. 'The commander-in-chief of our army is on the right.'

I accompanied him, and the moment that he presented his sword, General Washington, anticipating him said, 'Never from such a good hand.'

An officer of the New Jersey Line thought that

The British officers in general behaved like boys who had been whipped at school. Some bit their lips, some pouted, others cried. Their round, broad-brimmed hats were well adapted to the occasion, hiding those faces they were ashamed to show. The foreign regiments made a more military appearance, and the conduct of their officers was far more becoming men of fortitude.

Meanwhile, on the other side, Captain Graham of the 76th Foot remembered:

Drums were beat, but the colors remained in their cases – an idle retaliation for a very idle sight which had been put by our people on the American garrison of Charleston, and the regiments having formed in columns at quarter distance the men laid down their arms.

It is a sorry reminiscence, this. Yet the scene made a deep impression at the moment, for the mortification and unfeigned sorrow of the soldiers will never fade from my memory. Some went so far as to shed tears, while one man, a corporal, who stood near me, embraced his firelock and then threw it on the ground exclaiming, 'May you never get so good a master again!'

Nevertheless, to do them justice, the Americans behaved with great delicacy and forbearance, while the French, by what motive actuated I will not pretend to say, were profuse in their protestations of sympathy . . . When I visited their lines . . . immediately after our parade had been dismissed, I was overwhelmed with the civility of my late enemies.

Cornwallis wrote to Clinton from Yorktown on 20 October.

236

I have the mortification to inform your Excellency that I have been forced to give up the posts of York and Gloucester, and to surrender the troops under my command, by capitulation on the 19th inst. as prisoners of war to the combined forces of America and France.

Two days later Lafayette wrote to a friend:

The play, sir is over. Washington has given a dinner for British General O'Hara.

For the second time in the war, an entire British army was lost at one stroke and with it 7200 men, 264 cannon, 6658 muskets, 457 horses and over £2000 in cash. It need not have happened if Cornwallis had retreated before Washington and Rochambeau arrived, or if he had fully realised his total dependence on British command of the sea; or if Clinton's intelligence had warned him of Washington's move south; or if Rodney had not sailed to Britain from the West Indies, in the belief that Hood and Graves had enough ships of the line. But such is war and its fortunes. For fortune requires luck as well as audax.

De Grasse, Washington and Rochambeau conceived a master plan and carried it through by land and sea, over 1500 miles of country and sustaining it for two months; Washington after three years of Fabian tactics moved suddenly at speed and without hesitation; and the French co-operated admirably.

The British were understandably shaken by the news of the surrender as Sir Nathaniel Wraxall wrote in his memoirs.

The First Minister's firmness, and even his presence of mind, which had withstood the [Gordon] riots of 1780, gave way for a short time under this awful disaster. I asked Lord George [Germain] afterwards how he took the communication when made to him. 'As he would have taken a ball in his breast,' replied Lord George. For he opened his arms, exclaiming wildly, as he paced up and down the apartment during a few minutes, 'O God! it is all over!' – words which he repeated many times under emotions of the deepest consternation and distress.

Anna Rawle, Quaker stepdaughter of Samuel Shoemaker, a prominent Pennsylvania Loyalist, recorded the details of the memorable night of 24 October:

October 24 It is too true that Cornwallis is taken. [Colonel Tench] Tiligman is just arrived with dispatches from Washington which confirm it. B[enjamin] S[hoemaker] came here and shewed us some papers; long conversations we often have together on the melancholy situation of things.

October 25 I suppose, dear Mammy, thee would not have imagined this house to be illuminated last night, but it was. A mob surrounded it, broke the shutters and the glass of the windows, and were coming in; none but forlorn women here. We for a time listened for their attacks in fear and trembling till, finding them grow more loud and violent, not knowing what to do, we ran into the yard. Warm Whigs of one side, and [James] Hartley's of the other (who were treated even worse than we), rendered it impossible for us to escape that way. We had not been there many minutes before we were drove back by the sight of two men climbing the fence. We thought the mob were coming in thro' there, but it proved to be Coburn and Bob Shewell, who called to us not to be frightened, and fixed lights up at the windows, which pacified the mob, and after three huzzas they moved off. A number of men came in afterwards to see us. French and J. B. nailed boards up at the broken pannels, or it would not have been safe to have gone to bed. Coburn and Shewell were really very kind; had it not been for them I really believe the house would have been pulled down. Even the firm Uncle [William] Fisher was obliged to submit to have his windows illuminated, for they had pickaxes and iron bars with which they had done considerable injury to his house . . . In short it was the most alarming scene I ever remember. For two hours we had the disagreeable noise of stones banging about, glass crashing, and the tumultuous voices of a large body of men, as they were a long time at the different houses in the neighbourhood. At last they were victorious, and it was one general illumination throughout the town. As we had not the pleasure of seeing any of the gentlemen in the house, nor the furniture cut up, and goods stolen, nor been beat, nor pistols pointed at our breasts, we may count our sufferings slight compared to many others. Mr Gibbs was obliged to make his escape over a fence, and while his wife was endeavouring to shield him from the rage of one of the men, she received a violent bruise in the breast and a blow in the face which made her nose bleed. Ben Shoemaker was here this morning; tho' exceedingly threatened he says he came off with the loss of four panes of glass. Some Whig friends put candles in the windows which made his peace with the mob, and they retired. John Drinker has lost half the goods out of his shop and been beat by them; in short the sufferings of those they pleased to style Tories would fill a volume and shake the credulity of those who were not here on that memorable night, and today Philadelphia makes an uncommon appearance, which ought to cover the Whigs with eternal confusion . . . .

In France Louis XVI decreed:

All the inhabitants of Paris will illuminate on November 27 the fronts of their houses to celebrate with due respect the great victory gained in America, both by land and sea, over the English, by the armies of the King combined with those commanded by General Washington.

When the British marched out at Yorktown, the band played The world would be upside down:

> If buttercups buzzed after the bee,
> If boats were on land, churches on sea,
> If ponies rode men and grass ate the cows,
> And cats should be chased to holes by the mouse,
> If the mamas sold their babies to the gypsies for half a crown;
> Summer were spring and the t'other way round,
> Then all the world would be upside down.

And Philip Freneau wrote:

> When a certain great king, whose initial is G.
> Shall force stamps upon paper, and folks to drink tea;
> When these folks burn his tea and stampt paper, like stubble,
> You may guess that this king is then coming to trouble.
> But when a petition he treads under his feet,
> And sends over the ocean an army and fleet;
> When that army, half starved, and frantic with rage,
> Shall be cooped up with a leader whose name rhymes with cage;
> When that leader goes home dejected and sad,
> You may then be assured the king's prospects are bad.
> But when B. and C. with their armies are taken,
> This king will do well if he saves his own bacon.
> In the year seventeen hundred and eighty and two,
> A stroke he shall get that will make him look blue;
> In the years eighty-three, eighty-four, eighty-five,
> You hardly shall know that the king is alive;
> In the year eighty-six the affair will be over,
> And he shall eat turnips that grow in Hanover.
> The face of the lion shall then become pale,
> He shall yield fifteen teeth, and be sheared of his tail.
> O king, my dear king, you shall be very sore;
> The Stars and the Lily shall run you on shore,
> And your Lion shall growl — but never bite more.

1782–3

There never was a good war –
or a bad peace

On 22 February 1782 – which happened to be Washington's birthday – General Conway moved an address to the throne, urging 'a happy reconciliation with the revolted Colonies'. It was lost by only one vote. Two weeks later a stronger motion was passed.

The House would consider as enemies to His Majesty, and to the Country, all those who should advise, or by any means attempt, the further prosecution of the war on the continent of North America, for the purpose of reducing the revolting Colonies to obedience by force.

In March George III planned his abdication.

His Majesty during the twenty one years He has sate on the Throne of Great Britain, has had no object so much at heart as the maintenance of the British Constitution, of which the difficulties He has at times met with from His scrupulous attachment to the Rights of Parliament are sufficient proofs.

His Majesty is convinced that the sudden change of Sentiments of one Branch of the Legislature has totally incapacitated Him from either conducting the War with effect, or from obtaining any Peace but on conditions which would prove destructive to the Commerce as well as essential Rights of the British Nation.

His Majesty therefore with much sorrow finds He can be of no further Utility to His Native Country which drives Him to the painful step of quitting it for ever.

In consequence of which Intention His Majesty resignes the Crown of Great Britain and the Dominions appertaining thereto to His Dearly Beloved Son and lawful Successor, George Prince of Wales, whose endeavours for the Prosperity of the British Empire He hopes may prove more Successful.

Later, he wrote to the Earl of Shelburne:

I cannot conclude without mentioning how sensibly I feel the dismemberment of America from this Empire, and that I should be miserable indeed if I did not feel that no blame on that account can be laid at my door. And did I not also know that Knavery seems to be so much the striking feature of its inhabitants that it may not in the end be an evil that they will become aliens to this Kingdom.

On 31 March John Hamilton, a Charleston Loyalist, wrote to a London friend:

I was in a State Of Despondence for some time untill his Majesty's speech arrived when it revived my Spirits, but what was my astonishment when I Read Lord George G[ermai]n's and Lord North's speech in parliament; surely they can never be so weak as to give up this Country.

Our Country is lost in dissipation, luxury and faction. There is no publick Spirit or virtue left either to reward merit or punish offences. Remove all Such wretches from power and leav either Execution of affairs to the brave, zealous Loyalists, who have lost their fortunes and Risk'd their lives in defence of their King and Country; such are the men who will save their Country from Ruin and distruction . . .

Notwithstanding all our Misfortunes, Great Britain can never, must never relinquish America. The last man and shilling must be expended before she gives America her independence; if she looses America, she looses all her West Indies and must Revert again to her insular Situation, which hardly make her visible on the face of the Earth.

Some examples must be made. A General, an Admiral and others must pay for our Misfortunes; a Spirited minister must take place and an honest man who will reward merit and punish the offenders. Then we may Expect to become ourselves again, but not before a very great change is made.

I still flatter myself the war will be carried on with vigour in North Carolina and Virginia and a large reinforcement sent out this season. The inhabitants are tired of their French Connections and with the Tyranny of their Leaders which is more conspicuous than ever. It behoves the nation at large to interfere and prevent the Ministry from giving America her independence. Your Salvation depends on Spirited Exertions at present, if not and America is given up, Britain must become a Province of France and America.

There were many pointers to a British peace settlement. A new commander-in-chief was announced — on 23 February Sir Guy Carleton replaced Clinton, who was recalled to vent his spleen in bitter reminiscence. There came news of French victories in the West Indies — with the capture of St Kitts, Nevis and Montserrat and a serious threat to Jamaica; the British loss of Minorca, the siege of Gibraltar and clashes in India; there came also rumours that 'the citizens of London and Westminster had petitioned the king in the strongest terms to relinquish the American war'.

On 20 March Lord North resigned, to be replaced by the Marquis of Rockingham, with the pro-American Charles James Fox as Foreign Secretary and Shelburne as Secretary for the Colonies. Fox sent Thomas Grenville to open negotiations at Versailles, and Shelburne sent Richard Oswald, the former Scottish merchant and slave trader, to talk to Benjamin Franklin. Fox favoured immediate independence for the United States; Franklin sought the cession of Canada; Shelburne was against this and wanted debts met and the Loyalists compensated. The American commissioners refused, and insisted on fishing rights off Newfoundland.

In July, however, Rockingham died, Shelburne became Prime Minister and Fox left the Cabinet. In American eyes, Shelburne was less liberal, despite all his pro-American sympathies throughout the war. Washington concluded:

The death of the Marquis of Rockingham has given a shock to the new administration and disordered its whole system . . . That the King will push the war as long as the nation will find men or money admits not of a doubt in my mind.

The peace negotiations were not easy. In 1781 Vergennes had favoured a map that would have left Maine, New York and much of the south in British hands: he did not want a strong United States. France's ally, Spain, wanted the Mississippi south of the Ohio firmly under its own control. Franklin's fellow peace commissioners, John Adams and John Jay, suspected him of being dangerously pro-French. But on the fundamentals he never compromised: fishing rights, no compensation for Loyalists, no surrender on the western or the northern boundaries. Nor was it a case of holding on to the status quo for the continuing naval struggle was bringing Britain new advantages.

In April Sir George Rodney, with superiority in ships and guns, destroyed de Grasse's fleet en route to Jamaica, wrecking the flagship Ville de Paris, *on which, eight months before, the Yorktown campaign was planned. The battle was known as the Saints, from the narrow channel between Guadeloupe and Dominica. Rodney signalled Lord Sandwich at the Admiralty:*

YOU MAY NOW DESPISE ALL YOUR ENEMIES

On the same day, British and French ships fought an inconclusive battle off Ceylon in the Indian Ocean.

Back on land, Yorktown was certainly not the end — especially not for Washington, who left Rochambeau and his forces encamped near Williamsburg, and spent the winter in New Jersey and — yet again — facing Clinton along the Hudson. He did not believe the war was over. Greene still had a force bottling up the British in Charleston. When Washington returned to his troops — after a week at home at Mount Vernon — and established his headquarters at Newburgh in New York at the end of March, he faced the usual intractable problems. In spite of Washington's doubts, Carleton, who arrived in May, went ahead with his plans for the evacuation of southern ports.

The evacuation is not a matter of choice but of deplorable necessity in consequence of an unsuccessful war.

In July Savannah was evacuated. This sent a wave of alarm through still-Loyalist Georgia, which its gallant royal governor, Sir James Wright, thought had been 'shamefully neglected'. They complained about the speedy abandonment of Savannah, whose defences were strong; they complained still more loudly when it became clear that East Florida was to be returned to Spain in order to retain Gibraltar. There would be no haven for the Loyalists except the humid Bahamas or the icy wastes of Canada.

Loyalist sentiments stayed high also in the area of New York City and neighbouring New Jersey. Throughout the seven years a dirty little civil war had been waged along the Long Island Sound, in Connecticut and in Monmouth County, New Jersey. In March an artillery militia officer, Captain Joshua Huddy, was seized by Tory irregulars at Tom River, confined on a British prison ship and released to be hanged, on the charge that he had slain one of their leaders, Philip White. Captain Richard Lippincott was in charge of the execution. On Huddy's chest was pinned:

We, the Refugees, having long with grief beheld the cruel murders of our brethren . . . therefore determined not to suffer without taking vengeance . . . and thus begun, having made use of Captain Huddy as the first object to present to your view; and we further determine to hang men for men while there is a Refugee existing.

Below this was written: 'Up goes Huddy for Philip White.'

The 'Monmouth Retaliators' organised matching exercises and lamented Huddy's fate.

But Cap'n Huddy sho'd 'em how
　a Jersey boy could die.
They left his corpse a-hangin'
　as they hurried from the strand,
His corpse, to call for vengeance,
　to his Monmouth County band.

Washington requested Lippincott's arrest by Clinton. When he was released after a court-martial that found him guilty only of obeying orders, Washington ordered that a British officer should be chosen by lot to be executed in retaliation. The lot fell on nineteen-year-old Charles Asgill, the only son of Sir Charles Asgill. On his mother's pleading his cause to the French Foreign Minister Vergennes, Congress ordered his release. (In 1814 Asgill became a full general in the British Army.)

　Fighting continued in the Ohio valley and on the frontier, where Indians raided and where white men tried to secure Indian lands. A white massacre of ninety-six Delaware Indians led to reprisals. David Zeisberger recounts the massacre; Simon Girty, at the head of a motley group of Tories and Indians, describes the consequences.

March 7, 1782: The militia, some 200 in number, as we hear, came first to Gnadenhutten. A mile from town they met young Schebosh in the bush, whom they at once killed and scalped, and, near the houses, two friendly Indians, not belonging to us, but who had gone there with our people from Sandusky, among whom were several other friends who perished likewise. Our Indians were mostly on the plantations and saw the militia come, but no one thought of fleeing for they suspected no ill. The militia came to them and bade them come into town, telling them no harm should befall them. They trusted and went, but were all bound, the men being put into one house, the women into another . . . Then they began to sing hymns and spoke words of encouragement and consolation one to another until they were all slain, and the above mentioned Abraham was the first to be led out, but the others were killed in the house. The sisters also afterwards met the same fate, who also sang hymns together. Christina, the Mohican, who well understood German and English, fell upon her knees before the Captain, begging for life, but got for answer that he could not help her. Two well-grown boys, who saw the whole thing and escaped, gave this information. One of these lay under the heaps of slain and was scalped, but finally came to himself and found opportunity to escape. The same did Jacob, Rachel's son, who was wonderfully rescued. For they came close upon him suddenly outside the town, so that he thought they must have seen him, but he crept into a thicket and escaped their hands . . . He went a long way about and observed what went on.

June 12, 1782: Simon Girty arrived last night from the upper village (Half Kings's town) who informed me that the Delawares had burnt Colonel Crawford and two captains at Pipes-Town after torturing them a long time. Crawford died like a hero; never changed his countenance tho' they scalped him alive and then laid hot ashes upon his head; after which they roasted him by a slow fire. He told Girty if his life could be spared, he would communicate something of consequence, but nothing else could induce him to do it. He said some great blows would be struck against the country. Crawford and four captains belonged to the Continental forces. He [Girty] said fourteen captains were killed. The rebel doctor [Knight] and General Irvine's aid-de-camp [Rosenthal] are taken by the Shawanese; they came out on a party of pleasure.

In November, as a reprisal for Shawnee Indian attacks on the Kentucky frontier, George Rogers Clark and 1000 mounted riflemen routed the Shawnee near Chillicothe, Ohio, and burned their villages. It was a punitive act, since many had fled before he arrived. But it established strong American claims to territory in the west. It was also the last land action of the war.

In the same month the American commissioners signed a provisional – and secret – treaty of peace in Paris – without consulting the French.

Meanwhile on 14 December, 300 ships evacuated the British garrison in Charleston, 3800 Loyalists and 5000 Negro slaves sailing with them, and ten days later, having marched by easy stages from Virginia, Rochambeau's army embarked at Boston.

The winter of 1782–3 was unusually severe. Washington thought the army 'better organised, disciplined and clothed' than ever before, but was aware of the officers' view that Congress was indifferent to them. 'The temper of the army is much soured and has become more irritable than at any period since the commencement of the war,' he reported to Congress.

A committee of officers pleaded for payment of arrears in pay, settlement of food and clothing accounts, and assurance of half pay for life to the incapacitated and the retired as promised in 1780. When Congress rejected the officers' proposed commutation of the pension in exchange for six years' full pay, a meeting of general and field officers was called for 11 March. An anonymous address was circulated, highly critical of Congress. Washington was appalled and called a meeting of officers himself for 15 March. As Major Samuel Shaw reported, he drew from his pocket a letter from Congressman Joseph Jones of Virginia:

. . . that as a corroborating testimony of the good disposition in Congress towards the army he would communicate to them a letter received from a worthy member of that body and one who on all occasions had ever approved himself their fast friend. This was an exceedingly sensible letter, and while it pointed out the difficulties and embarrassments of Congress, it held up very forcibly the idea that the army should at all events be generously dealt with.

One circumstance in reading this letter must not be omitted. His Excellency, after reading the first paragraph, made a short pause, took out his spectacles, and begged the indulgence of his audience, while he put them on, observing at the same time that he had grown gray in their service and now found himself growing blind. There was something so natural, so unaffected in this appeal as rendered it superior to the most studied oratory. It forced its way into the heart, and you might see sensibility moisten every eye. The General, having finished, took leave of the assembly . . .

The news of the signing in November of the previous year of the provisional peace treaty came through a few days later. On 19 April — eight years to the day since Lexington — the cessation of hostilities was formally announced. The men went home, carrying their muskets, voted as a farewell gift by Congress, and with promissory notes only. Most of them went off without any last review. A few from Lancaster mutinied and marched on the State House in Philadelphia, where Congress was sitting. Not for the first time in the war that body moved out of town with speed.

Sergeant Joseph Martin got his formal dismissal on 11 June.

'The old man,' our captain, came into our room . . . and . . . handed us our discharges, or rather furloughs . . . I confess, after all, that my anticipation of the happiness I should experience upon such a day as this was not realized . . . We had lived together as a family of brothers for several years (setting aside some little family squabbles, like most other families); had shared with each other the hardships, dangers, and sufferings incident to a soldier's life, had sympathized with each other in trouble and sickness; had assisted in bearing each other's burdens, or strove to make them lighter by council and advice; had endeavored to conceal each other's faults, or make them appear in as good a light as they would bear. In short, the soldiery, each in his particular circle of acquaintance, were as strict a band of brotherhood as Masons, and I believe as faithful to each other. And now we were to be (the greater part of us) parted forever, as unconditionally separated as though the grave lay between us. This, I say, was the case with the most; I will not say all. There were as many genuine misanthropists among the soldiers . . . as of any other class of people whatever, and some in our corps of miners. But we were young men and had warm hearts. I question if there was a corps in the army that parted with more regret than ours did, the New Englanders in particular. Ah! it was a serious time!

Some of the soldiers went off for home the same day that their fetters were knocked off; others stayed and got their final settlement certificates, which they sold to procure decent clothing and money sufficient to enable them to pass with decency through the country, and to appear something like themselves when they arrived among their friends. I was among those . . . I . . . sold some of them and purchased some decent clothing and then set off . . .

Lieutenant-Colonel Benjamin Tallmadge, the strikingly handsome and daring dragoon officer who had managed Washington's secret service, kept a faithful record of the final days.

The troops now began to be impatient to return to their respective homes, and those that were destined for that purpose, to take possession of the city [of New York] . . . The twenty-fifth of November, 1783, was appointed for the British troops to evacuate the city and for the American troops to take possession of it. General Knox, at the head of a select corps of American troops, entered the city as the rear of the British troops embarked; soon after which the Commander-in-Chief, accompanied by Governor Clinton and their respective suites, made their public entry . . . on horseback, followed by the Lieutenant Governor and members of the Council . . .

And his diary revealed Washington's goodbye to his own 'family' in New York:

At twelve o'clock the officers repaired to Fraunces Tavern in Pearl Street, where General Washington had appointed to meet them and to take his final leave of them. We had been assembled but a few moments when His Excellency entered the room. His emotion, too strong to be concealed, seemed to be reciprocated by every officer present.

After partaking of a slight refreshment, in almost breathless silence, the General filled his glass with wine, and turning to his officers, he said, 'With a heart full of love and gratitude, I now take leave of you. I most devoutly wish that your latter days may be as prosperous and happy as your former ones have been glorious and honorable.'

After the officers had taken a glass of wine, General Washington said,

247

'I cannot come to each of you, but shall feel obliged if each of you will come and take me by the hand.'

General Knox, being nearest to him, turned to the Commander-in-Chief, who, suffused in tears, was incapable of utterance, but grasped his hand, when they embraced each other in silence. In the same affectionate manner, every officer in the room marched up to, kissed, and parted with his General-in-Chief.

Such a scene of sorrow and weeping I had never before witnessed, and hope I may never be called upon to witness again . . . Not a word was uttered to break the solemn silence . . . or to interrupt the tenderness of the . . . scene. The simple thought that we were then about to part from the man who had conducted us through a long and bloody war, and under whose conduct the glory and independence of our country had been achieved, and that we should see his face no more in this world, seemed to me utterly insupportable.

But the time of separation had come, and waving his hand to his grieving children around him, he left the room, and passing through a corps of light infantry who were paraded to receive him, he walked silently on to Whitehall, where a barge was in waiting. We all followed in mournful silence to the wharf, where a prodigious crowd had assembled to witness the departure of the man who, under God, had been the great agent in establishing the glory and independence of these United States. As soon as he was seated, the barge put off into the river, and when out in the stream, our great and beloved General waved his hat and bid us a silent adieu.

From the New Jersey shore Washington rode south to Philadelphia and then to Annapolis in Maryland where Congress was perforce sitting. To it he surrendered his commission.

The great events on which my resignation depended having at length taken place, I have now the honor of offering my sincere congratulations to Congress and of presenting myself before them to surrender into their hands the trust committed to me and to claim the indulgence of retiring from the service of my country.

Happy in the confirmation of our independence and sovereignty and pleased with the opportunity afforded the United States of becoming a respectable nation, I resign with satisfaction the appointment I accepted with diffidence – a diffidence in my abilities to accomplish so arduous a task, which however was superseded by a confidence in the rectitude of our Cause, the support of the supreme power of the Union and the patronage of Heaven . . .

Having now finished the work assigned me, I retire from the great theater of action, and bidding an affectionate farewell to this august body under whose orders I have so long acted, I here offer my commission and take my leave of all the employments of public life.

And for the Loyalists, who had guessed wrong? Some 80,000 went into exile, including Brant's Mohawks.

> To go – or not to go – is that the question?
> Whether 'tis best to trust the inclement sky
> That scowls indignant oe'r the dreary Bay
> Of Fundy and Cape Sable's rock and shoals,
> And seek our new domains in Scotia wilds,
> Barren and bare; or stay amoung the rebels,
> And by our stay, rouse up their keenest rage
> That, bursting o'er our now defenceless heads,
> Will crush us for the countless wrongs we've done them?
> Hard choice! Stay, let me think, – To explore our way,
> Thro' raging seas, to Scotia's rocky coast,
> At this dire season of this direful year.
> Where scarce the sun affords the cheerful ray;
> Or stay and cringe to the rude surly whigs,
> Whose wounds, yet fresh, may urge their desperate hand
> To spurn us while we sue – perhaps consign us
> To the kind care of some outrageous mob,
> Who for their sport our persons may adorn
> In all the majesty of tar and feathers;
> Perhaps our necks, to keep their humour warm,
> May grace a Rebel halter! – There's the sting!
> This people's, the bleak clime, for who can brook
> A Rebel's frown – or bear his children's stare
> When in the streets they point and lisp 'A Tory?'
> The open insult, the heart-piercing stab
> Of satire's pointed pen, or worse, – far worse –
> Committee's rage – or jury's grave debate
> On the grand question: 'shall their lives forsooth
> Or property – or both – atone their crimes?'
> Who'd bear all these calamities, and more
> We justly may expect, while Shelburne's shore
> Invites us to decide the case ourselves . . .
> Then let us fly, nor trust a war of words

Where British arms and Tory arts have failed
T'effect our purpose. On bleak Roseway's shores
Let's lose our fears, for no bold Whig will dare
With sword or law to persecute us there.

On 29 March Major Walter Dulany of the Maryland Loyalists, wrote to the commander-in-chief in New York, Sir Guy Carleton, about the prospect of being given a permanent commission, explaining his position thus:

My duty as a subject; the happiness which America enjoyed under the British government; and the miseries to which she would be reduced by an independence; were the motives that included me to join the British Army; nor are there any dangers, or difficulties that I would not cheerfully undergo, to effect a happy restoration. But at the same time that I acted, with the greatest zeal, against my rebellious countrymen I never forget that I was an American – If therefore, Sir, Independence should be granted, and the war still continued, I should deem it extremely improper to remain in a situation, obliging me to act either directly or indirectly against America.

Samuel Curwen wrote in his journal:

September 25 Arrived at Boston, and at half past three o'clock landed at the end of Long Wharf, after an absence of nine years and five months, occasioned by an execrable and never enough to be lamented civil war, excited by ambitious, selfish wicked men here and in England, to the disgrace, dishonour, disparagement and distress of these extensive territories. By plunder and rapine some few have accumulated wealth, but many more in numbers are greatly injured in their circumstances; some have to lament over the wrecks of their departed wealth and estates, of which pitiable number I am; my affairs having sunk into irretrievable ruin . . .

Friday, 10 June 1785 I again departed, presuming never more to repossess my late estate nor effects and twill be well if any part of them shall revert, and am this day June 10 at half past four PM going on board the ship *Astra* accompanied only by Mr Ward, intending for London, where and in the country or at least in some foreign parts, I must in the 70th year of my age spend the remainder of my days.

By the terms of the Treaty of Peace in 1783, Britain recognised the independence of the United States and accepted her western boundary as the Mississippi River; she conceded the right of navigation on the Mississippi and fishing rights off Newfoundland. Congress agreed to recommend to the individual states that they indemnify the Loyalists and pay their debts in Britain — but this was easy to say, hard to implement. In the end only Pennsylvania indemnified the Loyalist sufferers, but Britain itself was generous with land grants in Canada and £3 million in compensation. Spain regained the Floridas, for what value they might be to her, but not Gibraltar. France won some West Indian islands — and a huge debt, the full interest on which would be six years in falling due. For the Americans, with whom it all began, it was a total triumph.

Benjamin Franklin wrote to Joseph Banks from Passy on 27 July 1783:

I join with you most cordially in rejoicing at the return of peace. I hope it will be lasting, and that mankind will at length, as they call themselves reasonable creatures, have reason and sense enough to settle their differences without cutting throats; for, in my opinion, *there never was a good war or a bad peace.* What vast additions to the conveniences and comforts of living might mankind have acquired, if the money spent in wars had been employed in works of public utility! What an extension of agriculture, even to the tops of our mountains; what rivers rendered navigable or joined by canals; what bridges, aqueducts, new roads and other public works, edifices and improvements, rendering England a complete paradise, might have been obtained by spending those millions in doing good which in the last war have been spent in doing mischief; in bringing misery into thousands of families, and destroying the lives of so many thousands of working people, who might have performed the useful labor!

Index

Adams, Abigail 84
Adams, John 7, 9, 31–2, 64–5, 69, 84–5, 133, 154, 242
Adams, Samuel 11, 17–18, 21, 31–2
Ainslie, Thomas 59
Aitken, James (John the Painter) 136
Allen, Ethan 40–1
Amherst, Gen. Jeffery 16–17, 29, 30
Anburey Lieut. 100, 105–6
André, Maj. John 8, 85, 88–9, 204–8
Armstrong, Gen. John 167
Arnold, Gen. Benedict 7, 8, 40, 56–60 passim, 102–5, 107, 128, 140, 204–9, 216, 224
Asgill, Charles 244
Bancroft, Edward (Edwards) 130–1
Bangs, Isaac 68–9
Banks, Joseph 251
Barker, Lieut. John 25–6
Barré, Isaac 20
Barrett, Amos 25
Baum, Col. 100
Beatty, Lieut. Erkuries 173–4
Beaumarchais, Caron de 132–3
Bemis Heights 103, 103n, 128 see also Freeman's Farm, Saratoga
Blair, Francis 221
Bland, Marjorie 80–1
Boston 7, 9–12, 15–28 passim, 31, 33, 36, 43, 47, 50, 51–2, 54, 82, 152, 155, 245, 250
Bostwick, Elisha 79
Boucher, Jonathan 68
Boyd, Lieut. 173–4

Brandywine Creek 85–8, 154, 194
Brant, Joseph (Thayeadanegea) 102, 144, 146, 156, 172, 249–50
Brodhead, Col. Daniel 172, 175
Bunker Hill 33–9, 51, 154, 220
Burgoyne, Gen. John 30, 36–7, 70, 93–116 passim, 191, 219
Burke, Edmund 20
Burke, Thomas 87
Byron, Admiral John 151, 154
Cadwalader, Gen. John 122
Campbell, Col. Archibald 149–50
Campbell, Col. William 194, 197, 201
Carleton, Sir Guy 16–17, 42, 111, 242, 243, 250
Carlisle, Earl of 139–40, 210
Catawba River 213, 218–19
Chad's Ford 85
Champlain, Lake 40, 41, 56, 60, 137
Chaney, John 227
Charleston 60, 61, 63, 71, 175, 185–6, 187, 224, 228, 236, 243, 245
Charlestown 9, 28, 33, 35, 38, 51–2
Charlestown Neck 33, 35, 39
Chatham, William Pitt, 1st Earl of 129, 139, 143–4
Chaudière River 7, 57
Cherry Valley 146
Chesapeake Bay River 69, 84, 224, 228, 230, 235
Chesney, Capt. Alexander 198
Chester 85, 86
Chronicle, Maj. William 195, 197, 199
Clark, Maj. George Rogers 7, 147–9,

163–7, 245
Clark, Rev. Jonas 21–2, 24
Clark, Joseph 86
Clark, Peter 101
Cleveland, Col. Benjamin 197
Clinton, Gen. George 102–3
Clinton, Sir Henry 30, 37, 60, 61–2,
    102–3, 106, 109, 111, 113, 123, 124,
    138, 140, 149, 151, 153, 154, 169,
    170, 178, 181, 183–7, 202, 204, 206,
    220, 221, 222, 224, 225, 230, 234,
    235, 236–7, 242, 243, 244, 247
Clinton, Gen. James 172
Collier, Admiral Sir George 73, 169
Collins, James 197–8, 199–201, 213–15
Concord 7, 22–3, 25, 28
Conway, Henry 20, 170, 240
Conway, Gen. Thomas 122
Conyngham, Gustavus 140
Cook, Capt. James 162
Cornwallis, 2nd Earl 77, 80, 81, 82, 85,
    89–90, 181, 184, 186, 187, 190,
    192–3, 194, 195, 201, 213, 216–37
Cowpens 195, 213–16, 218, 227
Cresswell, Nicholas 81, 82–3
Crèvecoeur, Hector St John de 144–5
Cruger, John Harris 177
Curwen, Samuel 250
Dale, Lieut. Richard 159–62
Dartmouth, Earl of 142
Davidson, William Lee 190
Davie, William 190, 222
D'Estaing, Charles Hector Théodat,
    Comte 131, 151, 175, 176, 183
De Grasse, Admiral 228–9, 230, 237,
    242
De Kalb, Baron Johann 153, 193
Deane, Silas 122, 130–1, 132, 136
Delancey, James 156
Delaware River 7, 77, 78–9, 84, 90
Denny, Lieut. Ebenezer 233, 234
Dickson, William 221
Digby, Lieut. William 97
Dorchester Heights 29, 33, 55
Drinker, Mrs Henry 123–4
Du Portail, Louis 109, 122, 125, 184
Duct, Mathurin 136
Dulany, Maj. Walter 250

Dumas, Matthieu 235–6
Duncan, Capt. James 232
Dunmore, John Murray, Earl of 43–4,
    46, 69, 111, 156, 169
Eden, William 139
Effingham, Lord 139
Emerson, Rev. William 53
Erskine, Gen. Sir William 82, 123
Eutaw Springs 189, 226–8
Ewald, Johann 120
Fairfield 169–70
Fanning, Nathaniel 161–2
Farnsworth, Amos 33–5
Febiger, Col. Christian 171
Ferguson, Maj. Patrick 88, 183, 194–201
    passim, 216
Fishing Creek 190
Fogg, Maj. Jeremiah 173, 174–5
Fox, Charles James 20, 220, 242
France 123, 130–8, 140, 151–3, 154,
    157, 159, 202–4, 230, 242, 245, 251
Franklin, Benjamin 19, 39–40, 65–6,
    69–70, 90, 122, 130–4, 138, 140,
    150, 154, 157, 158, 162, 242, 251
Franklin, William 154
Fraser, Gen. 110
Fraunces' Tavern 8, 247–8
Freeman's Farm 103, 103n see also Bemis
    Heights, Saratoga
Freneau, Phillip 227–8, 239
Gage, Thomas 17, 18, 19, 21, 23, 27–8,
    29, 33, 35, 41–3, 111, 116, 138, 142
Gates, Gen. Horatio 54, 73, 103, 105,
    107–8, 111, 122, 153, 171–2, 191–3,
    194, 195, 201, 223–4
George III 7, 16, 18, 19–20, 44, 49, 65,
    68–9, 130, 240–1
Georgia 142, 150, 154, 175, 220, 224,
    243
Gérard, Conrad Alexandre 140
Germain, Lord George 14, 61, 70, 93,
    109, 143, 209–10, 224, 237, 241
Germantown 90, 131
Gilliland, Capt. James 233
Gipson, William 167–8
Girty, Simon 244–5
Glich, Lieut. 101
Gloucester 137, 231, 237

Graham, Capt. Samuel 231–2, 236
Grant, Gen. 154
Graves, Admiral Thomas 230, 237
Greene, Nathanael 48, 117, 118, 120,
    125, 153, 170–1, 191, 201–2, 207,
    213, 215–20 *passim*, 225, 226, 228,
    229, 243
Grenville, Thomas 242
Grey, Maj.-Gen. 88
Guilford Courthouse 167, 216, 218–20
Gum Swamp 192–3
Hale, Nathan 7, 49–50
Hale, Samuel 49
Hamilton, Alexander 118, 124–5,
    193–4, 233
Hamilton, Henry 147, 149, 164, 165–6
Hamilton, John 241
Hammill, Maj. Daniel 204
Hammond's Store 213
Hancock, John 11, 17, 21, 26, 31–2
Hanging Rock 190, 221
Hardy, Sir Charles 157, 159
Harris, Capt. 39
Harrower, John 40
Harvey, Capt. Moses 48–9
Hawkins, Sgt.-Maj. John 86
Hay, Maj. Samuel 89
Hazard, Ebenezer 69
Henry, John Joseph 57
Henry, Robert 199
Herkimer, Nicholas 102
Hewes, George 10–11
Hickey, Sgt. Thomas 49
Hobkirk's Hill 221
Hood, Admiral Sir Samuel 230, 237
Hopkins, Esek 137
Hopkinson, Francis 94–6, 113–14
Howe, Richard 69–70, 73, 151, 152
Howe, Gen. Robert 46, 149–50, 211
Howe, Gen. Sir William 8, 29, 33, 36,
    39, 43, 49, 55, 69, 71–85, 90–1, 93,
    109, 113–14, 123, 129, 150, 155
Huddy, Capt. Joshua 243–4
Hudson River 73, 99, 100, 106, 153,
    170, 187, 205, 211, 230, 243
Huger, Gen. Isaac 183
Hulton, Ann 38–9
Hunter, Lieut. Martin 51–2

Hutchinson, Peggy 155
Hutchinson, Thomas 9, 11, 77, 155–6
Hyde Parker, Commodore 150
Irvine, Col. William 89
Jackson, Andrew 221–2
James River 225, 228
Jay, John 242
Jefferson, Thomas 7, 64–5, 67, 156,
    166, 223–4, 226
Johnson, Col. Guy 142
Jones, John Paul 7, 140–2, 158–61
Jones, Joseph 245–6
Jones, Justice 82
Kaskaskia, Fort 147–9, 163
Keppel, Admiral Augustus 30, 136, 139
Kidder, Frederick 101–2
King, Lieut. Joshua 205–6
King's Ferry 170, 205
King's Mountain 194, 198–201, 216
Knox, Gen. Henry 55, 90, 118, 120,
    128, 232, 247, 248
Knox, Lucy 128
Knyphausen, Gen. Wilhelm von 85, 88
Lafayette, Marquis de 7, 122, 124, 125,
    152–3, 157, 158, 225, 231, 237
Lamb, Roger 8, 99–100, 109–10, 219
Laurens, Henry 44–5, 139–40, 151
Leach, John 51
Lee, Arthur 134, 225
Lee, Charles 53, 75, 91, 125–7, 204
Lee, Henry (Light Horse Harry) 171,
    219–20
Lee, Richard Henry 16–17, 63–4, 225
Lee, William 16–17
Lewis, Gen. Andrew 69
Lincoln, Benjamin 175, 176, 183–4, 232
Lippincott, Capt. Richard 243, 244
Livingstone, William (Hortensius) 115
Louis XVI 113, 202–3, 230, 239
McCrea, Jane 100
MacDonald, Flora 60, 61
McDowell, Col. Charles 197
McGinnis, Richard 145–6
Mackenzie, Capt. Frederick 8, 26,
    49–50, 150–1, 220
MacLean, Lieut.-Col. Allan 81–2
MacMahan, Isabella, Thomas 55
McMichael, Lieut. James 78

Mahan, Admiral 60
Marion, Francis 189–90, 220
Martin, Sgt. Joseph 125–6, 180–1,
    233–4, 246–7
Mason, George 163
Matthews, Gen. 169
Meigs, Private 57
Middlebrook 153, 154, 170
Miller, Rev. John 216
Mohawk Valley 102, 146, 156
Monck's Corner 183
Monmouth County 156, 243
Monmouth Courthouse 124–8, 151
Monroe, James 79
Montgomery, Gen. Richard 56, 58, 91
Montreal 56, 102, 111–13
Moore's Creek 60–1
Morgan, Gen. Daniel 103, 105, 116,
    204, 213–16
Morris, Lewis 73, 217
Morris, Robert 211–12
Morristown 80, 178, 211
Moultrie, William 61, 62, 150, 184–5
New Town 172–3
New York 9, 68–9, 74, 78, 80, 84, 102,
    106, 124, 138, 139, 142, 151, 153,
    155, 156, 170, 178, 183, 186, 208,
    220, 223, 224, 229, 230, 242, 243,
    247, 250
Newell, Timothy 55–6
Newport 152, 153, 181, 202, 204
Ninety-Six, Fort 186, 187, 190, 195,
    213, 220
Norfolk 45–6, 69, 169
North, Lord 9, 16, 18, 70, 130, 139,
    157, 241, 242
O'Hara, Brig. Charles 235–6, 237
Oliver, Peter 11–12
Oswald, Richard 242
Paine, Thomas 78
Panther, Wyandot 100
Paoli 88, 170
Parker, Capt. 7, 24
Parker, Admiral Sir Peter 60–3
Parsons, Samuel 204
Paulus Hook 171, 178
Percy, Earl 8, 25, 26, 28, 82
Peters, John 111–13

Philadelphia 9, 47, 84, 85, 90, 113–14,
    116, 123, 127, 128–9, 138, 140, 142,
    170, 204, 230, 246, 248
Phillips, John 156
Phillips, Maj.-Gen. William 223, 224
Pickering, Col. Timothy 85–6, 90
Pigot, Gen. Sir Robert 33, 152, 153
Pinckney, Maj. Thomas 176–7
Pitcairn, Maj. 23, 28, 38–9
Pockets, Andrew 190
Pontgibaud, Chevalier de 122–3
Popp, Stephen 233
Pownall, Thomas 139
Prescott, Col. William 35–6
Prévost, Gen. Augustin 149
Prevost, Col. Mark 175
Priestley, Joseph 20
Putnam, Israel 39
Putnam, Gen. Rufus 33, 204
Quebec 29, 57, 58–60, 95, 138, 142
Rall, Johann 79, 81
Randolph, Fanny 80
Rawdon, Lord Francis 54–5, 71, 192
Rawle, Anna 237–8
Redman, Polly 114
Reed, Joseph 74–5, 77
Reeves, Lieut. Enos 212
Revere, Paul 7, 21–3
Rhode Island 138, 152, 153, 183, 230
Riedesel, Baron 107, 108–9
Robin, Abbé Claude 203–4
Rochambeau, Comte de 202–4, 230,
    236, 237, 243, 245
Rockingham, Marquis of 242
Rodney, Caesar 66
Rodney, Sir George 209–10, 237, 242
Roush, George 91–3
Rush, Dr Benjamin 117–18, 204
Rutledge, John 69, 175
St Leger, Brig. Barry, 102
Sandwich, Earl of 19, 70, 135–6, 157, 242
Saratoga 103n, 106–7, 109–11, 129,
    131, 132, 191 see also Bemis Heights,
    Freeman's Farm
Sartine, Antoine de 135, 141
Savannah 149, 150, 175, 228, 243
Scott, Gen. Charles 126
Selkirk, Lord 141

Serle, Ambrose 8, 74, 123
Sevier, Col. John 194, 197
Sewall, Jonathan 50–1
Shaw, Maj. Samuel 121–2, 245–6
Shelburne, Earl of 241, 242
Shelby, Col. Isaac 194, 197, 199, 200
Shipley, Dr Jonathan 20
Shippen, Peggy 114, 128
Simcoe, Gen. 127, 226
Smith, Benjamin 184
Smith, William 205
Spain 138, 157, 159, 242, 243, 251
Stark, Col. John 101
Staten Island 8, 69, 71, 78, 82, 124, 178
Stedman, Charles 187, 217
Steele, Robert 37–8
Stephen, Adam 90, 118
Steuben, Friedrich von 119–20
Stirling, Gen. Lord 118, 124, 125
Stokes, Anthony 175–6
Stony Point 170–1
Stormont, Lord 136–7
Strahan, William 39–40
Stuart, John 143
Sullivan, Gen. John 85, 87, 116, 118,
    151–2, 172, 173, 174
Sullivan's Island 61–2, 183
Sumter, Thomas 189, 190
Sutherland, William 23
Tallmadge, Benjamin 207, 247–8
Tarleton, Col. Banastre 183–4, 186–7,
    189, 190, 194, 195, 201, 213, 215,
    216, 225–6
Thacher, Dr James 76, 97–9, 102–3,
    179–80, 207–8, 211, 230, 232–3
Thompson, Benjamin 53–4
Ticonderoga, Fort 40, 42, 55, 93, 95,
    97, 102, 111
Townshaw, Joseph 86–7
Trenton 79, 83, 90
Trumbull, John 29
Trumbull, Col. Jonathan 231
Tucker, Col. St George 218, 230–1, 235
Valley Forge 116, 124, 128, 144, 153, 154
Van Cortlandt, Col. Philip 233

Vance, David 194–7
Vaughan, Gen. John 80
Vergennes, Comte de 131–8, 242, 244
Vincennes 7, 147, 149
Virginia 9, 43, 63, 142, 143, 149,
    156, 166–7, 169, 187, 189, 216–17,
    223–4, 230, 231, 241, 245
Voltaire 133
Wabash River 7, 163–4
Wakefield, Capt. 103–5
Waldo, Dr Albigence 116–17, 120–1
Walker, Ben 119
Walpole, Horace 30, 93, 216
Warner, James, Jemima 57
Warren, Dr Joseph 17, 21–2, 39, 43
Washington, George 7–8, 30–4, 47–8,
    53–6, 60, 71–85, 89, 90–1, 107, 109,
    116, 120–2, 124, 126–7, 142, 144,
    151, 153, 155, 156, 167, 170–1,
    178–9, 180, 181, 191, 201–13, 220,
    227–49
Washington, Lund 47, 73
Washington, Martha (Patsy) 30–1, 80
Washington, Col. William 79, 213, 227
Wayne, Gen. Anthony 87, 88, 111, 112,
    120, 127, 128, 170–1
Webb, Lieut. Samuel 38
West Indies 134, 135, 138–9, 153, 154,
    175, 187, 229, 237, 242, 251
West Point 8, 153, 170, 205, 208, 211
Weymouth, Lord 136
White, John 153–4
White, Philip 243
Wickes, Lambert 140
Wilkinson, Eliza 187–9
Wilkinson, James 122
Williams, Col. Otho 191–3, 226–7
Wood, Sylvanus 23–4
Wraxall, Sir Nathaniel 237
Wright, Sir James 150, 175, 243
Wythe, George 137–8
Yorktown 8, 193n, 224, 228, 230–7,
    239, 242, 243
Young, Thomas 198–9
Zeisberger, David 244–5